The
Social
Dynamics
of Open Data

Edited by
François van Schalkwyk, Stefaan G Verhulst,
Gustavo Magalhaes, Juan Pane & Johanna Walker

AFRICAN
MINDS

Published in 2017 by African Minds
4 Eccleston Place, Somerset West 7130, Cape Town, South Africa
info@africanminds.org.za
www.africanminds.org.za

ISBN Paper 978-1-928331-56-8
ISBN eBook 978-1-928331-57-5
ISBN ePub 978-1-928331-58-2

Orders
African Minds
4 Eccleston Place, Somerset West 7130, Cape Town, South Africa
info@africanminds.org.za
www.africanminds.org.za

For orders from outside South Africa:
African Books Collective
PO Box 721, Oxford OX1 9EN, UK
orders@africanbookscollective.com
www.africanbookscollective.com

Contents

About this book

The chapters in this edited volume have all trodden the well-worn path from an opening call for abstracts to publication. The call in question was for the Open Data Research Symposium (ODRS), the second edition of which was held on 5 October 2016 in Madrid. ODRS 2016 was chaired by Stefaan Verhulst and François van Schalkwyk with the invaluable support of the organising committee comprised of Emmy Chirchir (Munster University), Katie Clancy (International Development Research Centre), Gisele Craveiro (University of Sao Paulo), Tim Davies (University of Southampton), Kyujin Jung (Tennessee State University), Gustavo Magalhaes (University of Austin Texas), Michelle McLeod (University of the West Indies), Stefania Milan (University of Amsterdam), Fernando Perini (International Development Research Centre) and Andrew Young (The GovLab, NYU Tandon School of Engineering).

ODRS is a bi-annual gathering designed to provide a dedicated space for researchers working specifically on open data to reflect critically on their findings, and to apply and advance theories that explain the dynamics of open data as a socially constructed phenomenon and practice.

The ODRS space is meant to shelter researchers from the ever-present demands for quick wins, short-term results, tweet-length findings and immediate impacts. This is not to suggest that researchers should be immune to considerations of relevance and transfer, but the International Open Data Conference (IODC) that follows on the day after the ODRS is perhaps the more appropriate place for researchers to dust off their business cards, brighten their brochures and have their two-minute sound bites locked and loaded.

Selecting the Papers

A total of 70 abstracts were received by the ODRS programme committee. All abstracts were reviewed by at least two peers recruited either from within the committee or from a pool of invited external experts. The review process followed a single-blind review process. In cases of conflicting reviews, a third, tie-break review was sought. Of the 70 abstracts received, 29 were accepted, and authors of accepted abstracts were invited to submit a full paper by a deadline of just under a month ahead of the Symposium. All 29 authors submitted full papers and 28 were able to present their research in Madrid.

The Symposium was designed such that the morning's parallel sessions consisted of paper presentations. The afternoon sessions were an opportunity for researchers to discuss a range of research-relevant issues such as available research infrastructure, methodologies for conducting research on open data, and 'getting to grips with the impact of open data'. A session was also convened to discuss the publication of the papers presented at the Symposium. In these discussions, novel approaches to publishing were blended with more traditional approaches. The goal was to test the best possible approach that would strike a balance between quality, prestige, speed and accessibility.

After the Symposium, the ideas that surfaced during the consultation on the preferred publication format were shared with all ODRS attendees via a Google Document. The outcome of this consultative process was agreement (if not consensus) to publish the papers as chapters in an open access edited volume within a year of the Symposium; that the editors would be from the ODRS programme committee but could include others who participated in the Symposium; that those who presented papers should be given the option to include their paper and could, without prejudice, seek alternative publishing options; and that all papers would be double-blind peer reviewed.

Following the Symposium, 24 papers were submitted for consideration, some of which were revised versions of the papers presented at the Symposium. The authors of these revised papers had used the feedback received from their peers at the Symposium to make improvements to their papers. The final selection of ten papers was based on the recommendations of the reviewers, the revisions made by the authors, and on determinations made by the editors regarding the papers' fit with the volume's overall focus on the social dynamics of open data. In addition, given that much of the existing research on open data is descriptive, the editors gave preference to papers that contribute to theory-building. A deliberate attempt was made during the review process to invite one reviewer with expertise on open data and a second reviewer more familiar with the non-data-specific concepts or the theoretical framework used in a paper. The editors received nine revised papers, and these are the papers that appear as chapters in this volume.

In addition to the nine research chapters, the co-chairs of the conference wrote a framing chapter which is published as the introduction to this volume.

About the papers in this volume

Transitioning from abstracts submitted in response to an open call to a collection of nine chapters that are in some way coherent in their content is well-near impossible, particularly if quality and relevance to a broadly defined topic area are the primary selection criteria. Remarkably, though, some content 'patterns' are discernible. The most obvious of these are, first, papers concerning the governance of open data (Canares; Gurin et al.; Vancauwenberghe and Van Loenen) and institutionalisation (Gonzalez and Heeks; Piovesan); and, second, papers that address the role of intermediaries in open data ecosystems (Enaholo; Maail; Fumega; Scrollini).

The chapters on governance and institutionalization make an important contribution to deepening our understanding of how governments, as socially constructed institutions, respond to external pressures for change. Piovesan's study of open data initiatives at the local government level in Europe concludes that there is a need to understand these initiatives within an evolving ecosystem, and that while resources and skills shortages account for some of the lack of progress observed, more important is the resistance to change 'because of cemented routines and risk aversion towards the exposure of their inner workings to the public'. Gonzalez and Heeks's study of the Chilean government's open data initiative shows the importance of taking into account how institutional dynamics may shape the trajectories of new initiatives. They acknowledge, however, the agency of senior politicians in institutional settings as having some influence over the development path of new initiatives. Consistent with the observed tension between compliance and innovation, they conclude that 'institutions may condition how initiatives are planned and implemented, but OGD [open government data] is not necessarily condemned to fully replicate those institutional trajectories. Indeed, the challenge to institutionalise OGD is to develop long-term policies that clearly state objectives, resources and responsibilities and, at the same time, evaluate dominant institutions and determine what the best approach is to overcome any constraining environmental conditions'.

The other three papers that fall within the same interest area steer away from a direct interest in the institutional context (although they acknowledge its significance) to focus on how to govern open government data initiatives within those contexts. Gurin et al. draw attention to governing the relationship between openness and privacy in order to realise the inherent benefits of open data while simultaneously protecting individuals' right to privacy. They conclude that 'a combination of strategies can make it possible to tap the value of granular, detailed data while managing privacy risks. While some strategies involve technical approaches, others are based on policy, data governance, community outreach and communication.' Vancauwenberghe and Van Loenen focus their attention on the specificities of governing spatial data, data that holds both commercial and public value. Their analysis shows how several countries in Europe have taken measures to engage actors outside the public sector in the governance of open spatial data infrastructures, and that policy changes reflect this shift to a more inclusive and open approach. Finally, Canares bemoans the absence of a more inclusive governance in the case of Jakarta: a city that aspires to be smart but not necessarily open. Canares contends that open data has an important role to play in making the governance of smart cities more open.

What emerges from the chapters on open data intermediaries is the varying proximity of intermediaries to other actors. Enaholo's chapter shows how Nigerian intermediaries – mainly civil society organisations (CSOs) – have over time become progressively professionalised, thus lubricating their engagement and interaction with government and donors. But with the closer proximity to those actors comes greater distance between those grassroots communities from which these CSOs emrged and whose insterests they served when they were founded. Scrollini explores the close working relationship between a CSO and government in Uruguay, catalysed by open data, and resulting in the co-production of an open data application in the health sector. Notable are the compromises made by both parties in the co-production process. Maail investigates how the relationships between data suppliers, intermediaries and data users change as a result of open data initiatives, and, he suggests, those relationships must constantly be maintained. Fumega's paper shows that proximity is not only a matter of distance or closeness between CSOs and other actors; there is also varying proximity between CSOs in different domains that share a common goal of government accountability. She argues for greater cohesion and co-operation between CSOs in the open government data and those in the right to information domains.

Common to the majority of chapters is the attempt by the authors to draw on existing theories applicable to open data in order to better explain the reasons for open data's successes and failures in contributing to a more equitable and just society. Without providing an exhaustive list of approaches taken by authors, notable are the use of path dependence theory (Gonzalez and Heeks), Offenhuber's ladder of participation (Canares), the concept of co-production as developed in theories on public management (Scrollini), and the combined use of the concepts of routines and satisficing with two models describing the social dynamics in the flow of open data and the diffusion of innovation (Piovesan).

We hope that this volume is more than an advertisement for the quality of research presented at the Second Open Data Symposium; we hope that each of its chapters makes a valuable and much-needed contribution to a better understanding of the social dynamics of open data.

The editors
October 2017

1.

The state of open data
and open data research

François van Schalkwyk & Stefaan G Verhulst

Open government data, and the attendant excitement over its potential, emerged as an asset for social good just under a decade ago. It rose to prominence on the back of related trends and developments, including the rise of big data, the arrival of new analytical methods to derive insights and innovations from that data, and deteriorating trust in public institutions that are the custodians of large datasets related to the functioning of government and the allocation of public resources. In addition, the relative success of open source and open innovation provided new models on how to create public value. The Obama administration's move to increase access to government data (in particular, its launch of the data.gov site) also played a part in increasing the visibility and the legitimacy of open data.

Eight years after the launch of that site, open data has entered the mainstream of both policy and activism. Around the world, in both developed and developing countries, at the national and local levels, governments have created or are planning open data programmes and portals. Open data projects are playing an increasingly important role in economic and social development, spurring progress in areas as varied as healthcare, education, banking, agriculture, climate change and innovation. A growing list of private companies, whose businesses have hitherto depended on *private* data, are also coming to recognise the potential competitive and social benefits of opening up that data; and we are witnessing the emergence of social enterprises that rely on open data to provide tools and services for the public good.

So where do we stand now? And where do we go from here? This introductory chapter outlines some reflections on current developments in the field, and considers how they may affect the state of open data and open data research in the years to come. It describes a wide variety of trends – some positive, some more cautionary. If there is one overarching message, it is that for all the excitement

1

and hype, there is still much that we don't know about the contributions of open data to social and economic development.

The theoretical potential of open data has been established; but much work remains to be done, many challenges need to be overcome, and several gaps in our understanding must be breached if open data is, in fact, to help solve complex social problems and improve people's lives.

One of the purposes of this volume is, in fact, to begin that process of filling in the gaps in our knowledge. Each of the nine chapters published in this volume, in its own away, adds to our existing and steadily growing understanding of how open data works. Through these contributions, we see the importance of social dynamics – be they institutional or otherwise – across the value chain of open data. It is important to remember that each of these examples represents a specific instance, in a specific setting. But it is slowly, through individual examples like these, that our overall understanding of the real impact of open data will advance.

Current trends and their implications for open data

Rise of populism and regime change

Donald Trump's rise to power and, more generally, the emergence of nationalist strongmen with limited faith in democracy around the world, is likely to affect the perceived value proposition and use of open data. Two aspects of Trump-style governance will have a particular impact: a penchant for secretive deal-making, and the debasement of knowledge, facts and evidence both in governance and in public discourse.

These trends and others have already led some to highlight the value of open data as a force for accountability and transparency, and, more generally, as a tool for the 'resistance'. (This trend is evident, for instance, in increased interest in the storage and archiving of existing government data.) Paradoxically, however, we believe that this heightened interest may prove counter-productive to the spread of open data as it elevates only one value proposition (i.e. transparency) above other, potentially less controversial or difficult value propositions such as increased innovation and economic growth. Similarly, if open data comes to be equivalent in the public mind simply with archiving government data, then its potentially much greater value as a tool for real-time decision-making may be overlooked or ignored.

Transparency and accountability are of course valuable and crucial goals. However, many years of research and practice has repeatedly indicated that governments are more likely to create open data projects if they believe it will also spur economic growth, improve the efficiency of public service delivery and lead to innovation. It is therefore essential to keep highlighting these value propositions, making clear the full range of benefits that can potentially be conferred by open data – beyond making governments accountable.

2

The emerging narrative of the 'dark side' of data

Several popular books, including Cathy O'Neil's *Weapons of Math Destruction: How Big Data Increases Inequality and Threatens Democracy*, have awakened some to the real and perceived threats posed by data. Primarily, these threats concern biases and various forms of inequality that may be inherent in and arise from a greater use of data and algorithms. While many of the concerns raised by these books are valid and important, there is also a great danger that these threats become the dominant trope in conversations and considerations of open data. Unfortunately, as a result of the increased negative connotations associated with data, the burden of proof for those who want to show its potential positive impact has become substantially higher than those who warn of data's risks. Most importantly, a narrative of 'destruction' (especially promoted by several progressive groups), while not exactly wrong, is simplistic and overlooks the many potential benefits of open data.

Partly as a result of this emerging 'destruction' narrative, data has become toxic among many non-government and other stakeholders. We are witnessing the rise of a burgeoning anti-data movement, one whose views are as simplistic and naive as those who have over-hyped and over-championed data. What's required is a far more nuanced and less polemical discussion about data. And, in order to make that discussion possible, we need policies, projects and research that are equally nuanced – that continue to increase access and use of data, yet that balance this against the need for more data responsibility and attention to the risks of data.

New data divides

None of the preceding discussion should be taken to indicate that we are minimising the risks. The challenges of using data are real, and among the most serious unintended consequences is the emergence of a new data divide that rides on, and in many ways exacerbates, the existing digital divide. The emergence of such a new divide is deeply ironic: after all, open data was intended as a tool for democratisation and empowerment. Yet, as with other assets, and as with technology in general, the understanding and the capacity to extract value from open data is not equally distributed. Those who may need data the most often don't realise the value data may have to improve their decision-making. Different skill-sets, and differential access to the tools required to store and analyse data, also mean that there is a very real risk that open data could reinforce existing inequalities and potentially create new ones.

What can we do to avoid such inequalities? Critically, all data stakeholders need to be as attuned to the *reality* of open data as the potential of open data. By this we mean that much greater attention needs to be paid to the actual, realisable possibilities of individuals and groups to access and extract meaning and insight

3

from data. Open data exists on a continuum of value: the final parts of the value chain, which involve extracting meaning, are as important as the earlier parts, which involve data collection and storage. It is not enough simply to make sure data is made 'open'. We need to ensure that people understand the questions data can answer and that they can use open data, either directly or indirectly.

The role of government is also key here, as it is government that holds the power to strike a balance between informational and human development; it is government that determines the corrective and redistributive policies required to create the conditions for balanced, inclusive development.

The 'magical thinking' of standards

As so often in the technology world, there is an emerging belief that open data as a field can only scale and become truly useful through a greater use of principles and standard-bearing bodies. For instance, the International Open Data Charter seeks to establish a set of standards, expectations and principles for how governments should publish their data. While standards and principles can of course be very useful to establish common expectations, it is also the case that they can hamper innovation and increase barriers to entry, especially among groups who may not have the requisite financial or institutional capacity to meet all requirements of a standard. This can be particularly problematic for countries from the developing world, or cities that want to make their data liquid yet lack the resources. Standards are generally set by early movers, which typically means more developed and resourceful countries; these standards can then set unrealistic or unfeasible expectations for 'late adopters'.

The concern is that, instead of scaling and promoting open data, standards and principles may ultimately hamper the exchange of data. Standards should not be seen as apolitical when their application is inevitably both political and varied across many social contexts. We need to remember that the ultimate goal is to improve people's lives by generating insights from data has been made accessible; not just compliance of principles and standards. In addition, a standard is only a standard, and only creates value, when it becomes widely accepted.

Understanding open data research

The preceding section outlines some key forces currently shaping the state of open data. But what is the state of open research – research that shapes our understanding of these trends and advances the field by providing new, empirically sound insights?

The first Open Data Research Symposium was held in Ottawa in May 2016. Selected papers from that Symposium were published in a special issue of the *Journal of Informatics* (JCI2016). The same journal published an earlier special issue in 2012 titled 'Community Informatics and Open Government Data' (JCI2012).

As far as we are aware, these are the only peer reviewed, edited volumes that focus exclusively on open data. Combined with this volume, *The Social Dynamics of Open Data* (SDOP), it may be instructive to explore what this small sample[1] of publications tells us about shifts in the open data research landscape (if anything). Of course, it is dangerous to talk of trends over a period of five years and across only three scholarly publications. To bolster those insights, we therefore also draw on a second sample of open government data research publications from the bibliographic index of the Clarivate Web of Science.[2, 3] While we acknowledge that the sample remains small – and, importantly, ignores all the research findings shared through other means, including the corpus of grey literature – such an analysis could nonetheless provide some insights into who is conducting research on open data, how they are writing up their research, and who is supporting that research.

How much research on open data is being published?
The sample of articles and chapters in the three publications focused exclusively on open data reveals little about the overall volume of research being published. The bibliometric data is more comprehensive but still excludes those journals (and books) not indexed in Clarivate's Web of Science as well as a vast body of grey literature. Google Scholar's indexing is more inclusive, but the data requires a level of checking and cleaning that is beyond the scope of this modest effort.[4] The data in the bibliometric sample of 216 pubclications do, however, show (1) a marked increase in the number of 'open data publications' from a modest 2 publications in 2008 to 86 publications in 2016, and (2) a rapid increase in the number of publication post-2010 (see Figure 1).

---

1 The sample of articles and chapters in the three publications focused exclusively on open data consisted of 22 chapters and papers in total: 6 in the 2012 special issue of the *Journal of Community Informatics*, 7 in the 2016 special issue of the same journal, and 9 in this publication. A total of 39 authors contributed to the chapters and papers in the sample.
2 The 'bibliometric sample' consisted of 216 journal articles, books and book chapters on open (government) data. The sample was generated by searching the Web of Science Core Collection for the 10-year period 2007 to 2016 using the search query "TI=('open data' OR 'open government data')" and limiting the search to the publication types 'article', 'book' and 'book chapter'. This returned 264 results. Results related to open science or open research data were removed to ensure a focus on open government data. The Journal of Community Informatics is not indexed by the Web of Science. Given that two of publications in the open data only sample were special issues of the *Journal of Community Informatics*, and that this volume has not yet been published, there is no overlap of publications between the two samples.
3 The collection, cleaning and analysis of the data relied on the primitive data skills of the lead author. The full dataset is available for verification and further analysis.
4 A search on Google Scholar using the same query and date range returned 17,100 results (search done on 14 September 2017).

Figure 1 Number of research publications on open government data indexed in the Web of Science 2007–2016 (n=216)

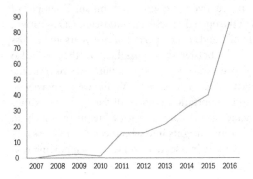

Where is research on open data being done?
The analysis[5] of the sample of open-data-only volumes shows that authors are mostly affiliated to universities (59%), followed by non-government organisations (30%) and research institutes (9%). Authors are most often and consistently affiliated to universities across all three publications (JCI2012 67%, JCI2016 43%, SDOP 56%).[6] Authors from non-government organisations, typically research-orientated, have emerged more recently (JCI2012 0%, JCI2016 36%, SDOP 44%), and those from research institutes (JCI2012 17%, JCI2016 14%, SDOP 0%), that is non-degree awarding private- or publicly-funded research organisations, have declined. Bibliometric data confirm that most researchers are based at universities (85%). However, only 1 corresponding author out of the 205 for which sufficient address data were available to make a determination as to their institutional affiliation, listed their affiliation as being a non-government organisation. In the case of research institutes, a proportion similar to that of the open data-specific publications was found at 8% (17). Other affiliations were also present in the bibliometric data: 3% (7) were from government and 2% (5) were from private corporations.

Who is conducting research on open data?
In terms of gender, 36% of all authors in the open data-specific sample were female. There were marked differences between the three publications with a sharp swing from predominantly female authors to predominantly male authors (JCI2012: Female 67%, Male 33%; JCI2016: Female 36%, Male 64%; SDOP:

---

5   The data was analysed using fractional counting in instances where a paper or chapter was multi-authored. For example, if there are three authors, each author is assigned a score of 0.33 and each author contributes fractionally to the variable being measured.
6   JCI2012 and JCI2016 refer to the issues of the *Journal of Community Informatics* published in 2012 and 2016 respectively. SDOP refers to this publication, *The Social Dynamics of Open Data*.

Female 17%, Male 83%). Determining the gender profiles for all authors using the bibliometric data was beyond the scope of this chapter as authors are not coded for gender in the Web of Science. However, using only corresponding authors and coding them for gender based on first names and a Google Search, 209 corresponding authors were identified as being either male or female. Of the 209 corresponding authors, 30% (70) were female.

No readily available data on the ages or career stages of authors were available for analysis.

Where are open data researchers from and how are they collaborating?

Most authors in the open data specific sample are from the Global North,[7] but only marginally so at 55% across all papers and chapters. However, closer analysis shows that representation of authors from the Global South was highest in the second special issue of the *Journal of Community Informatics* (71%). This is not surprising given that the focus of the special issue was on open data in developing countries. Authors from the Global South represent a much lower proportion in the other two publications (JCI2012 17%, SDOP 44%). This could be interpreted in two ways. First, that authors from the Global South are under-represented when topics aren't specifically focused on developing-country issues. Or, second, that there has been a positive shift from 17% to 44% in representation from the Global South when comparing the two publications that did not have a developing-country focus.

Bibliometric analysis shows that of 216 open data research publications, 88% (189) were published by authors in the Global North (using the corresponding author's address as an indicator of location). The trend data show that there is indeed an increase in the proportion of authors from the Global South, although the gap remains wide (see Figure 2).

What is more definitive, and worrying from a Global North–Gobal South collaborative point of view, is that for the 22 articles and chapters published in the publications focused exclusively on open data, there is not a single example of collaboration between authors of the Global North and the Global South. There is evidence of South–South collaboration in the case of two papers. In fact, collaboration in general is the exception. In the case of the first special issue of the *Journal of Community Informatics,* only 1 (16%) paper was co-authored, and in the *Social Dynamics of Open Data,* 3 (33%) papers were co-authored. The second special issue of the *Journal of Community Informatics* bucked the trend: all papers in that publication were co-authored. Bibliometric analysis of the larger sample of publications shows that the trend is for research publications on open data to be co-authored: 79% (170) publications were authored by two or more researchers, and the average number of authors per publication is 3.29.

---

7 Countries were assigned to the Global North or Global South using the following map: https://www.mapsofworld.com/headlinesworld/miscellaneous/division-global-north-global-south

Figure 2 Authors of research publications on open government data from the Global North versus those from the Global South (%, n=216)

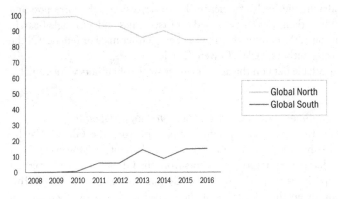

In terms of collaboration, the bibliometric data show that for the 213 publications for which author address data were available, 22% (47) of authors did not collaborate. Of those that did collaborate, 33% (71) did so with colleagues in the same organisation, 23% (49) collaborated with colleagues in the same country and 11% (23) collaborated across the region. Only 3% (7) collaborated between regions but within the same development region (e.g. collaboration between authors in the US and Europe), and marginally more (16, 8%) collaborated across development regions (i.e. North-South collaboration, e.g. between authors in Mexico and the US or between authors in Africa and Europe).

Figure 3 Collaboration between authors of publications on open government data indexed in the Web of Science 2007–2016 (n=213)

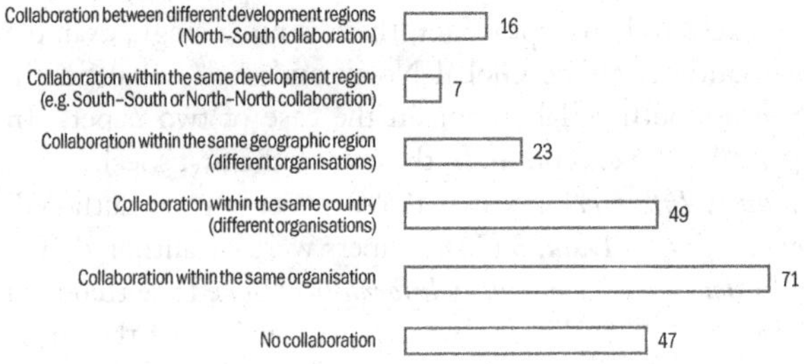

Collaboration between different development regions (North–South collaboration)	16
Collaboration within the same development region (e.g. South–South or North–North collaboration)	7
Collaboration within the same geographic region (different organisations)	23
Collaboration within the same country (different organisations)	49
Collaboration within the same organisation	71
No collaboration	47

The stereotypical open data researcher

Sex:	Male.
Age:	Unknown.
Employment:	University in the Global North.
Behaviour:	Most likely to co-author with colleagues at the same organisation.

Accessibility of research on open data
All three open-data specific publications are open access. The picture from a universal access point of view is less positive in the case of journal articles, books and book chapters indexed in the Web of Science – only 19% (40) of those publications are published under an open access licence. This finding reflects a key paradox of academic research on open data: while the focus is on the value of open access on society, the authors still decide to publish their findings in a manner that is antithetical to the principles and values of open data.

Who is funding research on open data?
All but one paper in the second special issue of the *Journal of Community Informatics* acknowledge funding support from the IDRC. In the case of the first special issue of the *Journal of Community Informatics,* only 1 (16%) paper acknowledges a funder (The Asia Foundation), and in the *Social Dynamics of Open Data*, 3 (33%) papers acknowledge funding (from the National Commission for Scientific and Technological Research [Chile], Microsoft, IDRC and Avina Foundation). The bibliometric data show that 32% (69) publications included funding acknowledgements. No single funding agency stands out, with the possible exception of the European Union: 20% (14) acknowledge financial support from the EU in one form or another (e.g. European Commission or the European Commission's Seventh Framework Programme). If funding agencies are classified by their geographic focus area, the data show that most funding comes from national science councils and funding agencies (44, 64%). This finding could account for the high levels of intra-organisational and intra-national collaboration in conducting research on open data.

The 'impact' of research on open data
The impact of the new knowledge produced by open data researchers can either be measured within science (i.e. its contribution to further knowledge production) or on society (i.e. the change brought about in society attributable to new knowledge). Neither is easy to measure.

The impact on knowledge production is typically measured in the form of citations. The more frequently a research publication is cited by other researchers, the greater the scientific impact of the publication. Figure 4 shows the number of citations for the sample of publications indexed in the Web of Science. It shows a marked increase in the number of citations, which is to be expected as the number of publications on open data increased. On average, each paper in the sample is cited 5.88 times. Normalisation for scientific field would need to be done to provide an indication of whether citations to open government data journal articles are high or low. At this stage, given the small number of publications and the difficulty of ascribing open data research to a specific scientific field makes such analysis difficult.

Figure 4 Number of citations in the Web of Science (n=213)

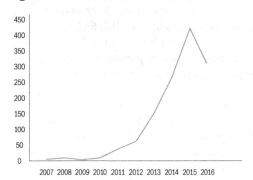

Disciplinary perspectives on open data
Open data is inherently an inter-disciplinary topic that straddles a wide variety of areas of social inquiry and research. An analysis of the subject area assigned to the publications in the Web of Science sample shows that the most frequent category by subject is computer science (80, 27%), followed by information science and library science (69, 23%), after which there is a significant drop in the frequency of other subject categories (see Figure 6). The Top 10 subject categories account for 75% (221) of all the subject classifications; non-technical disciplines in the Top 10 such as geography, government and law, social sciences, communication, and public administration only account for a combined 16% (47). This suggests that publications on open data are mostly technical in terms of their content. Conversely, there appears to be a very limited social perspective that is brought to bear on open data by researchers. Further analysis would need to be done to determine whether there are any correlations between subject classification and region (e.g. 'Are researchers in the Global South more attuned to social

dynamics?'), or between subject classification and institutional affiliation (e.g. 'Are non-university research more interested in exploring the social dynamics of open data?').

Table 1 Top 10 subject categories for open data publications indexed in the Web of Science (n=294)

Geography	5
Public Administration	6
Communication	7
Social Sciences - Other Topics	7
Telecommunications	7
Government & Law	8
Business & Economics	14
Engineering	18
Information Science & Library Science	69
Computer Science	80

Note: The number of publications (294) exceeds the number of publications in the sample (216) because a single publication may be assigned to more than one subject category.

Conclusion

The findings and analysis above bring us back to the relevance of this collection of chapters on the social dynamics of open data.

First, the bibliometric data show that there is a relative dearth of scientific literature that focuses on the social dynamics that hinder, constrain, enable, promote or propel the supply, (re)use and impact of open data.

The current tendency in much of the research is, quite simply, to *measure what is measurable*. In practice, this usually means focusing on volume or supply: measuring the amount of data, or number of datasets, that are being released or accessed. Such an approach fails to take into account the full range of factors – social dynamics – that determine the impact of open data, and overlooks the multiple axes along which open data operates. It also doesn't make us smarter about users and non-users. In addition, the problem with this approach is that, over time, researchers and policy-makers tend to start valuing what is measureable and simply what gets measured. This collection's focus on social dynamics goes some way in remedying this asymmetry.

Second, one might argue that the data on the classification of publications by subject is far from reliable as it is often difficult to categorise a topic such as open data, and that classifiers may default to more technical subject areas because of the perceived technicality inferred by 'data' at the expense of the social complexities inferred by openness. This may be true. And if it is, then combining several research publications on open data into a single volume brings to the attention of researchers, policy-makers and other stakeholders in a clear and unambiguous manner the social dimension of open data. In other words, the chapters in this collection will hopefully escape the fate of research papers that may well share a focus on social dynamics but are unfortunately buried by technically-biased classifications.

Third, while the social perspective appears to be under-represented, the citation data show that publications that deal with social dynamics are some of the most highly cited in the scientific community. This could be interpreted as a proxy indicator of the need for more empirical evidence on the social dynamics at work in contexts in which open data initiatives are conceived and implemented.

Open data is a networked movement and power in networks is corralled by the first-movers and consolidated by those with historically-endowed privilege. The networked nature of the global open data 'movement' is highly relevant in relation to unlocking the development benefits of open data. The network power of global movements, including the open data movement, will, as a structural feature of networks, continue to exclude by determining the rules of inclusion. Under such conditions, social development will fail. And it is the responsibility of research to provide the evidence that exposes the unintended exclusionary outcomes of open data, while simultaneously deploying theory as a tool to explain the observed outcomes in order to recalibrate open data initiatives such that they live up to their potential for creating a more equitable and just society.

Finally, open data has shown robust growth over the last decade, and its potential is now indisputable. But recent years have also shown a few tears in the seams. In particular, the current ideological or faith-based approach to open data, guided primarily by well-intentioned but under-informed enthusiasm, is starting to show its limits. Without more evidence and fact-based analysis, the case for open data – for data 'owners' to release it and for users to access it – may weaken, especially as the case of the potential harm starts to overshadow all debate. We need to develop a more rigorous and fine-combed analysis not only of why open data is valuable, but how it is valuable, and under what specific conditions.

The objective of the Open Data Research Symposium and the subsequent collection of chapters published here is to build such a stronger evidence base. This base is essential to understanding what open data's impacts have been to date, and how positive impacts can be enabled and amplified. We hope this collection provides a foundation for further and deeper research, and especially more evidence-based practice, and hope you will join us in building a community of open data researchers moving forward.

2.

The challenges of institutionalising open government data: A historical perspective of Chile's OGD initiative and digital government institutions

Felipe González-Zapata & Richard Heeks

Introduction

Open government data (OGD) has been globally endorsed given its promise of reshaping existing institutions. By opening up public records, governments can be more accountable, civil society can get involved in collaborative public policy-making or service delivery, and new business opportunities can be created (Davies et al. 2013). From this viewpoint, OGD is perceived as a one-directional influence: OGD's influence on existing institutions can help unlock these benefits.

However, opening up public records implies intervening in political spaces, thus OGD policies are rooted in a certain institutional arrangement (Davies & Bawa 2012); that is, a set of formal and informal institutions that are socially constructed (Scott 2013) frame OGD initiatives and determine to what extent they may be institutionalised. These trajectories may influence how OGD is adopted by governments and civil societies, and reflect that OGD institutionalisation is a socio-political (rather than purely technical) phenomenon. Currently, cross-sectoral OGD policies are led by central agencies which need to be sufficiently empowered, well-connected and resourced in order to push those agendas forward. Without that institutional backing, OGD initiatives are at risk of becoming one-off projects rather than long-term transformative policies.

Current research on OGD focuses more on the impact and capacity-building aspects of OGD agendas rather than their institutional origin. By acknowledging this research gap, this chapter analyses how OGD – as an initiative embedded into a certain institutional arrangement – can be explained by existing political institutions and decisions, specifically those currently leading and implementing

OGD initiatives. In order to study this influence, path dependence analysis is undertaken. Past decisions and their institutionalisation create political routes (Pierson 2000): trajectories with lock-in effects that are self-reinforced by feedback which is produced by existing institutions. This effect makes it more difficult to switch to a different trajectory, thus creating a path dependence in a particular institutional context. Among the several institutional trajectories exerting an influence on OGD (such as transparency, participation and data governance, among others), the focus of this chapter is the influence of preceding digital government institutions on OGD, taking Chile as a case study. In particular, our research consists of analysing how path dependencies that originated in the development of digital government institutions may determine Chile's current OGD policy outcomes. Led by the Modernisation and Digital Government Unit of the central government, OGD in Chile sits within a weak institutional environment. This digital government unit is preceded by a long institutional trajectory of public sector modernisation and e-government institutions, which may help explain why OGD has not fully taken off in the country to date.

With an overall purpose of analysing the influence of the digital government agenda on OGD by conducting path dependence analysis, the chapter is organised as follows: the following section provides a theoretical background on institutions and OGD, and on path dependence theory. Thereafter, the research methodology is defined, followed by the findings of this research, a discussion of the findings and concluding reflections.

Research background

Digital government institutions

Incorporation of digital technologies in the public sector has a long trajectory. ICT use in the public sector has been linked to efforts to modernise public service delivery and to manage efficiently large collections of data produced by public agents (Heeks 2006b). With the rise of new public management (NPM), those interventions gave birth to e-government policies to reduce bureaucracy and expand public service delivery (Heeks 2006b, Homburg 2004, Dunleavy 2006). However, ICTs have also been used in other areas, from basic public service delivery to more democratic areas of civil life. Digital technologies have been applied to incorporate civil society into participatory and collaborative public policies (Smith et al. 2011, Lathrop & Ruma 2010), thus widening its original use in the public sector – e-government – to a digital government paradigm: ICTs as enablers of different dimensions in state–society interaction.

Increasing cross-sectoral adoption of digital government practices requires formalisation of those practices within institutions to enable long-term intervention, facilitate coordination and provide resources (Heeks 2006b, Fountain 2001). An institutional framework for digital government can be

14

understood as a set of regulatory (laws or decrees governing digital technologies in the public sector), normative (specific ICT-related practices in public agencies) and cultural-cognitive (rationales/discourses awarded to ICTs) institutions to frame the development and operation of ICT initiatives in the public sector (Peters 2011). Institutional frameworks for digital government reflect on providing long-term resources, capabilities and political support/legitimacy to carry out cross-sectoral projects, and help reduce the influence of sectoral/individual rationales on the role of digital technologies in the public sphere (Heeks 2006b).

Different models of digital government institutional frameworks have been established to date (OECD 2016, Barros 2015), including: a) ministries for digital government, with high political legitimacy/authority and empowerment but less independent from dominant political ideologies; b) units or projects for digital government within a ministry, often highly dependent on the ministry's leadership and thus distant from top political support; and c) agencies for digital government, politically independent with higher levels of political stability but lower capacities to enact regulatory and normative digital-related institutions.

Selecting an appropriate model may determine the success of a digital government policy. Experts suggest that an independent agency or a ministry is more politically skilled and resourced to carry out long-term digital projects (OECD 2016, Barros et al. 2015). These institutional arrangements are more likely to obtain political legitimacy and support, to develop independent, long-term budgets, and to coordinate cross-sectoral strategies for digital development. By contrast, lower-level digital units are more focused on short-term initiatives and often lack political visibility and resources to carry out complex initiatives.

OGD and digital government institutions

The relationship between OGD and digital government can be theorised based on OGD's three foundational streams: open government, open data and government data. These three streams have a varying perspective on digital technologies but all see those technologies as fundamental: open government considers ICT as an enabler for transparency, participation and collaboration; open data represents technical standards and technological means to disclose datasets; and government data incorporates digital technologies to manage and use data created by public agents (Gonzalez-Zapata & Heeks 2015). Hence, OGD is a technological intervention of an intrinsic technological nature.

This aforementioned technological character of OGD has led, in some cases, to interventions being driven by digital government institutions (but also influenced by transparency and data governance-related institutions). Much of the advocacy and research on OGD claims that data disclosure opens up new opportunities to 'technologise' or 'digitise' the public sector by adopting 'open data by default' or 'open data by design' policies. These approaches often modify existing institutions by introducing: regulatory frameworks for data disclosure and management; technological platforms and standards or adoption of alternative practices to produce and manage public data; or new rationales for the role of public data in the relationship between state–society and data-intensive public policy (Gonzalez-Zapata & Heeks 2016). Thus, in all these new institutional forms there is a technological component that assumes an influence of OGD on existing digital government institutions. The influence of OGD on other institutions – such as those related to transparency and/or data governance – is also seen as important.

Other studies have made significant contribution to understanding OGD from an institutional theory perspective. Van Schalkwyk et al. (2016) study OGD under a series of variables that reflect its embeddedness in existing institutional arrangements and Styrin et al. (2017) analyse the institutional environment where OGD initiatives are implemented and acknowledge the role of these ecosystems in shaping current OGD outcomes. However, these and other studies on OGD do not pay significant attention to how these institutions have been constructed over time, nor the wider influence of digital government historical politics and political institutions on OGD.

Since OGD is embedded in existing ICT-related institutions, they may also play a significant role in determining how OGD policies are designed, implemented and operated. Hence, OGD and digital government institutions should be observed under a bi-directional relationship. Since OGD is rooted in a particular digital government institutional framework, certain institutional features may be inherited by OGD initiatives, thus constraining the disruptive character of OGD by following an existing institutional trajectory. Studying OGD under a historical institutional perspective facilitates understanding how these institutions have created paths over time that increase the likelihood that OGD will follow the same route and with similar outcomes. Consequently, our focus in this chapter is to attend to the reciprocal effect of historical digital government institutions on OGD.

Historical institutionalism and path dependency

Analysing the influence of digital government on the development of OGD involves paying attention to institutions. Institutions are universally accepted as 'rules of the game'; ways to regulate social life by enforcing formal/informal rules and to sanction violations according to social, rational and historical patterns (Scott 2013, Pierson 2004). Institutions are identified as stable but changing entities across time, with resilience being a key feature. They move and are moved by new social structures, thus adapting to new institutional environments. OGD initiatives can also be studied under institutional theory: they are framed by a series of legal and administrative rules to regulate data disclosure (regulatory institutions); diverse administrative practices and procedures to carry out data disclosure (normative institutions); and rationales and discourses to legitimise these initiatives (cognitive-cultural institutions) (Mahoney 2000, 2001).

Scholars have paid attention to understanding political phenomena by studying the historical formation of political institutions for a long time. By reviewing how institutions were formed in the past and how they have regulated social life through rules, practices and discourses, we can better understand how a policy is carried out or why it produces a specific impact. These concepts are foundational for historical institutionalism (HI), one of the three theoretical approaches of new institutionalism to study political and social formations through formal and informal institutions (Lowndes & Roberts 2013).

In particular, one of the ways to conduct HI research is through path dependence analysis (see Figure 1), which focuses on bringing past events and their formation sequences to light in order to understand those specific paths that are leading to observed outcomes over time. Path dependency is based on the premise introduced by Pierson (2000: 20) where 'what happened at an earlier point of time will affect the possible outcomes of a sequence of events occurring at a later point in time'. Path dependency reflects a lock-in effect: decisions taken in the past follow a particular route in determining where and how subsequent events occur, which makes switching to other alternative routes difficult and expensive. This lock-in effect is also reinforced by the feedback that existing institutions produce as an input in these trajectories (Thelen 1999). Hence, path dependency looks at historical events and patterns that produce lock-in events; in particular critical junctures that open up policy windows to create new or modify existing institutional trajectories, and help explain how future institutions are created and sustained across time.

Path dependency helps understand how change occurs in institutions: what events have the ability to have an influence in existing institutions in order to switch institutional trajectories (Mahoney 2000). Often these events are led by agents who promote and create new meanings that open up windows for disruption in institutional trajectories (Mahoney & Thelen 2010). Overall, path dependency analysis comprises of five steps:

1. Antecedent conditions: historical events which determine available policy options and shape selection processes;
2. Critical junctures: choice of a particular policy option among other alternatives;
3. Punctuated equilibrium: process of institutional stability disrupted by new critical events. It comprises two levels:
   a. Structural persistence: institutional production and reproduction of the selected policy;
   b. Reactive sequences: disruptive event(s) that may change lock-in of the selected option;
4. Outcomes: extent to which an institution is adopted as a consequence of path dependence.

In our research, path dependence analysis is used as a key methodological approach since it supports a critical understanding of the historical progression of digital government policies in Chile, helping explain current OGD implementation. Path dependence analysis for OGD thus requires studying key historical events in digital government in the country and how they affect further political institutions and policies such as OGD.

Figure 1: Path dependence theory

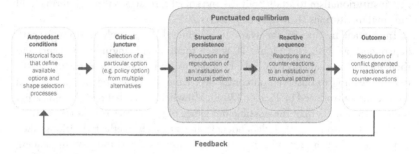

Methodology

This qualitative research investigates the historical influence of digital government policies and institutions on the development of OGD initiatives. In particular, we take the case study of Chile, its OGD initiative and its digital government trajectory. The recent political trajectory of Chile presents a rich development of new institutions after 17 years of dictatorship in order to boost the social, political and economic development of the country.

Currently, Chile follows a presidential governance system and a bicameral congressional legislature, with a stable democracy over the past 25 years. During these years, modernisation of the state through adoption of ICTs has been a significant element of digital policies across governments, by digitalising public service delivery or providing digital infrastructure.

Among these initiatives, Chile has been implementing an OGD stategy since 2011. To date, the OGD website datos.gob.cl comprises 2000 datasets from central government and an increasing number of local councils. These elements make Chile an interesting OGD case study. This chapter also covers Chilean digital government institutions from 1990 onwards, coinciding with Chile's return to democracy, for two reasons: first, covering the dictatorial period from 1973 to 1989 would significantly increase the amount of data to be analysed; and second, because the presence of ICTs in the Chilean public sector only began in earnest from the 1990s.

This chapter uses primary and secondary data sources. Fifty anonymous interviews with key actors involved in digital government and OGD were carried out in Chile during 2015. Interviewees were selected from five groups through the purposive sampling technique (Bryman 2008): politicians, public officials, public sector practitioners, civil society advocates and data users, and academics. While interviews represent the analytical core of this chapter, nine reports and official guidelines were used as secondary data sources to triangulate this evidence base, incorporating official views/discourses present in official documents. By transcribing all data as textual sources, these were analysed through template analysis (King 2012); by defining an initial template (list of codes derived from path dependence theory), textual sources were iteratively coded using NVivo10 to identify mis/match to the initial codes. A second and more refined template was then created with new codes developed during the first iteration, and applied again to the text until relevant findings were discovered.

Findings

Given that this chapter studies the impact of digital government institutions on OGD, we first conduct a path dependence analysis before analysing the impact of path dependence on OGD in Chile.

Path dependency of digital government institutions

This subsection follows a chronological structure according to the sequence of path dependence analysis. Three periods are identified: antecedent of digital government (1990–1994); critical junctures for digital government (1995–1999); and punctuated equilibrium (2000–2011). Finally, institutional outcomes are analysed.

Antecedent conditions for digital government (1990–1994)

With Chile back in democracy, the centre-left ruling coalition 'Concertacion' – led by President Patricio Aylwin – concentrated efforts on creating the conditions for stable and peaceful transition to a democratic system. Indeed, scholars agree that the key programmatic effort of Concertacion was to generate conditions for long-term governability (Boeninger 1997; Garreton 1995). Aylwin's government visualised that the Chilean state had to be modernised to enter into the global market, and awarded an operational role to digital technologies in those policies. Digital technologies thus became part of Concertacion's vision but were not much implemented over this period given the priority for social and political reforms. Other areas experienced a strong penetration of ICTs, such as the educational programme 'Enlaces' in 1992.

However, in 1994 Chile observed one of the most severe corruption cases in the country: Codelco, the world's largest copper producer and Chile's main public firm, was involved in a US$200m corruption case, and triggered a set of major political and administrative reforms (Araya & Barría 2008). In an attempt to safeguard Chile's incipient political stability and an increasing interest in subscribing to international trade agreements with key economic powers, Concertacion developed a major modernisation policy. This modernisation agenda – and the introduction of ICTs in public sector management – would only be designed and implemented during the second Concertacion administration led by President Eduardo Frei (1995–1999).

Critical junctures for digital government (1995–1999)

The risk of compromising Chile's incipient democracy and trust from both civil society and international investors triggered major political efforts to implement modernisation reforms. Added to Codelco's case, interest in trading with key global economies required improvement of Chilean institutions. Frei quickly organised a cross-sectoral committee for modernisation and reform of the public sector (Frei 1994), which suggested a series of key policies: improvements in civil service recruitment systems, a new procurement agenda, an incentive-based public policy programme, and reform in public service delivery based on ICTs, among others. This plan led to the creation of a second committee for e-government policies, coordinated by the Ministry of Economy, which developed a report with 61 initiatives to incorporate ICTs into Chilean public administration (Comisión Presidencial TIC 1999): an e-procurement system, one-stop shops for both citizens and firms, incorporation of electronic signatures and electronic documents, interoperability and digitalisation of public services, and a governmental intranet, among others. 'The agenda had a clear emphasis on promoting ICTs for bureaucratic and economic purposes' notes a former public official who worked on digital government.

However, this initial political impetus did not materialise into a formal, long-term institutional framework to sustain those initiatives. The agenda faced severe coordination and leadership issues: the government avoided the creation of a long-term unit or agency and relied on a cross-sectoral committee, fearing that sectoral ministries would not fully adopt the agenda. Iitiatives suggested by the committee were mostly pushed forward by a few empowered agents, but they lacked formal top political support to be implemented. Instead, interviewees observed that the political elite valued the powerful symbolism of the e-government agenda to transmit an image of modernity and efficiency concordant with major political programmatic priorities: 'Chile made use of ICTs to promote itself as a modern and efficient country, but there were mostly cosmetic changes rather than transformative interventions' highlights a public administration academic. Government also underestimated the institutional complexity of e-government: there was a clear absence of resources and regulatory-normative institutions to continue those initiatives over time (Ramírez-Alujas 2004). As a consequence, at the end of this period, the government intranet was the only project fully implemented, while political support focused on developing wider ICT-related public infrastructure, such as an expansion in internet connectivity.

This period is considered to be a critical juncture since it opened up a policy window for the development of a digital government trajectory; it also determined the foundational rationales and institutional framework for future digital government initiatives. The committee's report would become the navigational chart for future governments, but with no further institutional backing (in the form of regulations and aligned objectives/practices) to institutionalise it. The lack of formal institutions may be explained by dominant views awarded by the political elite to ICTs and e-government initiatives: ICTs were perceived as enabling tools to modernise the public sector with a powerful symbolism of modernity and efficiency, but were not associated with making major transformative reforms in Chilean bureaucracy: 'The challenge for Chile was to combine economic growth with an efficient public sector. We saw in ICTs an opportunity to foster both aspects' claims a former digital government public official. As a consequence, ICTs were promoted as innovative practices but, in reality, they represented mostly cosmetic changes to traditionally-embedded practices. Nonetheless, the outcome of this committee represented a transition in the country: although weakly, ICTs were introduced in Chilean public administration and became part of the common discourse around modernisation and economic growth, thus opening up a policy window for future interventions.

Punctuated equilibrium period (2000–2011)
Punctuated equilibrium is divided into two subsections: structural persistence (2000–2006) and reactive sequence (2007–2011).

Structural persistence (2000–2006)
In 2000, Ricardo Lagos took office as President of Chile. Urged by recurrent corruption cases and a political vision that ICTs may help address their negative impact, President Lagos gave the green light to continuing the implementation of the e-government agenda set in the previous term but realised that it required major political coordination. Hence, Lagos created a specialised programme at the Ministry-level Secretariat for the Presidency (SEGPRES), which assumed the coordination of all e-government initiatives through the Reform and Modernisation of the State Programme (PRYME) (2005). Moving e-government coordination to SEGPRES provided higher levels of empowerment and political legitimacy to those initiatives: SEGPRES is known as a key political ministry, close to the presidency and with sufficient legitimacy to carry out cross-sectoral initiatives. President Lagos promulgated special decrees for e-government, though these encouraged rather than legally framed those initiatives in Chile. According to a former digital government practitioner, 'This period is known as the golden age of e-government initiatives in Chile because there was significant political support.' Several initiatives materialised: an e-procurement system,

electronic tax systems, internal communication, and institutional websites, among others. These initiatives were consistent with the discourse of modernisation and reduction in the level of corruption present during this period, and thus were backed by sufficient political coordination, resources, and a clear mandate from the presidency (Lagos 2001).

Despite this positive momentum, there was no political will to institutionalise e-government in the form of a long-term agenda or formal agency within the government. PRYME was only a project-based programme for a specified period of time (SEGPRES 2007: 3), and much of the impetus for e-government came from the president himself rather than being fully backed by other cross-sectoral ministries or the political elite. Indeed, interviewees highlight that there was significant effort to obtain maximum local and international political reward from those successful initiatives, but significantly less disposition to run them in the long-term (see case of ChileCompra in Kleine 2013: 173). Hence, despite the presence of some political support, e-government-related institutions were not fully promoted, and efforts were concentrated on obtaining immediate outcomes. Interviewees also noted that, regardless of limited progression, this institutional framework was sufficient to operate key initiatives in digital government, while the government continued to gain an international reputation for the implementation of its e-government agenda.

The structural persistence period shows the progression of e-government initiatives in Chile, and how they were backed with political support and economic resources by President Lagos to consolidate a medium-term agenda during his presidency. Albeit valued by the government, e-government initiatives lacked an appropriate formal institutional framework. Despite political support, it was not sufficient to establish PRYME as a formal agency within the government; an issue that made this trajectory vulnerable to changing rationales around e-government and digital technologies.

Reactive sequence (2007–2011)
In 2006, President Michelle Bachelet took office. During the first year of her presidency, PRYME remained at SEGPRES and continued to implement a few pending projects from the past term, such as interoperability policies. However, at the end of 2006, Bachelet decided to cancel PRYME, and transferred all e-government initiatives to a new digital development unit at the Ministry of Economy (Secretaría de Desarrollo Digital 2010). Indeed, Bachelet perceived ICTs as enablers of economic growth, and partially disregarded the previous bureaucratic rationale (one of the key pending policies from PRYME was the recommendation to institutionalise the project in the form of a unit or agency, which did not occur during Lagos' term (SEGPRES 2007)): 'It seems that Bachelet underestimated the complexity of ICTs interventions. The movement to the Ministry of Economy was a clear mistake' notes an e-government academic.

With lower political legitimacy at the Ministry of Economy, e-government initiatives faced major political constraints during Bachelet's presidency, which affected other agencies' engagement. Interviewees agree that in the absence of the coordination legitimacy that SEGPRES had in the past, initiatives became much more complex to implement and required major political support and resources. Since these were not present during this period, e-government initiatives were reduced to a few sectoral projects.

Additionally, by awarding an economic meaning to the e-government agenda, Bachelet's government did not provide sufficient institutional resources to further expand and legitimise those initiatives. Notwithstanding this weak political foundation, the government developed a digital strategy for 2007 to 2012 (Comité de Ministros Desarrollo Digital 2007), which did correlate with a major emphasis on positive results from international e-government rankings (Heeks 2006a; United Nations 2008, 2010). However, the digital strategy was questioned by some stakeholders since it did not incorporate views from external agents such as civil society organisations or academia: 'Chile observes a systematic lack of active participation in the development of digital agendas. Besides, it seems that each government needs to reinvent the wheel. There is an evident lack of continuity in our digital strategies' (e-government academic). Critiques also focused on a lack of assessment of previous e-government efforts (such as PRYME) to plan future interventions. Interviewees highlight that e-government during this government exemplifies the nature of e-government initiatives in Chile: in the absence of formal regulatory and normative institutions, initiatives became more vulnerable to changing cultural-cognitive rationales, an issue that also revealed significant differences among sectoral ministries in ICT capacities, resources and infrastructure. Paradoxically, Chile continued to be regarded by the regional community as a leading country in digital government, thanks to key initiatives in public contracting, electronic invoicing and electronic tax declaration, among others.

In 2010, President Sebastián Piñera (centre-right) took office. Initially, e-government policies remained at the Ministry of Economy, but Piñera anticipated the complex political scenario that resulted from trying to lead those cross-sectoral initiatives from an isolated ministry. Thus, Piñera moved e-government back to SEGPRES and created the Modernisation and Digital Government Unit (MDGU). Piñera saw in MDGU an opportunity to deepen his rationale of bringing efficient practices from the private sector to public administration; one of the key reasons according to interviewees that further political and economic support was provided to the unit. MDGU also introduced an expansion from e-government practices to digital government by developing a four-year strategy based on three rationales: an efficient, citizen-centric and open government (UMGD 2011). Similar to other periods, this plan was not agreed upon with other stakeholders and did not assess previous e-government strategies. Coinciding with the global open government movement, MDGU assumed a leading role in the development of the Open

Government Partnership's (OGP) action plan by direct mandate of Piñera, who saw OGP as an opportunity to expand his regional leadership (OGP 2013): 'The President saw a good opportunity to became the Latin American Obama by supporting OGP. Added to the emphasis on efficiency, digital government was a good opportunity to promote himself in those areas' notes a former MDGU official. Chile's first action plan, similar to other countries, was concentrated on the digitisation of public services rather than participatory or collaborative initiatives, and thus helped to expand the initial rationale of efficiency through ICTs (Piñera 2012a). OGP gave major political visibility and legitimacy to MDGU (Gobierno de Chile 2012).

However, MDGU faced institutional constraints similar to those of the past. Although politically empowered, the unit did not receive any further formal institutional backing, remaining solely a project. This barrier caused MDGU's programmatic priorities to be based on maximising political reward for making visible its agenda and facilitating budget renewal, thus focusing on quick-wins rather than long-term strategies: 'Given MDGU is a project, it needs to become politically visible to gather politicians' attention. Our budget needs to be justified every year according to the results of our initiatives. There is an emphasis on short-term results' (MDGU practitioner). Besides, the weak institutional framework meant that the unit had to 'supplicate' to public agencies to convince them to engage in those initiatives, thus often reproducing existing ICTs' asymmetries: already-active agencies engaged with new initiatives, while less-resourced agencies were reluctant to participate.

Overall, the reactive sequence period shows how institutions responded to changes experienced during structural persistence. The transition to President Bachelet represents a change in the trajectory as digital government initiatives received lower levels of political support, institutional resources and funding. In this institutional framework, initiatives thus relied on sectoral efforts to overcome the lack of central political leadership. In addition, in the absence of a strong institutional framework, initiatives became vulnerable to changes in dominant political rationales and priorities, such as changes in leading agencies (for example, SEGPRES versus Ministry of Economy).

Institutional outcomes

Studying the institutional trajectory from 1990 to 2011 shows that the institutionalisation of digital government initiatives in the form of long-term, sustainable, formal and informal institutions is limited. In the absence of these institutions, digital government initiatives did not spread as initially expected but achieved a sufficient operational level to maintain the presence of ICT-related policies. Three institutional paths can be observed from this historical review:

- *Institutional path of de-institutionalisation and politicisation of ICTs:* The trajectory of digital government shows that ICT-related initiatives in the public sector have often not been backed with a strong institutional framework – in the form of regulation, long-term resources and political support – thus making them vulnerable to politicisation. Much of the disruptions seen in digital government trajectory come from direct presidential support and are subservient to other programmatic priorities such as reduction of corruption, entry into global institutions, or to project an image of modernity and efficiency. Indeed, as the evidence indicates, this institutional trajectory has significantly been shaped by the meanings different presidents have awarded to digital government across the years – from modernisation tools to enablers of economic growth. Presidents, as agents challenging existing institutional structures, had a major impact on conditioning digital government progression according to the meanings they awarded to this agenda. The influential role of presidents in defining digital government's agendas helps understand why digital government has followed an irregular trajectory during the period of study. Also, ICTs have also been commoditised by emphasising their technicality rather than their social nature, often being (incorrectly) perceived as an easy way to solve complex problems and as a source of political reward.

- *Institutional path of demonstrating modernity and efficiency through ICTs:* Since the introduction of digital technologies has been historically linked to modernisation efforts, initiatives have been systematically linked to an increase in the efficiency of Chilean public agencies – ICTs with bureaucratic purposes. While reduction of bureaucracy had a significant impact on Chileans' quality of life, there was no use of ICTs for democratic purposes, such as participatory and collaborative initiatives. Efforts in this area came from transparency and accountability initiatives, which did not emerge as part of any national digital government strategy.

- *Institutional path of emphasis on quick-win initiatives rather than long-term policies:* Evidence suggests a degree of short-termism by developing successive digital working plans/agendas, rather than developing and agreeing on a long-term strategy for digital government in Chile. Every government developed a brand-new strategy, but without properly assessing past experience to increase institutional learning. Thus, efforts were concentrated on developing quick-win initiatives, often reaching a sufficient operational level but lacking higher levels of appropriation and coordination with sectoral agencies.

One key question to answer is why these paths have occurred, and how they were reinforced over time. Evidence suggests that Chilean government was a 'victim of its own success'. As the country's digital government policies were successful and well-known to the local and international communities (United Nations 2003; 2010; 2012; Barros 2016), different administrations did not anticipate the need to improve domestic institutions in digital government. The existing format was sufficient to implement and operate these initiatives and to boost the country's political dividends. Hence, the reputation and success of a series of policies in digital government during this period acted as institutional feedback to reinforce these paths across years. Based on this historical analysis of digital government institutions, in the following subsection we reflect on the particular way these have influenced the development of OGD in Chile.

Influence of digital government institutions on OGD

Historical overview of OGD in Chile

OGD started in Chile in 2011. With the creation of MDGU, several public technologists were recruited, including those leading ICT-enabled transparency in previous presidential terms. These technologists saw in OGD an opportunity to deepen those transparency-related policies. However, OGD also received direct political support since Piñera saw an opportunity to increase his regional leadership in policies with significant global and local attention: 'the President gave direct support because it was important to become the first country in the region to have a national OGD website' notes a former MDGU official.

The initial publication approach was to deploy a functional platform as soon as possible. Anticipating the complex scenario to coordinate a cross-sectoral initiative from a unit with no further political legitimacy, MDGU extracted several existing datasets from sectoral agencies' websites without any further consultation. Once published, MDGU communicated their participation by letter to those agencies. The launch of the platform was also timed to coincide with Chile's first OGP action plan. Although already functional, MDGU included OGD publication in this plan to give more political visibility to the initiative. Interviewees at MDGU state that this quick approach helped Chile to become the first country in the region to have an OGD website, rhetoric that was often present in several interviews with OGD practitioners. In 2012 Chile had a functional OGD website – datos.gob.cl – with around 1000 datasets from several public agencies.

The initial take-off of OGD in Chile was reinforced by a presidential directive for open government and OGD. Piñera enacted a similar directive to that of Obama in 2009, which provided significant initial political backing to the initiative (Piñera 2012b). However, interviewees questioned the extent of the directive as it encouraged rather than regulated data disclosure in the country. The directive requests public agencies to release up to five datasets of social value, but it does not incorporate any further means of control. It does not provide any further operational structure within public agencies; OGD practitioners within sectoral agencies may be transparency or civil society participation officials, CIOs, etc. OGD life-cycles were not included, allowing public agencies to see OGD as a one-off initiative. The directive offers a minimum level of institutionalisation (unless the decree is formally derogated, OGD continues to be implemented) but it is insufficient to make it sustainable: 'the directive was made relatively soft so we did not have to compromise public agencies in tasks they were not able to fulfil' (former MDGU practitioner). Interviewees highlighted that this weak decree is the result of a dominant rationale to become the first regional country to have such a presidential backing for open government and OGD. A more complex directive would have required a long negotiation period with other public agencies and further political legitimacy that MDGU did not have. Indeed, interviewees stated that the dominant rhetoric to make Chile the first regional country to have such a presidential backing for open government and OGD sped up data disclosure but, at the same time, constrained its institutional framework.

During this term, MDGU did not set any policy to foster data publishing and reuse, and relied solely on the presidential directive and a technical guidance note (UMGD 2013). Besides, the directive did not incorporate any further policy to make effective use of those datasets, hence OGD became a disclosure-only initiative. The reality after its implementation was that agencies published under a minimum-effort scheme. Datasets were of poor quality and were rarely updated. Given the limited institutional framework provided to OGD, the challenge then became to re-engage with those agencies and create stable data disclosure practices. MDGU relied on its limited political legitimacy to try to 'evangelise' those agencies which did not continue to publish data. The rationale to convince them was that OGD would reduce bureaucratic externalities of active and passive transparency processes by giving priority to disclose most requested information in OGD formats (Gonzalez-Zapata & Heeks 2016). However, those datasets were not necessarily the ones with more social value or which helped unlock accountability and economic growth. In this process, MDGU found significant resistance from public agencies to open up their data, and it was not politically backed and resourced to develop more binding strategies. At the end of 2013 there were 1100 datasets, just 100 more than in 2011 and with insufficient quality levels.

In 2014, Michelle Bachelet took office again after four years. Contrary to past terms, MDGU remained at SEGPRES and their policies continued as during Piñera's term, but the agency lacked the political legitimacy conferrred to it in the preceding government. Similar to the previous term, MDGU did not develop any working plan or strategy for OGD in Chile and relied solely on past practices and the presidential directive. However, the change of government unveiled the weakness of the institutional framework for OGD. For instance, most sectoral data publishers were sacked for political reasons, thus data publication cycles were broken. Given that data publishing occurred on an informal basis (datasets and update cycles were at the discretion of each sectoral agency) there was an absence of dataset updates during 2014: 'the change of government exposes how weak the initiative was: we lost all the connection and advances made during the first two years' (MDGU official). Besides, MDGU did not have any formal way to exert control over those sectoral agencies, using again an 'evangelisation' strategy based solely on their political legitimacy and good connection with sectoral data champions. In this process, MDGU organised OGD introductory sessions and training to leading sectoral data publishers; a strategy that was not followed in the previous term.

As a result of this historical trajectory, Chile presents a weak OGD initiative. The initiative has been focused mostly on data disclosure, while policies to foster reuse and data-intensive policy-making have not been incorporated to date. Evidence from data reuse comes from MDGU itself by developing three applications for public service delivery.

Chronologically, OGD shows two momentums. During Piñera's term, the initiative achieved regional and global renown by quickly deploying an OGD platform with a high number of datasets. However, the lack of long-term policies and appropriation by public agencies meant that the initiative lost political momentum once Bachelet took office. This analysis is consistent with international OGD assessments such as the Open Data Barometer. In its 2016 edition, the Barometer showed that Chile, after leading OGD in Latin America, had one of the most dramatic drops in the ranking (from 15th to 30th), explained by lower scores in readiness and data availability (World Wide Web Foundation 2016).

Path dependency of digital government institutions on OGD

As a result of this historical trajectory, OGD has not been institutionalised in Chile to date. Evidence suggests a significant influence from digital government institutions on the ideological and operational ways in which OGD has been developed to date. While other institutional paths may be influencing OGD (indeed, transparency and data governance trajectories also have a significant and complementary role in OGD's development) this analysis and historical review provides interesting reflections regarding the role of the digital government trajectory in the OGD institutionalisation process in Chile.

Considering the aforementioned three institutional paths emerging from digital government institutions, path dependency can be observed in OGD:

* *Institutional path of de-institutionalisation and politicisation of ICTs:* Consistent with the trajectory of digital government, OGD shows a weak institutional framework as well as an emphasis on the political benefits that the initiative may bring to the government. MDGU has developed a limited institutional

28

framework for OGD, mainly given its limited empowerment and limited political legitimacy within the public sector. Indeed, the directive framing OGD does not include regulatory institutions that empower MDGU to operate OGD, and encourages rather than frames its implementation. Similar to the paths observed in digital government institutions, the meanings and emphasis awarded by different presidents in each of their terms are critical in implementing OGD. While President Piñera provided political support to implement OGD as he anticipated that Chile may assume a leadership position at regional and global levels, President Bachelet partially relegated the digital government agenda and, consequently, OGD policies. Presidents have influenced OGD's institutional trajectory by providing or limiting political support and legitimacy for its adoption and appropriateness. Interviewees emphasised this politicisation to justify the quick take-off of OGD in Chile and its limited progression over time. However, this support did not empower MDGU to deepen OGD practices or to create a more robust, systemic initiative.

• *Institutional path of demonstrating modernity and efficiency through ICTs:* The politicisation of OGD may be explained by dominant rationales in MDGU to promote ICTs in the public sector. Much of the political backing from President Piñera came from introducing 'a new way of governance' based on modernity, efficiency and managerial practices from his past entrepreneurial experience, but also to distance himself from mainstream governance practices that produced much of Chilean dissatisfaction with politics. Hence, his government provided major political support for the digitisation of public services (the main outcome from MDGU in his term) as well as OGD to deepen a discourse of efficiency and ICT-based policies. This rationale was also used to encourage public agencies to engage with OGD by reducing transparency-related externalities, such as significant workloads of passive and active transparency.

• *Institutional path of emphasising quick-win initiatives rather than long-term policies:* Similar to the digital government trajectory, OGD shows a predominance of short-term initiatives to speed up its take-off instead of policies which clearly state responsibilities, roles, funding and, most importantly, long-term objectives regarding how and why public datasets should be opened up. Initial efforts were concentrated on having a functional platform with as many datasets as possible in a short time, but there was a lack of further policies to make effective use of them, or to deepen dominant rationales further than reducing bureaucracy, such as an expansion of democracy, economic growth or innovation, among others. This weak framework was reinforced by an official directive which did not incorporate any of these elements and forced public agencies to release a minimum number of datasets as soon as possible. As a consequence, there was a limited adoption by most public agencies.

Similar to the digital government trajectory, evidence suggests that the Chilean government did not deepen its OGD policy framework given that the adopted model was sufficient for the purposes the agency outlined. Chile gained quick international reward for being the first regional country to implement an OGD initiative, as well as for having a dedicated directive with top political backing. The political benefits obtained were sufficient to sustain this operational model for OGD, acting as positive feedback that reinforced the paths outlined above. The approach undertaken by MDGU was sufficient to have a basic, operative OGD initiative, while deepening the existing institutional framework was disregarded (Gonzalez-Zapata 2016). However, during the period of OGD implementation, evidence suggests that Chile's digital government reputation was fading; the country observed how other regional countries continuously obtained positive assessments given their comprehensive approach to implementing digital government policies, as has been the case for Uruguay and Colombia (Barros 2016, United Nations 2014). Outside the period of study, the current digital government status in Chile has led the government to request a study from the OECD in order to provide a new institutional framework (OECD 2016). However, no political advances been observed in this direction to date.

Conclusion

Several institutions and institutional trajectories can influence OGD, such as those relating to transparency, data governance, digital government, and civil society participation, among others. These institutions can both facilitate and constrain OGD, thus affecting its institutionalisation process. This chapter solely addresses the influence of past decisions in digital government institutions on OGD implementation in Chile. Path dependency is observed in the rationales and regulatory institutions in digital government that determine how OGD is promoted and implemented, thus constraining its institutionalisation process in Chile to date.

Three influences of the trajectory of digital government on OGD are observed through this analysis – deinstitutionalisation and politicisation of digital initiatives, demonstrating modernity and efficiency through ICTs, and emphasis on quick-win initiatives rather than long-term policies. One key outcome shown by this research is that the institutional nature of OGD is embedded in existing, long-term institutional politics. Much of the advocacy and discourse supporting OGD speaks of the transformative power that data disclosure produces. Indeed, evidence suggests that OGD can help unlock disruptive, positive outcomes in some circumstances. However, one has to consider that OGD initiatives themselves carry, and likely reproduce, the very institutional features they attempt to transform. While existing digital government institutional trajectories may act positively in cases where digital government initiatives are part of a robust, cross-sectoral policy framework, they may be also acting as a constraint to develop impactful and transformative OGD initiatives where those institutions are limited and vulnerable to political ideologies. The case of Chile shows how a long trajectory of short-termism and politicisation of ICT-based initiatives can be reflected in OGD and, as a consequence, has a major role in its limited institutionalisation. This case highlights the influential role that presidents have in shaping the digital government trajectory and in OGD progression. Although we do not attempt to conduct a detailed study on institutional entrepreneurs, findings do reveal that OGD's trajectory is also shaped by the meanings and leadership awarded by the top executive political level, introducing change in that trajectory by either providing or restricting political backing to this initiative.

Results of this research show the relevance of taking existing dominant institutions into account to develop successful OGD initiatives, as well as the key role that top political agents play in the way OGD is developed. Certainly, existing institutions may condition how initiatives are planned and implemented, but OGD is not necessarily condemned to fully replicate those institutional trajectories. Indeed, the challenge to institutionalise OGD is to develop long-term policies that clearly state objectives, resources and responsibilities and, at the same time, evaluate dominant institutions and determine what the best approach is to overcome any constraining environmental conditions. Given that OGD faces institutional constraints which may reduce its transformative power, it should be understood under an institutional change perspective: how OGD initiatives may help gradually change the institutions they belong to, and the role that key actors play in such a dynamic. Path dependency observes that institutions recurrently face change and stability across time, and adapt themselves to those new environmental conditions. Future research may look at studying OGD from a perspective of gradual institutional change, as well as understanding the interaction of dominant institutional logics from OGD-related institutions. Additionally, further insights may be obtained from studying the role of other institutional entrepreneurs in introducing change at tactical or operational levels. Institutional theory is thus shown to be a suitable lens to understand the politics of OGD and to help develop more realistic and appropriate OGD interventions.

Acknowledgements

This research is part of Felipe González-Zapata's doctoral studies at the Centre for Development Informatics, University of Manchester, UK. The research is funded by the National Commission for Scientific and Technological Research (CONICYT) of the Government of Chile – Becas Chile.

About the authors

FELIPE GONZALEZ-ZAPATA holds a PhD in Development Policy and Management from the Centre for Development Informatics, University of Manchester, UK. He has a background in computer science and information systems. He has been a researcher and consultant on OGD since 2012. His doctoral research examined the relationships between politics, power and OGD in Chile. E-mail: felipegonza@gmail.com

RICHARD HEEKS is Chair in Development Informatics at the Global Development Institute, University of Manchester, UK; and Director of the Centre for Development Informatics. He has published several books on government, ICT and development, including *Reinventing Government in the Information Age* (1999), *Implementing and Managing eGovernment* (2006), and *Information and Communication Technology for Development* (2017). His research interests are data-intensive development, e-resilience and e-sustainability, digital development, and the digital economy in developing countries.

REFERENCES

Araya, E. & Barría, D. (2008). Modernización del estado y gobierno electrónico en Chile 1994-2006. *Buen Gobierno* 5(2): 80-103

Barros, A. (2016). Algunas reflexiones con nueva versión del eGov UN. [online]. http://www.alejandrobarros.com/algunas-reflexiones-con-nueva-version-del-egov-un/

Barros, A. (2015). Desarrollo digital, ¿qué institucionalidad tener? [online]. http://www.alejandrobarros.com/desarrollo-digital-que-institucionalidad-tener/

Barros, A., Campero, T. & Cabello, P. (2015). *Estudio para la Gobernanza Digital en Chile*. Santiago: Enable

Boeninger, E. (1997). *Democracia en Chile: Lecciones para la gobernabilidad*. Santiago: Editorial Andrés Bello

Bryman, A. (2008). *Social Research Methods*. 3rd edn. Oxford: Oxford University Press.

Comisión Presidencial TIC (1999). *Chile: Hacia la sociedad de la información*. Santiago: Comisión Presidencial 'Nuevas Tecnologías de Información y Comunicación'

Comité de Ministros Desarrollo Digital (2007). *Estrategia digital 2007-2012*. Santiago: Gobierno de Chile

Davies, T. & Bawa, Z.A. (2012). The promises and perils of open government data. *The Journal of Community Informatics* 8(2)

Davies, T., Perini, F. & Alonso, J.M. (2013). Researching the emerging impacts of open data ODDC conceptual framework. Washington DC: ODDC-World Wide Web Foundation

Dunleavy, P. (2006). *Digital Era Governance: IT corporations, the state, and e-government*. Oxford: Oxford University Press

Fountain, J.E. (2001). *Building the Virtual State: Information technology and institutional change*. 1st ed. London: Brookings Institute

Frei, E. (1994). *Instructivo Presidencial 06 sobre creación de Comité Interministerial para la Modernización del Estado*. Santiago: Gobierno de Chile

Garreton, M. (1995). Redemocratization in Chile. *Journal of Democracy* 6(1): 146-158

Gobierno de Chile (2012). *Plan de Acción 2012-2014 para la OGP*. Santiago: SEGPRES

Gonzalez-Zapata, F. (2016). Open Data Barometer 3rd edition: Regional report for Latin America. Washington DC: World Wide Web Foundation. www.opendatabarometer.org

Gonzalez-Zapata, F. & Heeks, R. (2016). The influence of the transparency agenda on open government data in Chile. In *Proceedings of the 6th International Conference for E-Democracy and Open Government*, CeDEM 2016. pp. 156-163

Gonzalez-Zapata, F. & Heeks, R. (2015). The multiple meanings of open government data: Understanding different stakeholders and their perspectives. *Government Information Quarterly* 32(4): 441-452

Heeks, R. (2006a). Benchmarking eGovernment: Improving the national and international measurement, evaluation and comparison of eGovernment. Manchester: University of Manchester

Heeks, R. (2006b). *Implementing and Managing eGovernment*. 1st edn. London: Sage

Homburg, V. (2004). E-government and NPM: A perfect marriage? In *Proceedings of the 6th international conference on Electronic Commerce*. pp. 547-555

King, N. (2012). Doing template analysis. In G. Simon & C. Cassel (eds.), *Qualitative Organizational Research: Core methods and current challenges*. London: Sage

Kleine, D. (2013). *Technologies of Choice?: ICTs, development, and the capabilities approach*. Cambridge MA: MIT Press

Lagos, R. (2001). Instructivo Presidencial 05 sobre gobierno electrónico. Santiago: Gobierno de Chile

Lathrop, D. & Ruma, L. (2010). *Open Government: Collaboration, transparency and participation in practice*. 1st edn. Sebastopol: O'Reilly

Lowndes, V. & Roberts, M. (2013). *Why Institutions Matter: The new institutionalism in political science*. 1st edn. London: Palgrave Macmillan

Mahoney, J. (2001). Path-dependent explanations of regime change: Central America in comparative perspective. *Studies in Comparative International Development* 36(1): 111-141

Mahoney, J. (2000). Path dependence in historical sociology. *Theory and Society* 29: 507-548

Mahoney, J. & Thelen, K. (2010). *Explaining Institutional Change: Ambiguity, agency and power*. Cambridge: Cambridge University Press

OECD (2016). *Digital Government in Chile*. Paris: OECD Publishing

OGP (2013). Chile and Open Government Partership. http://www.opengovpartnership. org/countries/chile

Peters, B.G. (2011). *Institutional Theory in Political Science: The new institutionalism*. 3rd edn. London: Continuum

Pierson, P. (2000). Increasing returns, path dependance and the study of politics. *The American Political Science Review* 94(2): 251-267

Pierson, P. (2004). *Politics in Time: History, institutions and social analysis*. Princeton: Princeton University Press.

Piñera, S. (2012a). *Instructivo Presidencial 02 sobre Digitalización de Trámites Públicos*. Santiago: Gobierno de Chile

Piñera, S. (2012b). *Instructivo Presidencial 05 sobre gobierno abierto*. Santiago de Chile: Gobierno de Chile

PRYME (2005). *Agenda de Gobierno Electrónico*. Santiago: Gobierno de Chile.

Ramírez-Alujas, A. (2004). *El Proceso de Reforma del Estado y Modernización de la Gestión Pública en Chile: Lecciones, experiencias y aprendizajes (1990-2003)*. Madrid: Instituto Nacional de Asuntos Públicos

Scott, W.R. (2013). *Institutions and Organizations: Ideas, interests, and identities*. London: Sage

Secretaría de Desarrollo Digital. (2010). *Plan de Acción Digital 2010-2014*. Santiago: Ministerio de Economía, Fomento y Turismo

SEGPRES (2007). *Informe Final de Evaluación: Programa de Reforma y Administración del Estado (PRYME)*. Santiago: Gobierno de Chile

Smith, M.L., Elder, L. & Emdon, H. (2011). Open development: A new theory for ICT4D. *Information Technologies & International Development* 7(1): 3-9

Styrin, E., Luna-Reyes, L.F. & Harrison, T.M. (2017). Open data ecosystems: an international comparison. *Transforming Government: People, Process and Policy* 11(1): 132-156

Thelen, K. (1999). Historial institutionalism in comparative politics. *Annual Review of Political Science* 2: 369-404

UMGD (2011). *Estrategia de Gobierno Electrónico 2010-2014.* Santiago: Gobierno de Chile

UMGD (2013). *Norma Técnica para Publicación de Datos Abiertos en Chile.* Santiago: SEGPRES

United Nations (2014). *E-Government survey 2014.* New York: United Nations

United Nations (2012). *E-Government survey 2012.* New York: United Nations

United Nations (2010). *UN e-Government survey.* New York: United Nations

United Nations (2008). *UN e-Government survey.* New York: United Nations

United Nations (2003). *World Public Sector Report 2003: E-government at the crossroads.* New York: United Nations

Van Schalkwyk, F., Willmers, M. & Schonwetter, T. (2016). Institutionalising open data in government. *SSRN.* DOI: 10.2139/ssrn.2925834

World Wide Web Foundation (2016). *Open Data Barometer 2015.* Washington DC: World Wide Web Foundation

3.

Beyond standards and regulations: Obstacles to local open government data initiatives in Italy and France

Federico Piovesan

Introduction

Despite national and supranational directives and growing interest in the potential of data-driven analysis, the majority of local public administrations have failed to implement progressive open government data (OGD) agendas. The aim of this study was to collect anecdotal evidence about how local public administrations (PAs) in Italy and France have initiated OGD agendas, what difficulties they have encountered, and how they have tackled them.

The study was motivated by the idea that 'open data needs to go local' (World Wide Web Foundation 2015). The research conducted attempts to shift the focus beyond the 'usual suspects', namely legal and technological issues, to include a perspective that looks at the individuals that are supposed to implement the OGD agendas, and at their inter- and intra-office interactions within local PAs.

A preliminary framework is proposed to help inform the empirical research by offering a common framing to the diverse experiences discussed both in the literature and interviews. The framework is based on interdisciplinary literature that integrates two concepts from evolutionary economics, namely routines (Coriat & Dosi 1995) and satisficing (Simon 1955) with the open data dynamics model (Helbig et al. 2012) and the multi-level perspective from science and technology studies (Martin 2014).

Following the presentation of the framework, the literature is reviewed – covering a wide range of legal, social and technical obstacles that hinder OGD agendas – and observations gleaned from 14 interviews about local OGD initiatives in Italy and France are presented. While anecdotes are far from being a complete representation of reality, they may nuance our understanding of the dynamics involved in changing information management within public administrations.

Both Italy and France have national OGD agendas with dedicated agencies in charge of drafting and implementing reforms. At the time of writing, France's national ranking in terms of open data was higher than that of Italy.[1] However, the research presented in this chapter shows significant differences between PAs within both countries, which suggests that national benchmarks partly overlook the intricate dynamics underlying each initiative.

OGD implies restructuring how public employees collect, process and archive data, as well as how PAs manage and share information. This chapter explores seven issues interfering with the successful implementation of OGD agendas: privacy, data ownership, economic obstacles, interoperability, release order, real-time data, and lack of resources.

Three main findings emerge: the impact of cultural factors on organisational change; the need for more research about implementation costs, the economic and social impact of OGD, and privacy issues; and the disregard for the perspectives of users.

The chapter starts by introducing the theoretical framework and the methodology. It then reports on the empirical findings (stemming from the comparison between literature and interviews) before moving on to a discussion of the study's key findings. The chapter ends by highlighting the limitations of the approach before concluding.

Theoretical framework

The theoretical framework adopted is composed of an interdisciplinary set of concepts that attempt to include the perspectives of relevant stakeholders; address the diverse dynamics that regulate their interactions; and account for the context in which OGD initiatives are embedded.

After providing a working definition of OGD, two concepts are introduced – routines and satisficing – that describe how public organisations and employees can interact with the changes in habits and procedures required by OGD agendas. In the following section, the open data dynamics (ODD) model by Helbig et al. (2012) discusses the activities and forces that surround OGD supply. Finally, this section borrows from Martin's (2014) multi-level perspective to frame the evolution of open data dynamics within their socio-political context.

OGD is public sector information (PSI) that has been released online in compliance with the open definition. According to the European Commission (2003) PSI, includes 'any content whatever its medium (written on paper or stored in electronic form or as a sound, visual or audiovisual recording) when produced by a public sector body within its mandate'[2] or, in other words, a

---

1   Based on the 2015 editions of the Global Open Data Index (http://index.okfn.org) and of the Open Data Barometer (http://opendatabarometer.org).

2   The original PSI directive excluded 'documents held by public service broadcasters and their subsidiaries [...]; documents held by educational and research establishments [...]; and doc-

common repository of knowledge whose collection, management and archival is largely financed through tax-payer money.

Making PSI available online is important for ethical and practical reasons since OGD can fuel social and economic innovation. Indeed, there are mainly four dimensions that are usually covered in the literature and raised by OGD advocates (see, for example, Davies 2010, Davies & Bawa 2012, Gray 2014, Janssen et al. 2012). The first is transparency, since open public information provides access to indicators of government performance. Second, OGD can foster positive economic spill-over as it fuels the market for data-driven products and services, which can promote entrepreneurship and employment. The third reason is improved efficiency as PAs are likely to be the first re-users of OGD in order to improve resource allocation and make public services more effective. Finally, OGD can be a tool for citizen empowerment thorough co-design, co-creation and co-development of innovative responses to public needs. As Gray (2014) observes, however, usually 'social justice, equality and other values take the backseat' in high-level political speeches, official communications and policy documents about OGD. Nevertheless, related initiatives are often considered as a building block of open government practices (Lee & Kwak 2012).

Routines and satisficing

Both routines and satisficing come from evolutionary economic theory. While the former describes the recurrence and evolution of practices within organisations, satisficing frames sub-optimal decision-making as a product of bounded rationality.

Nelson and Winter (1982) used routines as the unit of analysis in their theory of economic change. Over the years, routines have held many 'complementary yet different meanings in economics and business literature' (Becker 2003). This research draws from Coriat and Dosi (1995), whose conceptualisation presents two characteristics useful to the research. First, routines are inherently collective, as opposed to the individuality of habits. Second, routines have a double nature since organisations use them to learn how to undertake tasks and solve problems while also employing routines as a tool to govern and coordinate.

Coriat and Dosi (1995) sought to understand why so-called 'superior' organisational forms[3] diffuse slowly (or not at all) within industries and across countries. 'Firms are crucial (although not exclusive) repositories of knowledge' and routines are the building blocks of their competences; hence 'competences do not only involve problem-solving skills concerning the relationship between

---

uments held by cultural establishments [...].' Details may change in subsequent versions and national directives.

3 The paper examined built on a number of previous studies that investigated a variety of private companies whose 'superiority' was defined in terms of higher competitiveness and innovative outputs.

the firm and the outside environment, but also skills and rules governing internal relationships' or, in other words, competences emerge from the consolidation of collective routines (Coriat & Dosi 1995). Moreover 'firms are behavioural entities embodying specific and relatively inertial competences, decision rules and internal governance structures which, in the longer term co-evolve with the environment in which they are embedded' (Coriat & Dosi 1995: 11). It follows that the problem-solving and governance routines that form an organisation's competences cannot be transferred easily to other organisations due to what the authors call 'partial tacitness', namely the complexity of absorbing 'inertial competences' that emerged and evolved over time within a specific environment (Coriat & Dosi 1995).

Coriat and Dosi connect the resulting inflexibility to literature on path-dependency and lock-ins (for example, the work of Freeman 1982, Rosenberg 1985, Dosi et al. 1988, Saviotti & Metcalfe 1992). For this study, public administrations that do not operate in competitive markets and are subject to centralised forms of control – meaning that routines in local PAs can be influenced by directives from national agencies – are not included. Routines are expected to prove valuable in explaining heterogeneous performance across local administrations because centralisation and lack of competitiveness may hinder an organisation's capacity to change routines and thus build new competences.

While routines can help explain barriers to innovation within an organisation, satisficing frames the habits of individuals and the challenges involved in changing their daily routines.

Simon (1955) used satisficing to explain decision-making in circumstances where there is no clear optimal solution. The word comes from the combination of satisfy and suffice, and thus represents a compromise between the best solution and the available cognitive resources. Simon referred to bounded rationality to describe how individuals are most often unable to evaluate all potential outcomes with sufficient precision because they do not know the probability of each outcome and possess only limited memory. For this study, insufficient data literacy and/ or skills, lack of time, or unwillingness to change one's habits can affect the development of OGD agendas because workers may satisfy when complying with data-related practices.

To provide some concrete examples with respect to the literature on OGD, in their case studies, Helbig et al. (2012) highlighted elements of reluctance to change, low willingness to share information, risk aversion, power dynamics and internal conflicts. Wirtz et al. (2016), on the other hand, used a cognitive science approach to explore cultural barriers to OGD implementation in Germany. They examined five barriers and concluded that the most influential ones were risk aversion from public – which can be related to a low willingness to step out of defined routines – and the potential damage that increase transparency may bring to the administration.

Open data dynamics

Helbig et al. (2012) describe the dynamics surrounding OGD as an information polity: 'a collection of stakeholders, data sources, data resources, information flows, and governance relationships involved in the provision and use of government-held and non-governmental data sources.'[4]

The OGD information polity is composed of knowledge stocks, information flows and feedback loops. Knowledge stocks are entities that accumulate or deplete over time. Information flows, on the other hand, define the rate at which a stock can change, and are influenced by a variety of factors that entail various activities, some more objective than others.

On one side of the spectrum lies automated data collection, for example when electronic devices send temperature measurements to a weather database. On the other end, there is collection that relies heavily on the collector's judgement, such as medical data on a patient's mental status. It follows that 'usability of data, or its fitness for use, depends in large part on the nature of the encoding processes and data management practices' (Helbig et al. 2012).

Data owners exercise governance on their respective sources – i.e. the data they collect – and resources – i.e. the devices and infrastructure used to gather, store and retrieve knowledge. Owners also hold the responsibility to make information 'fit-for-use' before they publish it online, which entails anonymisation; removing meaning conflicts (i.e. describing data in a way that is understandable to people lacking the domain knowledge of public employees, including technical jargon); and being mindful of the adverse consequences that may damage data providers and/or users, or result in pressures to hide data.

While data owners exercise governance on their data and infrastructure, public institutions also exercise governance on the information environment – namely the 'different contexts from which data is extracted, encoded, and otherwise made visible'. Governance involves 'formulating policies; initiating social and technical processes; regulating standards, meaning and interpretation; and adding value' (Helbig et al. 2012).

Moreover, governance can be reciprocal: providers affect users through data provision, incentives, sanctions and persuasive methods, but users can affect governments through political processes and direct participation in decision-making (for example, through advocacy, shifts in consumer behaviour or social mobilisation).

This reciprocity of both information flows and governance reinforces the notion that stakeholders should strive for mutual collaboration.[5] Dawes (2010) considers

---

4 Data resources are defined as the tools (such as software, networks, platform, and organisational arrangements) that a data-holder uses to provide data.

5 Chignard (2009) introduces three concepts to describe the public perception of society with respect to OGD and government. The *famille liberale* considers the opening of public information as a mean for civil society to press the public sector and to promote economic actors. The *famille*

stakeholders in an information polity as stewards of primary (governmental) and secondary (non-governmental) data sources, who 'share responsibility for data accuracy, validity, security, management, and preservation' – in other words making data 'fit-for-use' can be a collaborative endeavour between primary and secondary users.

Finally, Helbig et al. (2012) introduce feedback loops as a significant process of open data dynamics. Feedback loops contain endogenous knowledge that travels through the system and that, through iteration, can influence future actions. A loop can be reinforcing when it tends to strengthen its initial input, thus leading to the growth or collapse of a specific set of practices. On the other hand, balancing loops counteract the initial action and resist change.

One way to initiate feedback loops is to engage external actors (i.e. secondary users). Most studies examined in my review, however, do not mention the importance of systems to collect and react upon feedback from secondary users who, on the other hand, could help by signalling mistakes and missing observations or support data maintenance.

Open data advocates often claim that sharing public knowledge will lead the community of potential re-users to propose innovative solutions, unthinkable if information was kept under some form of restricted access. Hellberg and Hedström (2015) confronted this idea in their sixth myths of open data:[6] 'the myth of public interest in the reuse of open public data. The open government agenda, as well as research on open data, often takes citizen interest in open data for granted. We believe that not everyone is interested in using public data, even if they have the necessary resources and competences.' However, as Zuiderwijk and Janssen (2014) point out, there is need for more research focusing on the perspective of users.

Multi-level perspective

The multi-level perspective (MLP) was originally developed in science and technology studies to describe the diffusion of innovations in complex socio-technical systems.[7] Figure 1 shows how innovations can be conceptualised as aggregates of factors that simultaneously co-evolve through different levels of diffusion – from niches to the landscape level – while facing resistance from the current status quo.

---

liberale-libertaire sees OGD as a mean for citizens to exercise their right to inspect and control the public sector, which is generally seen as flawed and corrupt. Finally, the famille participative sees open data as an opportunity for citizens to collaborate with, rather than oppose, the public administrations.

6 They refer to the work of Janssen et al. (2012) who advanced the other five myths.

7 Geels (2002), for example, applies it to the transport sector when analysing the shift from horse-drawn carriages to automobiles. More recent research uses MLP to imagine possible trajectories from our current carbon-intensive system to one where renewable energies are predominant (for example, Foxon et al. 2010, 2013).

Figure 1 Multi-level perspective

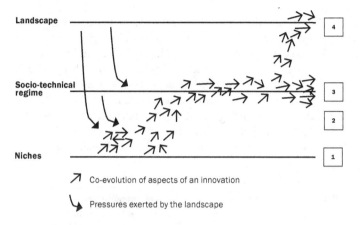

⬈ Co-evolution of aspects of an innovation

↳ Pressures exerted by the landscape

Source: Martin (2014)

Innovations develop in niches, outside the mainstream and are mainly supported by far-sighted groups and individuals. As they diffuse more widely, innovations approach the socio-technical regime, which is defined by prevailing technologies, rules and practices. Finally, the landscape level consists of super structures, rules (both normative and explicit) and artefacts that are deeply embedded in the fabric of society – such as prevailing political ideology, institutions, economic paradigms and socio-cultural values.

While previous sections discussed the nexus between stakeholders, information stocks, contextual pressures, and reinforcing or balancing dynamics that form the OGD ecosystem within each organisation, the MLP frames how the evolution of such ecosystems interacts with external forces, where system stability and innovation result from dynamic interactions of social and technical factors within and between each level (Martin 2014).

Within the limited temporal scope of this study, OGD in local public administrations most likely exists within niches and one would not expect to observe a significant evolution through these levels. Martin (2014), however, referred to resistance to innovation coming from the landscape level since OGD can be considered as a 'disturbance to existing practices, in that they alter some combination of technical, political, and social factors that influence governance'. Hence, the MLP was used to frame pressures (such as economic and political ideologies) that guide individual decision-making without being part of internal policy or management guidelines.

41

Methodology

For this study, a literature review of previous empirical studies covering PAs in different European countries is combined with observations gleaned from 14 interviews with individuals involved in OGD initiatives in Italy and France.

Empirical studies were examined and selected between November 2014 and February 2015. Four studies in particular presented a collection of obstacles categorised according to the authors' own criteria, as show in Table 1. To aid comparison with data collected during the interviews, the last column reports the categories (each labelled with a number) used to classify obstacles in the study. None of the studies was about Italy, and only one includes a French case.

Table 1 Summary of previous studies

Author(s)	Countries	Methodology	Obstacle Categorisation
Janssen et al. 2012	NL	Literature; interviews; workshops	[1] Institutional; [2] Task complexity; [3] Use and participation; [4] Legislation; [5] Information quality; [6] Technical
Martin et al. 2013	DE, FR, UK	Case-study (DE, FR); literature analysis (UK)	[1] Governance; [2] Economic issues; [3] Licence and legal framework; [4] Data characteristics; [5] Metadata; [6] Access; [7] Skills
Barry & Bannister 2014	IR	Literature review; interviews	[1] Economic; [2] Technical; [3] Cultural; [4] Legal; [5] Administrative; [6] Risk-related
Martin 2014	UK	Survey	[1] Digital technologies; [2] User practices; [3] Public management; [4] Institutions; [5] Resources

Interviews took place between February and April 2015. Previous to that, the researcher took part in two public events dedicated to OGD. The first was *Spaghetti Open Data 2015* in Bologna, Italy, and the other was *Infolab*, organised by the Paris-based think tank *Fondation Internet Nouvelle Génération* (FING). Attendance allowed the researcher to familiarise himself with the OGD communities in both countries.

The aim was to interview people who worked for or collaborated with public administrations that implemented OGD agendas or were in the process of doing so. To approach interviewees, the researcher used a combination of email questionnaires and snowball sampling. First, an email was sent to all the contacts gathered during the two events, introducing the research goals and presenting a short questionnaire. Some initial questions were used to collect information on each respondent's job, affiliation and role within their organisation.

Both at the beginning and at the end of the questionnaire, respondents were offered the opportunity to discuss each question in more detail during an in-person interview or a call (either through phone or Skype). Finally, at the end of an interview, each respondent was asked whether they knew other people who could be contacted.

Table 2 provides the final list of participants, their nationality, a letter to identify them in the following sections, and relevant information about their organisation, job position and OGD initiative. While the sample is relatively small and more interviews were conducted on the Italian case, all respondents had enough experience within their organisation to be considered as qualified respondents.

One semi-structured interview was conducted per participant, during which respondents were asked to share their experiences about their local OGD project. The aim was to gather specific knowledge on their information sharing procedures; the obstacles encountered during OGD campaigns; and (when applicable) how these were addressed or what strategies each interviewee would suggest. Each interviewee was allowed to steer the conversation to prevent bias on the part of the researcher and to avoid any suggestion on relevant obstacles, though this approach may have limited the number of issues discussed (this and other limitations are presented below). Finally, each participant was asked to confirm the statements included in a draft version of this text one month after being interviewed.

Table 2 List of participants in the order they were interviewed

Country	Code	Role	Organisation's function	Scope	Age of OGD programme
IT	A	Dispute office	Collect taxes and revenues	Municipality < 100,00	None
IT	B	Administrative	Social security	Municipality < 100,00	3 years (March 2012)
FR	C	Head of OGD division	Think tank	-	Not relevant
IT	D	Head of IT services	Local government	City < 400,000	4 years (2011)
IT	E	Programme manager	Public ICT service provider	Province > 500,000	3 year (2012)
IT	F	IT Director	Environmental protection	Region	Not yet started (end of 2015)
IT	G	Researcher	Scientific research	National	5 years (2010)
FR	H	Innovation and R&D manager	Telecommunications	International	10 years (2005)
IT	I	Head of innovation management	Local government	Municipality < 15,000	1.5 years (late 2013)
IT	J	Manager of OGD initiative	Local government	Province > 500,000	3 years (2012)
FR	K	Director of OGD Initiative	Local government	Province > 1,500,000	2 years (early 2013 + 1-year pre-phase)
FR	L	Director of OGD Initiative	Local government	Region < 7,000,000	4 years
IT	M	Director of Open Data	Local government	City > 600,000	2 years
IT	N	Consultant, PhD in privacy and cyber security	Consultancy, research	Province > 500,000	3 years (2012)

Findings

Seven categories of obstacles emerged during the interviews: privacy, data ownership, economic obstacles, interoperability, release order, real-time data and lack of resources. Each of them was mentioned by at least two interviewees and all but one (i.e. real-time data) were also found in the four empirical studies presented in the previous section.

Following Zuiderwijk and Janssen (2014) there was an expectation to find those high-level impediments mentioned in the literature and more detailed anecdotes from the interviews. Hence, findings were combined by providing in each of the following sections a summary of the literature (as tables) and a discussion of the anecdotes collected through the interviews. The former are discussed in more detail when complementary with the discussion prompted by the latter.

Privacy

Table 3 Literature review of obstacles relating to privacy

Janssen et al. 2012	Martin et al. 2013	Barry & Bannister 2014
[1] Unclear trade-off between public values	[3] Personal data and privacy	[6] Data protection
[4] Privacy violation	[6] Need to identify	
[4] Security		

Martin 2014
[3] [4] Government organisations face challenges balancing privacy concerns with the public interest when opening up data
[1] [3] [4] Government organisations face legal barriers, such as data protection law, that prevent the opening up of data

Almost all respondents considered privacy to be a key obstacle to their initiative. For example, D and G mentioned two examples related to educational data. The former, who works in a small-town PA, needs data from the Ministry of Education to offer basic services to students and their families. The latter, on the other hand, works in a publicly-funded research centre and is captivated by the potential of big data from schools and online education platforms. However, neither one can access educational data due to privacy regulations.

'Privacy can be a double-edged sword,' explained N, a cyber-security researcher that offers consulting services to his local PA. 'Think for example of an open business registry with information about restaurants that include their owners' names. While restaurant being included means that owners renounce some of their privacy, they may care more about free advertisement from a mobile application about local restaurants. However, that same data could be aggregated with other information (for example, from social networks) that may lead to unforeseen privacy violations, like targeted marketing.'

E argued that privacy is sometime used as a smoke screen to avoid data opening. For instance, his office does not publish the list of recipients of social aid as open data, although the law does not consider it sensitive information and that same list is published in PDF format.

When it comes to privacy, usually local administration does not exercise much governance on the information environment: national and supranational institutions are the ones that influence policy. Data owners, on the other hand, are responsible for properly anonymising whatever data they make public.

Three interviewees (D, G and J) affirmed that their OGD platforms are currently unfit to host sensitive information. In their opinion, platforms should allow restricted access to specific datasets so that only public employees or third parties that abide by non-disclosure agreements (such as researchers) would be able to re-use that information.

Solutions (or compromises) must account for several variables (like the type of data released) and allow for flexible opt-in and opt-out possibilities. OGD portals that allow public-worker identification can help to hide sensitive information from the public but sound cybersecurity would still be necessary since data will be vulnerable to attacks once it is released.

According to N, however, solving simultaneously the legal and technical nature of privacy issues is not sufficient: 'the very architecture of the Internet makes this a trans-disciplinary problem. Currently there is no clear answer: you either renounce a part of your privacy or refrain from sharing the information.'

Data ownership

Table 4 Literature review of obstacles relating to data ownership

Janssen et al. 2012	Martin et al. 2013
[1] Emphasis of barriers and neglect of opportunities	[1] The relevant administrative level
[2] Duplication of data, data available in various forms, or before/after processing resulting in discussions about what the source is	[3] Licence is not open enough
	[3] Heterogeneous licenses across datasets
	[3] Stacking of rights
[3] Threat of lawsuits or other violations	[3] Rights on data already engaged
[4] Dispute and litigations	[3] Rights on data are stacked
[5] Lack of information	[3] Legal framework concerning data in general
[5] Lack of accuracy of the information	[3] Intellectual property
[5] Incomplete information, only part of the total picture shown or only a certain range	[3] Not uniform licences
[5] Obsolete and non-valid data	[4] Decrease in the quality of data
[5] [Essential] information is missing	[4] Data are dependent on the state
	[7] Misinterpretation of data

Barry & Bannister 2014	Martin (2014)
[4] Litigation and liability	[1] [3] Government organisations do not have
[5] Security	comprehensive data inventories, and so face
[6] Abuse and fraud	challenges in identifying the data they could
[6] Misinterpretation	make open
[6] Errors	[3] Individuals and groups within government
[6] Consequences	organisations perceive significant risks of open
	data being misused
	[1] [3] Individuals and groups within government
	organisations view many existing datasets as
	poor quality and unsuitable for making open
	[1] Limited interoperability between ICT systems
	impedes the release and use of open data
	[1] [2] [4] Potential open data users will be
	more concerned about the stability and quality
	of open data

Five participants (D, I, J, K and M) mentioned opaque data ownership as an obstacle. G's public research centre, for example, faces issues related to data ownership when publishing research based on information sourced from different organisations. 'When we publish a map of seismic risk across Italy – which is composed of different layers of information coming from several organisations – the result of our work should be published as open data. However, we can only share the aggregate map because each of the layers that make up the map was not released as open data. The other option would be to draft an individual agreement with each original data owner,' he explained.

Another interviewee discussed how data ownership is inevitably connected to responsibility and how organisations will bear any adverse consequences that may derive from opening certain datasets. 'This can be a huge deterrent to release' said F, who works for an environmental monitoring agency, while explaining how geo-referenced data can lead to unpleasant consequences when, for instance, higher pollution levels are observed on or close to private land. Regardless of validity, land owners that consider that data as harmful may sue the organisation that published it. 'Things are even more complicated when companies own the land,' he added.

Uncertainties about data quality and resulting legal repercussions can be used as a smoke screen to prevent information release. 'In my experience risk aversion is a stronger deterrent than loss of power over valuable information,' said J, who proposed a 'best-effort policy for newly published data-sets', according to which PAs have an initial period where the adverse consequences of improperly published information are less burdensome.

According to Conradie and Cohenni (2014), ownership is affected by hierarchy of data storage, data collection practices, and use of data. Public agencies may use data that is key to their function but was not produced internally – i.e. they are primary re-users of another organisation's data. It may then be unclear who owns the information that the PA may eventually derive from that data.

J and E both suggested that a system for inter-agency data requests could address the reticence to publish due to opaque or partial ownership. On one hand, inter-agency communication would clarify opaque ownership while written agreements would distribute liability. On the other, it would also provide a good starting point for linking databases.

In K's organisation, it is assumed that all information should be published and each office evaluates the legal fitness of their datasets. Class A data presents no risk; class B presents unclear risks (and is therefore published in formats that do not easily lend to machine processing like PDF and DOC); and class C data presents substantial risk and is not made available. Datasets are then passed onto the president's office, whose final approval is necessary in any case.

'By categorising risks before release, our managers can focus only on problematic datasets,' he explained. In K's case, new routines were introduced to distribute governance on primary sources (namely data produced by the organisation) throughout different offices, though this remained an isolated case across both the literature and the interviews.

Economic obstacles[8]

Table 5 Literature review of economic obstacles

Janssen et al. 2012	Martin et al. 2013
[1] Revenue system is based on creating income from data	[2] Sustainable business model for the production of data
[1] Fostering local organisations' interests at the expense of citizen interests	[2] Endangering the business model of companies already re-using the data
[3] Having to pay a fee for the data	[2] Inappropriate pricing for re-users
	[2] Endangering current business model of administration
Barry & Bannister 2014	
[1] Fees and funding	[4] Formats require proprietary/paying software
	[7] Privatisation of benefits

Martin 2014
[1] [3] [5] Government organisations that open data can no longer use the data as a bargaining tool with other organisations
[3] [5] Government organisations will lose financial income by opening up data, as they currently generate revenue from some data

Most examples related to economic obstacles discussed during the interviews were connected to datasets characterised by high potential for re-use,[9] with Italian respondents unanimously agreeing that there were *de facto* blocks to the

---

8   The obstacles discussed in this section relate to the resistance towards an economic model based on open knowledge as opposed to intellectual property rights. Problems related to lack of financial resources are discussed below.

9   All are included in the list of valuable data by the Open Data Index (http://index.okfn.org/dataset/).

release of datasets such as cadastral data (owned by the Land Registry Office), company registries (Chamber of Commerce) and income data (Tax Revenue Office). In France, only the company registry was not open at the time of the interviews (OKFN 2014).

J gave an example about public transit data, the opening of which proved extremely laborious due to incumbent agreements between her municipality's transport office and a private company that planned to use that data for their services. Eventually the agreement was renegotiated and the data released.

E had a similar experience with meteorological data: while his administration was committed to release meteorological data, the adjacent province (which shared the meteorological station with E's municipality) was committed to protect its business models based on the sale of weather data to private companies. 'As long as private companies are willing to pay for PSI, things will hardly change' he added when talking about location data (including postal codes which are open in France but not in Italy). D shared her own example about cadastral data, for which her office 'had to undergo long negotiations before obtaining a one-time bulk download from the local Land Registry Office, though nothing could be agreed about updates'.

On K's platform, all data can be accessed for free. However, 'there has been an internal debate for some time now about whether we should charge for high-resolution pictures from the local museum's artworks'. In K's opinion, it was unclear whether potential revenues would be worth the cost of setting up a sales infrastructure to monetise on the interest of art enthusiasts. H faced similar doubts when explaining how his 'organisation's first attempt to engage with open data failed because, not understanding the value of reuse, we asked customers to pay for it'.

In E's province, the PA can manage cadastral data independently and thus could experiment with an alternative model. Since the change, everyone can access a 'basic' datasets through the province's OGD portal that is updated every six months. Users who need 'valuable' documents, on the other hand, still need to request them through conventional means (at a price).

By introducing a new routine, and challenging the conventional model that prioritises revenues from PSI provision, E's organisation reduced the volume of requests that its employees must handle while allowing them to focus on those users who were more likely to pay: 'After an initial investment – mainly for quality checks on the first dataset published – resources were diverted to more profitable activities.' E underlined how this 'resulted in a positive impact on our agency's revenue'.

Economic obstacles are prominent both in the literature and interviews. They include some of the most significant barriers to openness because they involve multifaceted issues that are connected to each socio-political context. For example, strong reluctance to publishing an organisation's information may be due to perceived risks to their current funding model and/or control and power over valuable information.

Interviews show how reluctance may be due to consolidated routines promoting the idea that sharing one's knowledge can lead to loss of revenue, or how incumbent public–private partnerships complicate or impede opening PSI. While in the former case resistance comes from the landscape level, the latter shows substantial obstacles (namely a commercial contact) that exist at the socio-technical level. And while one may be overcome through a shift in political will, the second requires innovative models such as the model experimented with in E's organisation. E's experimentation initiated a feedback loop that resulted in a positive impact on the organisation's allocation of resources. One cannot ignore, however, that it was made possible by a mix of willingness to experiment new routines and models of data governance that most Italian PAs, who do not own cadastral data, would not be able to replicate.

Benefits from experimentation, however, may not always be so clear, as shown in K's and H's experiences. Case studies could help compare returns and costs of managing a sales infrastructure, thus highlighting benefits and risks of data opening according to data type and organisational arrangements.

While political will is necessary to overcome reluctance and to define data ownership in a more transparent way, some datasets are more expensive to maintain than others. Agencies could charge for curated datasets with legal value or APIs, while experimenting with electronic payments might induce reluctant agencies to consider data release (and also reduces the costs of maintaining the sale infrastructure).

Interoperability

Table 6 Literature review of obstacles relating to interoperability

Janssen et al. 2012	Martin et al. 2013
[1] No uniform policy for publicising data	[1] Inconsistency in public bodies
[2] Duplication of data, data available in various forms, or before/after processing resulting in discussions about what the source is	[1] Risk of quartering: States/greater region/ Europe
[3] Registration required before being able to download the data	[3] Restrictive access
[4] Prior written permission required to gain access to and reproduce data	[4] Data available in heterogeneous formats
[6] Fragmentation of software and applications	[4] Only part of data is available
[6] Legacy systems that complicate the publicising of data	[4] Data buried in silos
	[4] Incompatible with other data
	[4] Incompatibility with other applications
Barry & Bannister 2014	[5] Lack of single standard to describe datasets
[2] Standards	[5] Lack of consistent standards
[4] Legislation	[6] Balance between free access and the need to know the use of data
[4] Licensing	[6] Need to register
	[5] Metadata unstructured

According to interviewees, lack of interoperability stems mainly from two problems. The first relates to outdated ICT infrastructure and incompatible software hindering data exchange. The second relates to heterogeneous bureaucratic procedures that can slow down daily exchanges of information, with offices bearing most of the consequences.

For A – who works in a local branch of the national tax authority – getting basic information such as a citizen's address (held by the local municipality) can take from a few hours to several days: 'It really depends on who picks up the phone.' Information is then sent via fax or PDF, and A needs to extract it manually. His agency has lost ongoing legal disputes due to delays in similar exchanges.

B works for the national social security agency and often needs to exchange information with the tax authority.[10] The flow of information works well from the social security agency to the tax authority while the other way around is 'complex and time-consuming' (and to her knowledge, no one can really explain why).

Another aspect that emerged is a lock-in with ICT service providers. Many Italian PAs outsource their IT software and service to in-house companies.[11] According to J 'if you want to change your information management structure you must take these businesses into account' who hold key knowledge about the PA's ICT infrastructure and whose contract with the public sector is often vital to their business.

Different publishing practices can also be an issue. With budget data, for instance, most PAs employ different layouts that hinder comparability and thus the re-use of such information.[12] One respondent also mentioned the risk of quartering between big urban centres and smaller cities while two more argued that data from smaller urban centres has low value unless it is aggregated with that of adjacent cities.

What emerges from the interviews is that interoperability will remain a complicated goal as long as OGD practices and technical standards do not reach a stable socio-technical regime. Most participants agreed that updating or changing software is hardly considered a priority in their PA and, while open source solutions (like CKAN) are free and allow customisation, implementation still requires time and trained personnel.

Incumbent agreements with ICT providers cannot be ignored: J's example shows socio-technical practices in the public sector can also be contrary to what one would expect from organisations influenced by market logics (cf.

10 INPS (the social security agency) provides *Agenzia delle Entrate* (tax authority) with information on workers' contracts and their duration, which are used to verify whether company revenues correspond to the human capital they employ. On the other hand, the tax authority gives INPS income data, which is used to verify that social transfers match earnings.

11 In-house companies are financed with public money while being managed as private companies (for example, their shares are traded on the stock market, hence they must be profitable).

12 To create the *Open Bilanci* platform (http://openbilanci.it) 'several expenses had to be harmonised and aggregated in order to allow for historical and geographical comparisons' (Openpolis 2014).

previous section). Hence, interoperability is not only a matter of homogeneity in technological standards that can be overcome mainly through software updates. It can also be hindered by a tradition of public agencies with diverse internal routines and whose communication regimes with other administrations vary considerably.

For these reasons, the implementation of OGD agendas might vary across municipalities and guidelines should nudge towards open and sustainable practices while accounting for differences in resource availability. OGD advocates (both internal and external ones) could take a mediating role on both technical and communication matters between ICT departments and/or providers and data-owning offices. While the latter may lack data processing skills, they possess domain knowledge that can promote re-use, for example, through meaningful metadata. In J's opinion 'we are facing a paradigm shift and a generational shift simultaneously: old and new should collaborate, and probably need to be protected from the logic of the market'.

Release order

Table 7 Literature review of obstacles relating to release order

Martin et al. 2013	Martin 2014
[1] Public policies not consistent	[1] [3] Government organisations own large amounts of data and so face capacity challenges when reviewing, releasing, and maintaining open data
Barry & Bannister 2014 [5] Policy	[3] [5] Government organisations lack a coherent vision for funding open data and promoting open data use

In K's organisation employees have to categorise datasets before opening them; data is then released according its degree of risk. In J's administration, on the other hand, each office was asked to publish at least one dataset (they could freely choose which) to let employees familiarise themselves with the new routines involved in data release. Consequently, they focused on ownership and liability issues on a case-by-case basis, which in some cases slowed the process down but allowed intra- and inter-office knowledge transfers that were valuable in subsequent experiences.

The two other interviewees discussed data priority work in organisations that publish fewer data types. While in G's public research centre releasing data is part of their mandate, there is no plan (to his knowledge) to release administrative data. F (who works in an environmental monitoring office) explained that 'in my experience, it is better to start with data from electronic sensors; then move onto data that needs to be validated in a laboratory; and finally data about checks on areas that include private land'.

There is little discussion about data priority in the literature, and only four respondents addressed this problem – but it could be useful, especially for PAs who approach OGD for the first time, to have guidelines on which data to open first. E proposed data catalogues – listing all the information agencies hold and what they can release as OGD – as a potential solution to help PAs understand where to focus their efforts in early phases. These may also represent an opportunity to categorise data according to its risk; pilot projects with non-problematic data could allow employees to familiarise themselves with OGD routines while avoiding risk. While the first phases are most demanding in terms of cost and effort, maintenance and updates also require resources. E mentioned how the 'most downloaded datasets eventually become the better-curated ones'.

Real-time data

While three interviewees mentioned this issue, none of the examined papers from the literature discussed it. F talked about issues with water-level monitoring, arguing that releasing data in real-time may lead to unforeseen consequences, such as faulty sensor signalling imminent emergencies and panic spreading before the agency can confirm accuracy. G referred to similar issues when talking about data from the National Institute of Geophysics and Volcanology. Finally, E talked about highway traffic data and explained how data from sensors in Italian highways is published once a year, thus preventing a wide range of meaningful re-uses.

Although previous literature does not discuss real-time data, the volume and relevance of information whose collection is automated through electronic sensors will increase as the number and variety of devices expands. As 'smart city' initiatives become more prominent, electronic sensors will be used to measure, among others, traffic (both human and vehicles), resource consumption and environmental data in both urban and rural areas (Greenfield 2013).

The examples discussed in the interviews show how different data sources require appropriate contextualisation and legal framing. Agencies may refrain from data release due to potential meaning conflicts or wrong observations. In some instances – as with sensors that can signal imminent emergencies – fear of legal repercussions could obstruct important innovations such as automatic monitoring.

F thinks that 'real-time data could be published with a 24-hour delay, leaving time for human validation before releasing any information'. In case of emergency, the administration would have time to take preventive action before informing citizens. E proposed a more open solution, saying that PAs could involve citizens in monitoring data validity. Hence, real-time data could be accompanied by a disclaimer alleviating the PA's responsibility for faulty sensors, while validated data would be released after official confirmation.

Lack of resources

Table 8 Literature review of obstacles relating to lack of resources

Janssen et al. 2012	Martin et al. 2013
[1] No resources with which to publicise data (especially small agencies)	[2] The cost of opening data
[2] Lack of ability to discover the appropriate data	[2] Benefits and return on investment
[2] Focus is on making use of single datasets, whereas the real value might come from combining various datasets	[1] Devolution: fragmented resources
	[2] Lack of cashable savings
	[2] Implementation costs: hardware and software
[3] No time to delve into the details, or no time at all	[5] Incomplete metadata
[3] Unexpected escalated costs	[5] Not enough information on data formats
[3] No time to make use of the open data	[7] Language barrier
[3] Lack of the necessary capability to use the information	[7] Unfamiliar with metadata
[3] No statistical knowledge or understanding of the potential and limitations of statistics	[7] Need of domain expertise
[5] Unclear value: information may appear to be irrelevant or benign when viewed in isolation, but when linked and analysed collectively it can result in new insights	**Martin 2014**
	[5] The absence of an evidence base demonstrating the value of open data makes it challenging to create compelling business cases for open data projects
[5] Too much information to process and not sure what to look at	[3] [4] Government organisations are not empowered to develop markets for open data
[6] Data must be in a well-defined format that is easily accessible: while the format of data is arbitrary, the format of data definitions needs to be rigorously defined	[1] [3] [5] In government organisations delivering open data the IT costs are high
	[3] [5] There are limited efforts and resources dedicated to promoting open data to potential users
[6] Lack of meta standards	[3] [5] Potential open data users lack the specialist knowledge required to interpret the data
[6] No standard software for processing open data	[1] [5] Government organisations lack the expertise in the technologies required to deliver open data
Barry & Bannister 2014	[3] [5] The business case for open government data projects must be made within the context of reductions in public spending and the scope of public services
[1] Resource constraints	
[2] Technical capacity	

Three types of resources were discussed during the interviews: financial resources; technological resources (more advanced software, hardware and network infrastructure); and human resources (including skills and willingness to invest effort in OGD activities). These often overlapped: for example, several Italian interviewees confirmed that a prolonged under-investment in technological infrastructure led to slower machines, outdated software and, more importantly, technicians unaccustomed to technologies necessary to set up and maintain OGD platforms.

K had an arguably atypical experience: 'Our office had a substantial budget that we could use to hire an external consulting company that helped define and plan key aspects of our initiative'.[13] While in his opinion this approach delivered satisfactory results, its cost may not be sustainable for most public agencies, especially small organisations whose budgets are fiscally constrained by an austerity-led socio-political regime.

E and J's agency followed a different strategy with less ambitious goals, namely starting by opening one dataset per office, as described above. Although they incurred lower costs (around a tenth compared to K's programme) problems had to be dealt with as they emerged, resulting in more resources being invested in their OGD project.

M's experience is at the opposite end of the spectrum with respect to K's. His local OGD initiative was set up by volunteers: 'Thanks to the ongoing development of open source software, widely applicable legal tools, and open guidelines we had the necessary tools to set up a platform based on sustainable standards that will result in lower adaptation costs in the future'. His experience, however, was very demanding in terms of time and effort by volunteers, making it hard to replicate.

The resources that can be invested in technical advancements vary in each municipality and ICT expenses are seldom a priority in financially constrained organisations. In some cases, they may also depend on incumbent agreements with ICT service providers. Hence, precise estimations are complicated by a lack of comprehensive cost-benefit analysis coupled with the diversity of local experiences.

Time constraints can also be a problem. In K's agency, where substantial resources were invested in preparatory activities aimed at improving data awareness, several employees reportedly considered OGD-related tasks unnecessary or of low priority and were thus not able to comply with requests from the OGD department 'due to lack of time'. Sometimes, even when individuals showed interest in OGD-related activities, their managers would pressure them to focus on tasks they considered more important.

Technical resources should be addressed according to needs and availability of funds. Open-source software can be a less expensive or free option, does not imply the commitment to proprietary solutions and promotes interoperability in the long term. However, changing technological tools means changing routines, which will inevitably require an investment of human resources.

When financial resources are available, organisations can hire new employees or revise agreements with incumbent ICT service providers to gain technical expertise. The absorptive capacity of an organisation will affect how easily new technologies can be integrated with current routines. Employees at all levels need to master the activities necessary to open PSI, including data collection

---

13 € 300 000 for a department of 1.5 million people. Consultancy services included legal issues, technical solutions, data governance, database inventory, platform prototyping, and a communication plan – both internal to raise employees' awareness and external to engage the local community (mainly through social networks).

(for example, including contextual information as metadata), data processing (for example, respecting the requirements for open format tabular datasets) and data release on the platform (for example, licensing). On the other hand, public administrations are already endowed with domain experts: employees that, while 'data illiterate', understand the context where data is collected. Hence, while technical expertise is necessary to set up and maintain platforms, contextual knowledge is key to provide meta-information that will foster re-use. Workshops, regular cross-office meetings and promotional activities can help bridge between diverse set of skills.

Discussion

In this section, the focus is on three main reflections that emerged from the comparison of the interview data and from the literature within the framework of study: the importance of cultural factors in organisational restructuring; the need for further research about diverse issues in implementing OGD agendas; and a 'non-result', or in other words something that none of the participants mentioned: the perspectives of users.

Organisational restructuring through cultural change

There was a recurring theme in most of the interviews: implementing OGD agendas implies that consolidated organisational routines – those determining how individuals carry out their tasks, how they communicate and interact with each other, and how manager-level employees approach change – need to change. Relevant practices span across all the different phases of opening PSI and, in turn, impact each organisation's knowledge stocks and flows as well as feedback loops that promote or impede change (Helbig et al. 2012). According to the MLP, on the other hand, cultural obstacles are framed within landscape pressures, defined as artefacts that are deeply embedded in the fabric of society – such as prevailing political ideology, institutions, economic paradigms and socio-cultural values (Martin 2014).

Relevant examples were discussed with respect to data ownership issues (risk aversion), economic obstacles (moving away from sales-based revenues), interoperability (need for increased collaboration between old and new practices), and lack of resources (internal resistance due to public workers not understanding or not agreeing with the value of open data.). For example, both respondents and the literature mention lack of willingness or time to delve into OGD activities. According to some, this was due to low data literacy, lack of resources (both financial and human), or unwillingness to change habits. Hence changing routines may not be enough. Workers need to invest considerable effort in learning and assimilating new routines, and this requires a shift in their beliefs: they must consider OGD activities valuable.

In such cases, satisficing can help explain how people tend to protect 'business as usual' routines. With OGD activities dispersed along the public information value chain, employees may satisfy when collecting or processing data. For instance, they may not include full contextual information (i.e. metadata) because it seems tedious and unnecessary. Executives may also satisfice when, while being committed to share their organisation's knowledge, they press their employees to focus on other tasks.

The fact that OGD practices are still at the niche level also plays a role: as a respondent remarked 'it is hard to advocate for a radical change in routines when the public value that can be derived from OGD is yet to be proven'. Most participants also mentioned a broadly defined 'human factor' as a key to success throughout different parts of the interviews.

Based on the experiences collected, one can see how support from political leaders can help to legitimise new routines. Moreover, promotional and training activities (such as events and workshops) can help address doubts among employees and increase the absorptive capacity of those directly in charge of OGD collection and maintenance.

Despite cultural obstacles, four interviewees were convinced that OGD introduced significant changes to the routines of their organisation. Increased dialogue across offices was a prominent example, which led to improved internal efficiency and was positively valued by most employees. Two participants recounted how 'several months after our OGD project had started, employees from different offices (among whom there used to be no communication) were signalling mistakes about their data and sharing advice on how to solve them'.

Organisational knowledge management also appears to be affected by personal and power relations within and across departments. While routines are the building blocks of an organisation's knowledge, conflict and power dynamics are also cemented in its structure. Since OGD agendas can lead to data owners losing control over the information they produce and the revenues they can earn from data, new initiatives are likely to face strong resistance and conflicts at all levels: from relationships between employees in local administrations to political struggles across agencies.

Some PAs have taken a proactive approach to the issue by setting up a dedicated department or team that manages communication and coordinates activities.[14] OGD teams could map internal actors and their relations (both professional and personal); propose OGD supervisors within each department or office; work closely with external stakeholders to understand what datasets are in demand; and define organisational tools (for example, software, workshops, guidelines) for information opening activities. Moreover, these offices can help address doubts harboured by all stakeholders and promote cooperation among employees.

---

14 Examples include dedicated offices led by so-called 'open data evangelists' in the US and the 'chief data officers' in France.

Further research

Since OGD is still at a niche level and research on local contexts is still in development, some of the issues discussed during the interviews highlighted the need for additional experimentation. Few organisations, however, possess the resources (and perhaps political will) to risk venturing into 'uncharted waters', as one interviewee put it. Moreover, some issues cannot be decided at the local level.

As regards privacy issues, for example, case studies can to help clarify risks and benefits involved in opening different types of data. There is a need for analysis on the trade-offs between protecting one's information and the public interest.[15] Sensitive information could be provided to those who agree not to disclose it; lest governments lose opportunities for data-driven research.

Research is necessary to quantify the financial and human resources required to deploy OGD programmes as well as to release and maintain datasets. Moreover, there is a demand for clearer accounts of the economic and social impacts of OGD as fiscal constraints remain a major obstacle to OGD initiatives.

The Open Data 500 network, for example, investigates how SMEs in selected countries are using OGD in their businesses, and shows the aggregate impact on national economies.[16] However, case studies accounting for the efficiency gains derived from OGD-related routines (similar to the example on cadastral data discussed above) are still lacking.

Finally, sharing know-how will lead to improved guidelines for requesting data (both across agencies and from external actors) and changing internal routines. These can be adapted from previous works that are published under non-restrictive licenses. Examples include *Bordeaux Metropole*'s guide to citizen data requests;[17] the Open Government Implementation Model of the city of Vienna, which offers a tool to categorise data risk (Krabina et al. 2012); and *The Open Data Handbook* (Open Knowledge Foundation 2015).

Finally, the most recent Italian national guidelines provide both technical and legal guidance as well as laying out organisational tasks and responsibilities.[18] In the drafting of the latest edition, external stakeholders were consulted about how to improve the new guidelines, opening to a collaborative framing of the Italian OGD environment.

---

15 See McCann and Green's (2013) definition of public interest as 'not intended as public attention, but instead [as] interests like democratic accountability, justice and effective oversight'.
16 OpenData500 is a research project by the GovLab at NYU (http://www.opendata500.com).
   The Italian edition of the project can be found at: http://www.opendata500.com/it/. There is no
   similar initiative in France.
17 See http://www.bordeaux-metropole.fr/sites/default/files/guide-demande-open-data_0.pdf.
   Something equivalent could advise public workers about inter-agency data requests and ownership determination.
18 The latest 2016 edition can be found at: http://www.dati.gov.it/sites/default/files/LG2016_0.pdf.

The perspectives of users

Within my framing of the open data dynamics model, secondary users (namely external actors operating outside public institutions) were included as a force that can initiate positive feedback loops that promote change of routines but also support maintenance of OGD repositories through reciprocal governance. Indeed, throughout the interviews, a number of issues arose where involving users could help address (at least in part) some of the obstacles.

For example, interviews that discussed economic obstacles and/or release order issues, mentioned a difficulty in deciding whether all available PSI should be open at once (perhaps unrealistic in most of the cases examined) or that more valuable datasets should be prioritised. Choosing *a priori* which datasets are valuable, however, is not a simple task; collaborative data catalogues that integrate user-driven feedback could help PAs understand which datasets they should focus on in the early phases.

M's experience – where a group of volunteers started and maintained the local OGD initiative – shows how expertise can be harnessed to some degree from the local community. This is more likely to be a rare scenario rather than a replicable experience and user engagement cannot be predicted nor included in assessments of available resources.

Though the strong focus on the supply-side of this study coupled with semi-structured interviews may have limited the scope of the analysis, interviewees maintained a rather inward perspective on OGD-related issues. While one participant lamented how hard it can be to justify further investment on experimental ventures that do not show results in the short term, none considered cultivating the user community as a necessary step. Users could signal mistakes in the data, request more information and meta-information, thus cuing public workers about how to improve collection and processing activities. This may also give a sense that their efforts are being valued.

Limitations

The goal of this research was to provide concrete examples of the obstacles encountered by PAs that engaged in OGD programmes, at either municipal or provincial level. By using a strongly qualitative approach, it aimed to integrate a theoretical framework with a more pragmatic perspective. There are, however, important shortcomings that should be accounted for.

A first limitation is the relatively small set of respondents and the unbalanced division of participants between the two countries under study, with 11 Italian interviewees and only 4 from France. The majority of Italian examples meant that interesting anecdotes could not be compared with the French socio-political context. For example, in the section discussing economic obstacles, it is highlighted how several valuable datasets (for example, cadastral, location, weather forecasts) are still largely unavailable as open data in Italy. Since this does not apply to their context, French respondents did not mention related issues. Understanding what resistances OGD advocates north of the Alps may have faced in releasing similar data, could nuance an understanding of the factors that impede data opening.

The choice of using semi-structured interviews may have also limited the number of issues discussed. While fluid conversations prevented researcher bias from influencing respondents, these might have focused on the problems that seemed most relevant at the time of the interview. Moreover, by examining only the supply side of OGD provision none of the interviewees discussed issues related to lack of user engagement.

Moreover, interviews lasted between one and two hours. Comparable literature did not specify the duration of their engagement with participants – in this research project one session per participant was conducted. While all interviewees were asked to confirm the statements included in the text one month after the interview, some issues may have been solved and new ones may have arisen since the end of the research period (i.e. June 2015).[19]

Finally, a few considerations on the theoretical framework. The combination of interdisciplinary theories helped to develop an understanding of the different experiences gleaned from the interviews within a common frame of analysis. A number of conceptual tools were chosen in an attempt to provide a more nuanced understanding of the OGD ecosystem. Routines and satisficing illustrate the decision-making processes of organisations and individuals respectively, while the open data dynamics model represents how knowledge stocks and information flows are influenced by wide range of activities and pressures. Finally, the multi-level perspective framed the diffusion of open data within its socio-technical context.

The open data dynamics model and the MLP were useful to explain the internal and external factors that affect knowledge management within PAs. Organisational knowledge management is, however, also affected by personal and power relations within and across departments. In this respect, approaches like the one proposed by Van Schalkwyk et al. (2016) provide a more comprehensive description of the connections between internal and external pressures.

Further research and more data collection is needed to refine the structure of the framework. For example, there are broad concepts that require a more rigorous definition (for example, those related to the 'human factor'). A second round of more structured interviews would also allow for delving into aspects that were not discussed by many participants (for example, release order and real-time data), or by none at all (like the perspective of users).

---

19 For example, at the time of writing (September 2016), France has actually stopped releasing data about land ownership and location (http://index.okfn.org/place/france/).

Conclusions

The aim of this study was to collect anecdotal evidence about how local PAs in Italy and France have initiated OGD agendas, what difficulties they encountered and how they may have tackled them. During the interviews, the perspective was informed by a preliminary theoretical framework that explored the different dimensions involved in making PSI available online – namely individuals, organisations and the socio-political environment in which they operate – and by a comparison with other empirical studies that explored similar issues in different European countries.

This approach was used in the hope that anecdotes, when combined with a theoretical framework, could help nuance the current understanding of PAs complex dynamics. In accordance with the literature, significant legal and technical barriers to the release of PSI were found. Moreover, there is an important cultural dimension that affects the restructuring of knowledge management in public administrations. Despite knowledge's increasingly crucial role for economic and social development, sharing PSI implies loss of control and revenues and political and conflict dynamics are resisting this shift.

The study's qualitative approach led to the emergence of three key results: the importance of cultural factors in organisational change; the need for further research about implementation costs, economic and social impact, and privacy issues; and the lack of efforts devoted to understanding the perspective of users. The latter point proves that PAs can still draw from their local communities. By encouraging feedback, they can crowdsource contributions for data collection and maintenance. Private companies and entrepreneurs can help to lead the development of data-driven products and services while civil society and citizens can pool resources to create innovative solutions to public problems and promote government legitimacy through monitoring initiatives.

The results presented in this chapter, although far from being generalisable, offer cues for reflection on the pragmatic obstacles to OGD diffusion and implementation at the local level. This research confirms the need to understand OGD initiatives within an evolving ecosystem composed of stakeholders that, despite their seemingly different incentives, can benefit from increased cooperation and open knowledge. What emerges is the image of organisations that lack financial resources and technical know-how, and while more open knowledge management models could help, PAs tend to resist change because of cemented routines and risk aversion towards the exposure of their inner workings to the public.

Acknowledgments

I would like to thank all the interviewees who agreed to be part of this research, as well as all those who contributed with their insights and experience. I would also like to thank the reviewers who were an invaluable help to the improvement of this paper.

About the author

FEDERICO PIOVESAN is a doctoral student in urban and regional development at the Interuniversity Department of Regional and Urban Studies and Planning (DIST), Polytechnic of Turin. Federico researches the relationships between communities and their urban spaces in emerging digital societies. Currently his main focus is the impact that ICT is having on participatory processes. E-mail: federico.piovesan@polito.it

REFERENCES

Barry, E. & Bannister, F. (2014). Barriers to open data release: A view from the top. *Information Polity* 19(1,2): 129–152. DOI:10.3233/IP-140327

Becker, M.C. (2003). The concept of routines twenty years after Nelson and Winter (1982): A review of the literature. *DRUID Working Paper* No. 3-6. Copenhagen Business School, Department of Industrial Economics and Strategy/Aalborg University

Coriat, B. & Dosi, G. (1995). Learning how to govern and learning how to solve problems: On the co-evolution of competences, conflicts and organizational routines. *IIASA Working Paper WP-95-006*. Laxenburg: International Institute for Applied Systems Analysis

Davies, T. (2010). Open data, democracy and public sector reform. http://www. opendataimpacts.net/report/

Davies, T.G. & Bawa Z.A. (2012). The promises and perils of open government data (OGD). *Journal of Community Informatics* 8(2)

European Commission (2003). Directive 2003/98/EC of the European Parliament and of the Council of 17 November 2003 on the re-use of public sector information. http:// eur-lex.europa.eu/LexUriServ/LexUriServ.do?uri=CELEX:32003L0098:EN:HTML

Gray, J. (2014). Towards a genealogy of open data. *SSRN*. https://ssrn.com/ abstract=2605828 or http://dx.doi.org/10.2139/ssrn.2605828

Helbig, N.C., Cresswell, A.M., Burke, G.B. & Luna-Reyes, L. (2012). *The Dynamics of Opening Government Data*. Albany NY: Centre for Technology in Government. https://www.ctg.albany.edu/publications/reports/opendata/opendata.pdf

Hellberg, A.-S. & Hedström, K. (2015). The story of the sixth myth of open data and open government. *Transforming Government: People, Process and Policy* 9: 35-51. DOI:10.1108/TG-04-2014-0013

Janssen, M., Charalabidis, Y. & Zuiderwijk, A. (2012). Benefits, adoption barriers and myths of open data and open government. *Information Systems Management* 29: 258–268. DOI:10.1080/10580530.2012.716740

Krabina, B., Prorok, T. & Lutz, B. (2012). Open government implementation model. Vienna: Centre for Public Administration Research. http://www.kdz.eu/de/file/11433/download

Lee, G. & Kwak, Y.H. (2012). An open government maturity model for social media-based public engagement. *Government Information Quarterly* 29: 492-503. DOI:10.1016/j.giq.2012.06.001

Martin, C.J. (2014). Barriers to the open government data agenda: Taking a multi-level perspective. *Policy Internet* 6: 217–240. doi:10.1002/1944-2866.POI367

Martin, S., Foulonneau, M., Turki, S. & Ihadjadene, M. (2013). Risk analysis to overcome barriers to open data. *Journal of e-Government* 11(1): 348-359

Open Knowledge Foundation (2015). *Open Data Handbook*. http://opendatahandbook.org/

Simon, H.A. (1955). A behavioral model of rational choice. *Quarterly Journal of Economics* 69: 99-118

Van Schalkwyk, F., Willmers, M.A. & Schonwetter, T. (2016). Institutionalising open data in government. *SSRN*. DOI: 10.2139/ssrn.2925834

Wirtz, B.W., Piehler, R., Thomas, M.-J. & Daiser, P. (2016). Resistance of public personnel to open government: A cognitive theory view of implementation barriers towards open government data. *Public Management Review* 18: 1335-1364. DOI: 10.1080/14719037.2015.1103889

World Wide Web Foundation (2015). Open Data Barometer (2nd edn). http://www.opendatabarometer.org/

Zuiderwijk, A. & Janssen, M. (2014). Open data policies, their implementation and impact: A framework for comparison. *Government Information Quarterly* 31: 17-29. DOI: 10.1016/j.giq.2013.04.003

4.

Governance of open spatial data infrastructures in Europe

Glenn Vancauwenberghe & Bastiaan van Loenen

Introduction

Since the 1990s, public administrations in Europe and worldwide have invested considerable resources in the development of infrastructures for promoting, facilitating and coordinating the exchange and sharing of geographic data (Dessers et al. 2011). A crucial driver in the development and implementation of these spatial data infrastructures (SDIs) in Europe was the 2007 INSPIRE Directive establishing an Infrastructure for Spatial Information in the European Community (European Commission 2007). The INSPIRE Directive aims to overcome the major barriers affecting the availability and accessibility of geographic data through the development of a European spatial information infrastructure, based on the creation, operation and maintenance of the national spatial data infrastructures in Europe. While the original focus of most of these spatial data infrastructures was on promoting and stimulating data sharing within the public sector, in recent years several countries and public administrations started to make a shift towards the establishment of a more 'open' spatial data infrastructure, in which also businesses, citizens and non-governmental actors are considered as key stakeholders and beneficiaries of the infrastructure.

The launch of national open data agendas and the implementation of related initiatives in several European countries was an important driving force in the development of these open SDIs. At the same time, they also brought a need for alignment between national open data and SDI policies. The move towards more open spatial data infrastructures also created additional challenges related to the governance of the SDI, as new and additional governance approaches and instruments had to be implemented. In order to engage different stakeholder groups, including data users and producers outside the public sector, and take into account their needs and requirements, the scope of traditional governance structures, mechanisms and processes had to be expanded.

The central research question this chapter aims to answer is: Which governance instruments are adopted for governing open spatial data infrastructures in Europe? The chapter provides an analysis of how several European member states have been dealing with the governance of their open spatial data infrastructures since the adoption of the INSPIRE Directive in 2007. In the next section of this chapter, a brief introduction is provided to the concepts of open spatial data infrastructures and governance of these infrastructures. The third section describes the official INSPIRE reporting process and introduces the four spatial data infrastructures that will be analysed in this chapter. In the fourth section, the analysis is presented of how different governance instruments are introduced and implemented for the governance of these open spatial data infrastructures. The chapter ends with a discussion of the main findings in the fifth section and some conclusions and recommendations for further research in the sixth and final section.

Towards open spatial data infrastructures

Since President Obama's Memorandum on Transparency and Open Government announcing the creation of a transparent and collaborative government (Obama 2009), the concepts of open government and open data have attracted considerable attention from researchers, practitioners and decision makers. Open government data became a very popular topic in many parts of the world, including Europe, Australia, New Zealand and Asia (Wirtz & Birkmeyer 2015). In Europe, the Digital Agenda for Europe (European Commission 2010) and the revised Public Sector Information (PSI) Directive (European Commission 2013) encourage governments to stimulate content markets by making public sector information available in a non-discriminatory, transparent and effective manner, minimising barriers to reuse public sector information. It is hoped that the greater availability of interoperable public data will catalyse the secondary use of such data, leading to the growth of information industries and greater government transparency. A large part of government data can be considered as geographic or spatial data, i.e. data that refer to a location on the earth (Van Loenen 2006). Typical examples of spatial data are topographical maps, address data, road data and hydrographical data (Groot & McLaughlin 2000, Nedovic-Budic et al. 2011). These and other types of spatial data are becoming increasingly important in society, as most of the societal, environmental and economic challenges that governments, businesses and citizens are facing, require spatial understanding and insight (see Janssen 2011). It has been claimed that the economic value of billions of Euros will be created by the reuse of open government spatial data alone (Pira International et al. 2000, Dekkers et al. 2006, Forneveld 2009, Vickery 2011). Therefore, several types of spatial data were top-listed by the European Commission and the G8 for release as open government data due to the high demand from re-users (Cabinet Office 2013, European Commission 2014). It is not surprising that calls for free access to spatial data played a particularly important role in the formation of a number of open data initiatives, including the UK (see Saxby 2011). Access to these high-value spatial datasets is, until very recently, primarily provided through national spatial data infrastructures.

In the past 20 years, public authorities in all parts of the world have invested considerable resources in the development of spatial data infrastructures. A spatial data infrastructure (SDI) can be defined as a collection of technological and organisational components oriented towards facilitating and coordinating spatial data sharing (Vancauwenberghe et al. 2014). Among the key components of an SDI are the data, metadata, standards, access networks, policies, legal framework, funding and governance (GSDI 2012, McLaughlin & Nichols 1994). The original focus of SDI developments worldwide was on promoting and stimulating data sharing within the public sector. Governments were the central actors in the development and implementation of spatial data infrastructure, since they are the major producers and users of spatial information (Janssen 2010). Data sharing with organisations and individuals outside the public sector for a long time remained limited, as the mechanisms and instruments to support and facilitate this type of sharing were missing (Vancauwenberghe et al. 2014).

Several authors have suggested and explored the introduction of a new generation of more user-driven spatial data infrastructures and the need to redefine or expand the SDI concept (e.g. Van Loenen 2006, Masser 2009, Budhathoki et al. 2008, Hendriks et al. 2012, Coleman et al. 2016). Some authors considered the involvement and engagement of other stakeholders such as private companies, non-profit organisations, research institutions and also citizens to be essential to the realisation of a successful spatial data infrastructure (McLaughlin & Nichols 1994, Wehn de Montalvo 2001, Van Loenen 2006), while others argued for combining open data and SDI principles to optimise public sector information reuse (Van Loenen & Grothe 2014). The concept of open spatial data infrastructures expresses the need to open existing spatial data infrastructures to non-government actors. To begin with, open spatial data infrastructures involve the application of the principles of open data to spatial data, and making available spatial data for free to all potential users. These spatial data should also be license-free, machine processable and released in timely manner to the widest range of users in an open format (OpenGovData 2016). In addition to opening up spatial datasets to businesses, citizens and other users, open spatial data infrastructures also include the provision of different types of spatially enabled e-services to these citizens and businesses (Latre et al. 2013). The provision of data and services to non-government actors can be seen as opening the main outputs of the infrastructure to other parties. Another way of opening the infrastructure is by allowing other stakeholders to contribute to and participate in building the infrastructure. This means also businesses, research institutions, citizens and other stakeholders should be able to add their own data and components to the infrastructure. The contribution of non-government actors to the development and implementation should go further than the traditional contribution, i.e. working as contractors for public administrations and providing services to these administrations (Vancauwenberghe et al. 2014). In other words, open spatial data infrastructures require a redistribution of data production activities among different types of organisations and users (Budhathoki et al. 2008). Open spatial data infrastructures can only be realised by putting in place processes, methods and tools that stimulate and enable non-government actors to add their own datasets and other components to the infrastructure. Ideally such an open SDI is embedded in the general data infrastructure of a country (cf. Gray & Davies 2015, Kitchin 2014).

Governance of open spatial data infrastructures

A key challenge in the establishment of open spatial data infrastructures is the governance of the infrastructure. Governance of SDIs is essential to the implementation of different SDI components in a coordinated and consistent manner (Craglia & Johnston 2004). The implementation of an open SDI is not only about opening spatial data, but also about organising and governing the infrastructure in an open manner, and considering non-government actors as important stakeholders. In order to take into account the needs and requirements of different stakeholder groups, data users and producers outside the public sector should also be involved in the governance of the SDI (De Kleijn et al. 2014). The governance of spatial data infrastructures deals with the adoption of structures, procedures and instruments for managing the relationships and dependencies between all involved actors, units and organisations. The central challenge of governance is reconciling collective and individual needs and interests of different stakeholders in order to achieve common goals (Box 2013). Governance of open data infrastructures requires expanding the scope of stakeholders to include the private sector, research bodies and other actors outside the public sector, to actively promote bottom-up and participative processes and to find the appropriate mechanisms and instruments to enabled the participation of these non-government actors (Georgiadou et al. 2005).

In open government and open data research and practice the importance of appropriate governance structures, mechanisms and processes is widely recognised (e.g. Lee & Kwak 2012, Martin et al. 2013, Jetzek 2016). Martin et al. (2013) identified governance as one of the seven risk areas in the development of open data initiatives. Particular risks related to the governance are inconsistencies in public policies, a lack of dialogue between producers and users, fragmentation between different administrative levels and the reluctance of civil servants. In their development of an Open Government Maturity Model, Lee and Kwak (2012) argue that appropriate governance structures are essential for governments aiming to reach the highest level of open government. In her in-depth analysis of the Basic Data Programme in Denmark, Jetzek (2016) identified four governance tensions in the implementation of an open data infrastructure and four governance strategies that were used in Denmark to address these challenges. In several open data assessment frameworks and initiatives, governance is considered as a key element for determining the readiness of the infrastructure (e.g. World Bank Group 2015, Ubaldi 2013). However, despite the recognition of governance as a key component in the development of open data policies, so far little is known about the governance of open data and the different governance models used for open data policies (Lämmerhirt 2017).

Governance of public authorities and policies is one of the key topics in public administration research and practice, and several methods and approaches have been used for analysing governance in the public sector (Lynn et al. 2000, Bevir et al. 2003, Andresani & Ferlie 2006). For the analysis of the governance of open spatial data infrastructures, in this chapter the approach introduced by Verhoest et al. (2007) for describing and analysing trajectories of specialisation and coordination in the public sector is followed. Verhoest et al. (2007) focus on the instruments – and underlying mechanisms – that are adopted over time to enhance the alignment of tasks and efforts of organisations within the public sector. A classification is made of both management and structural instruments for coordinating and governing the relationships between public bodies. Management instruments include strategic planning and evaluation, financial management, culture and knowledge management and mandated consultation or review systems. Structural instruments are: reshuffling of competences and/ or lines of control; establishment of coordinating functions or entities; regulated markets; systems for information exchange; negotiation bodies and advisory bodies; entities for collective decision-making; common organisations; and chain management structures. The aim of this chapter is to explore how these and other governance instruments are used for managing the relationships and dependencies with actors and organisations outside the public sector with the aim of realising a more open spatial data infrastructure.

Methodology and selected cases

The central research question this article aims to answer is: Which governance instruments are adopted for the governance of open spatial data infrastructures in Europe? To answer this research question, an explorative analysis is made of the development and implementation of spatial data infrastructures in three European countries and one region: The Netherlands, Slovenia, Luxembourg, and Flanders (Belgium). The study is based on a document analysis of relevant publicly available documents on the development and implementation of the national spatial data infrastructure and the implementation of INSPIRE in each of these four cases.

67

Document analysis

Key documents in the analysis are the official reports on the implementation and use of infrastructures for spatial information that have to be submitted by all EU member states every three years. According to the INSPIRE Directive, EU member states have to monitor and report on the implementation and use of their infrastructures for spatial information. The content of the monitoring and reporting is defined in detail in Commission Decision 2009/442/EC of 5 June 2009 on monitoring and reporting of INSPIRE. While monitoring follows a quantitative approach and includes the establishment of the list of spatial datasets and services of the member states, INSPIRE Reporting follows a more qualitative approach, as member states need to provide information on five areas: coordination and quality assurance; contribution of stakeholders to the functioning and coordination of the infrastructure; the use of the infrastructure for spatial information; data sharing arrangements between public authorities; and cost and benefit aspects. The country reports contain information on many different aspects of the governance approach implemented in the different countries, and different types of governance instruments that can be used to govern the infrastructure.

Reporting started in 2010, with a first set of reports on the status of the MS spatial data infrastructures and INSPIRE implementation in 2009. A second round of reporting was coordinated in 2013, providing information on the status and evolution of the infrastructure between 2010 and 2012. In May 2016, a third set of country reports was submitted by the member states, covering the period 2013 to 2015. As reports now are available for three periods, the analysis also addresses changes in the adopted instruments between 2009 and 2015. In addition to these official country reports, other policy documents were analysed, including implementation strategies, legislation and other official reports. Also, information, results and findings from other studies on SDIs in Europe and the national SDIs of the Netherlands, Flanders, Luxembourg and Slovenia were included in the analysis. Examples of these are the INSPIRE/SDI State of Play Study (KU Leuven/SADL 2011a, 2011b, 2011c) the SmeSpire study on the involvement of the private sector in the implementation of INSPIRE (Vancauwenberghe 2013) and the UN-GGIM Country profiles (UN-GGIM 2016).

An important reason for selecting the four cases was the availability of information on the most recent SDI developments. While the first two editions of all official INSPIRE country reports have been translated into English, only four countries decided to submit the final version of the report in English: Belgium, Slovenia, Luxembourg and the United Kingdom. Since the latest UK report was rather concise and did not contain information on all the relevant topics, it was decided not to include the United Kingdom in the analysis. In Belgium, its regions are responsible for the implementation of the INSPIRE

Directive, and currently no overarching national spatial data infrastructure is in place. The decision was made to include only the regional SDI of Flanders, which can be seen as one of the most advanced regional SDIs. Besides Flanders, Slovenia and Luxembourg, the Netherlands was added as a fourth case, since the 2015 INSPIRE report and other reports were available in the mother tongue of the researchers.

Selected cases

Netherlands

In the Netherlands, the political responsibility for implementing the national spatial data infrastructure, but also INSPIRE lies with the Minister of Infrastructure and Environment. While it is the Ministry of Infrastructure and Environment that acts as the principal and budget holder of the SDI, the technical implementation of the infrastructure is delegated to Geonovum. The Ministry of Infrastructure and Environment also set up an INSPIRE steering committee, of which the main parties concerned in the SDI are members, and which is advised by a consultative group. Among the most important spatial data producers in the Netherlands are the Cadastre; the Ministry of Infrastructure and Environment; the Ministry of Economic Affairs, Agriculture and Innovation; the Ministry of Defence; the Netherlands Meteorological Institute (KNMI); Statistics Netherlands (CBS); provincial governments; district water authorities; and municipalities. In 2011, the Ministry of Infrastructure and Environment adopted an open data policy for the entire ministry, and by 2015 all data of the ministry and its departments had to be made open (Netherlands Ministry of Infrastructure and Environment 2012). The ministry responsible for open data and access to public sector information, however, is the Ministry of the Interior and Kingdom Relations. In 2013, this ministry presented a vision and associated plan for action for open government in the Netherlands (Kabinet 2013a, Kabinet 2013b), followed by a national open data agenda (Kabinet 2015). From 2013 to 2016 the Ministry of Economic Affairs established an open data breakthrough team composed of representatives of the public sector, private sector and academia. This team lobbied for open data, investigated barriers in PSI reuse and organised open data innovation rallies to bridge open data supply and reuse. While the National GeoRegistry has been the central access point to spatial data in the Netherlands since 2009, open spatial data from the National GeoRegistry are harvested by the Dutch Open Data Portal, which was established in 2011.

Slovenia

The legal framework for establishing and functioning of the spatial data infrastructure in Slovenia is determined by the Infrastructure for Spatial Information (ISI) Act of 2010. Different stakeholders cooperate in the Republic of Slovenia in the development of the national spatial data infrastructure and the implementation of the INSPIRE Directive. These especially include data providers at the national level, such as the Ministry of the Environment and Spatial Planning, the Ministry of Infrastructure, different bodies affiliated to both ministries, and also several other ministries. The Surveying and Mapping Authority, which is affiliated to the Ministry of the Environment and Spatial Planning, is a key actor in the coordination and implementation of the infrastructure, as it is responsible for the tasks of the national INSPIRE contact point, but also for the development and management of the national geoportal and the national metadata information system. The Slovenian intersectoral INSPIRE project group was established as the strategic body authorised to steer the measures for sharing spatial datasets and services related to these data and implementing the INSPIRE Directive in practice. The project group offers guidance and assistance to individual public authorities managing spatial data and services, so that such data and services comply with the provisions of the ISI Act and the INSPIRE Directive. While the development of the national SDI was originally included in the National eGovernment Strategy, a specific SDI strategy was drafted for the period 2016–2020. However, integration with other relevant policies and strategies was still considered to be essential.

Luxembourg

In the Grand-Duchy of Luxembourg an interdisciplinary and inter-ministerial task force was created to prepare and manage the development and implementation of the national spatial data infrastructure (LSDI). Leadership of this task force was in the hands of the Administration of Cadastre and Topography (ACT), who was and still is responsible for most spatial data available in the Grand-Duchy. All other public bodies dealing with spatial data in Luxembourg are closely linked to the 'LSDI' task force, and provide delegates to the Coordination Committee of the LSDI. The Coordination Committee acts as a steering committee of all the activities concerning the creation, updating, management and distribution of spatial data. From the start, the committee followed a strongly collaborative and open approach, and until now still has not adopted an official set of rules. The Luxembourgish geoportal is considered to be the technical backbone of Luxembourg's SDI. All the datasets and services that are relevant for INSPIRE can be discovered on this geoportal and in its metadata catalogue, visualised in the map viewer of the geoportal, and accessed or downloaded through web services. Since 2016, INSPIRE data are also accessible through the national open data portal. The establishment of this portal was one of the key open data developments in Luxembourg, together with the adoption of new open data legislation.

Flanders (Belgium)

Because of the federal structure of government in Belgium, four parties are responsible in Belgium for implementing the INSPIRE Directive: the federal government, the Walloon Region, the Flemish Region and the Brussels Capital Region. These four parties all have their own spatial data infrastructure, and are responsible for the coordination and implementation of INSPIRE within their own territory and jurisdiction. Currently there is no overarching spatial data infrastructure in Belgium. In Flanders, the Dutch-speaking northern region of the federal state of Belgium, a framework for cooperation to develop a government system for geographical information was formulated in 1995. This framework, which is currently named 'SDI-Flanders', aimed to optimise the production, the management, exchange and use of spatial data in Flanders. The GIS decree of 2001 and the SDI Decree of 2009 provided the legal framework for the partnership. All public administrations in Flanders, including the departments of the Flemish government, the Flemish public agencies, the provincial authorities and the municipalities, are considered to be members of this partnership. All partners are required by decree to contribute their geographical data to the GDI. Within the partnership 'SDI-Flanders', the regional Agency for Geographic Information Flanders (AGIV) was for a long time responsible for the operational coordination and exploitation of the Flemish SDI. While the development of the regional SDI already started in 1995, the first step towards a Flemish open data policy was taken in 2011, with the approval of the concept note on open data. In 2016, the Agency Information Flanders was created, integrating the AGIV into one main agency responsible for all government data.

Table 1 provides an overview of the legal and policy framework on spatial and open data, the leading organisations and the access points to data in the four cases.

The table shows how, in most cases, spatial data policies and open data policies were developed and implemented separately from one another. In most cases, also the organisations in charge and coordinating the work of other public administrations are different. However, an important development to align and integrate spatial data and open data policies recently took place in Flanders, with the integration of the bodies for coordinating both policies into one single agency, responsible for all types of government data. Also, important to note is the timing of the different initiatives. Especially in the Netherlands and in Flanders, initiatives and policies to promote the sharing of spatial data were implemented many years before an open data agenda and associated policies were introduced. Nevertheless, in some cases there also are clear linkages between the two domains and their legislation, policy documents and policy initiatives.

Although the focus of this chapter is not on the alignment between spatial data policies and open data policies, certain links between both and the efforts to integrate them will be addressed in this analysis, especially if they contribute to the realisation of a more open spatial data infrastructure.

71

Table 1 Policy framework, legal framework, leading actor(s) and main access point(s) for spatial data and open data in the four cases

	The Netherlands	Slovenia	Luxembourg	Flanders
Policy framework				
Open data	Vision and Action Plan on Open Government (2013a, 2013b)	Part of the Public Administration Development Strategy 2015–2020	Part of the Digital Luxembourg Initiative (2014)	Concept Note Open Data (2011) and Flemish Action Plan Open Data (2013)
Spatial data	GIDEON: Key geo-information facility for the Netherlands (2008) replaced by 'Partners in GEO' Vision (2014)	Originally part of eGovernment strategy 2013–2015, now eSpatial strategy 2016–2020	Luxembourg SDI (LSDI) project (2007)	SDI-plan 2011–2015 and Strategic programme 'Map of Flanders' (2012)
Legal framework				
Open data	Government Information Act (2006) changed to the Law on the reuse of public sector information (2015)	Public Information Access Act (ZDIJZ-E) (2006, amended in 2015)	Law on the reuse of public sector information (2007, amended in 2016).	Decree on the reuse of public sector information (2007, amended in 2015)
Spatial data	National INSPIRE law (2009) & Decision INSPIRE (2009)	Spatial Information Act (2010) & Amending the Infrastructure for Spatial Information Act (2015)	National INSPIRE law (2010, amended in 2014)	GIS Decree (2001) & SDI Decree (2009)
Leading actor(s)				
Open data	Ministry of the Interior and Kingdom Relations, Ministry of Economic Affairs, Ministry of Infrastructure and Environment	Ministry of Public Administration	Ministry of State	Coordination Cell Flemish eGovernment, now Agency Information Flanders
Spatial data	Ministry of Infrastructure and Environment, Geonovum	Ministry of the Environment and Spatial Planning, Surveying and Mapping Authority	Administration of Cadastre and Topography	Agency for Geographical Information, now Agency Information Flanders
Main access point(s)				
Open data	Data.overheid.nl (launched 2011)	Open Data Portal Slovenia (launched 2010)	Data.public.lu (launched 2016)	Flemish Open Data Portal (launched 2010)
Spatial data	National GeoRegistry (launched 2009) Public Services on the Map (launched 2011)	National INSPIRE geoportal (launched 2011) and several thematic portals	ACT's geoportal (launched 1997)	Flemish geoportal Geopunt.be (launched 2013)

Analysis of the governance of open spatial data infrastructures

This section discusses the use of different instruments to govern the relationships with non-government actors in the SDI and to engage these non-government actors in the development and implementation of the SDI.

Netherlands

Both the coordination structure and the strategic planning and management of the implementation of the SDI reflect the ambition to develop an open SDI. The most recent policy document, the 'Partners in Geo' vision, is a shared vision of both the private, academic and public sector on the future of the geo-information domain in the Netherlands, in which open data is put forward as a key strategic priority (Bregt et al. 2014). Since Partners in Geo, the coordination structure fits 'the golden helix' construct with equal representation from the public sector, private sector and academia. The Top Team, consisting of the chairman of the public GI-Council, the president of the association of GI businesses and the chair of the Netherlands Centre for Geodesy and Geo-Informatics, discusses strategic issues. The tactical level is addressed by the strategic council, again with equal representation from the public sector, private sector and academia.

From the first stage of INSPIRE implementation, actors outside the public sector were closely involved in decision-making on the development and implementation of INSPIRE in the Netherlands (VROM/Geonovum 2010). The central steering committee of INSPIRE is advised by a consultative group, in which both INSPIRE data providers and users are represented. The consultative group is considered to be a main factor in the quality assurance procedure of the INSPIRE programme in the Netherlands, as the group examines the main results delivered by the INSPIRE programme and advises the steering committee on the implementation of the programme. The chair of the consultative group is a member of the steering committee.

Already in the first stage of INSPIRE implementation, the conclusion was drawn that important barriers to sharing and use of spatial data were related to the conditions for use, which often were not transparent, not harmonised and difficult to understand (VROM/Geonovum 2010). Therefore, the Netherlands started with the development of the *'Geo Gedeeld'* framework, which included a proposal to harmonise conditions for use (Van Loenen & Van Barneveld 2010). In the second phase of INSPIRE implementation, after 2010, the *'Geo Gedeeld'* framework was implemented as the standard license framework for INSPIRE data in the Netherlands. In 2014, it was decided to bring the Dutch INSPIRE data policy in line with international standards, and to apply where possible the Creative Commons framework (I&M/Geonovum 2016). A 'Creative Commons, unless' principle was introduced, which means governments now, for INSPIRE data themes, have to apply one of the Creative Commons licenses when making their data available, unless they want to impose specific conditions that the Creative Commons framework does not cover. In that case, they have to apply the *'Geo Gedeeld'* framework.

In 2011, the ambition was set in the Netherlands to make access to all public spatial data by definition unconditional and free of charge, and the development of an open data policy was considered to be essential for achieving this ambition

(I&M/Geonovum 2013). The Minister for Infrastructure and Environment declared in 2011 that it would open all government data under the remit of the Ministry of Infrastructure and Environment by 2015 at the latest. At the same time, the national 'Open Data Programme' was launched by the Minister for the Interior, as part of which the Dutch Open Data Portal (data.overheid.nl) was launched, providing access to a large number of open datasets, including the datasets from the National GeoRegistry. All spatial datasets that are included in the National GeoRegistry and that can be classified as open data, are harvested by the National Open Data Portal. As a result, almost half of the open data in the Netherlands are spatial data. According to a report of the Dutch Algemene Rekenkamer (2014) approximately 95% of all spatial data in the Netherlands are available as open data.

Already in the preparation of INSPIRE implementation, the Netherlands started with estimating and measuring the costs and benefits of INSPIRE (VROM/Geonovum 2010). In 2009, a cost–benefit analysis was carried out on the implementation of INSPIRE in the Netherlands, in which a comparison was made of two alternative implementation models: a basic model, in which the impact of INSPIRE on organisations managing geo-information is kept minimal, and a collective model, in which all organisations managing geo-information in the Netherlands should make their data INSPIRE compliant (Ecorys & Grontmij 2009). The analysis was based on the information supplied by various relevant parties (both data providers and users) from a number of (theoretical) use cases. The results of the cost-benefits were repeated and updated in the 2013 report, focusing on INSPIRE implementation between 2010 and 2012 (I&M/Geonovum 2013). The updated cost–benefit analysis demonstrated that the costs of INSPIRE implementation were significantly higher than was originally estimated (see Ecorys 2016). The main reasons for this were the lack of experience in implementing INSPIRE in 2009 and the complexity of INSPIRE. In addition to the assessment of the costs and benefits of INSPIRE, several cost–benefits analyses were undertaken in the Netherlands of particular spatial datasets, such as topographic data and elevation data (Bregt et al. 2013, 2016).

Slovenia

In Slovenia, the implementation of a more open spatial data infrastructure mainly took place in the latest phase of INSPIRE implementation and reporting. In the first years of INSPIRE implementation, private partners were considered to be relevant actors in the SDI, but only in the role of contractors of technically demanding tasks in establishing and operating the Slovenian SDI (Petek et al. 2010). Businesses could play an important role in the standardisation and harmonisation of data during data collection and maintenance processes. Good practices and experiences in other countries raised the awareness of the potential role of private companies as providers of value-added services on top of the public sector data. However, to make this possible in Slovenia, the limited access to spatial data had to be re-examined and regulated, with the aim to provide non-government actors access to the data. The lack of a long-term and stable funding model was, however, seen as an important barrier in opening spatial data to actors outside government (Government of the Republic of Slovenia 2013). Therefore, the focus of the SDI in Slovenia for a long time remained on data-sharing among public sector bodies, and especially these public sector bodies were represented in the SDI governance structure. Such a structure did not exist in the first phase of INSPIRE implementation, and was implemented after 2010 with the 'Intersectoral INSPIRE Project Group' (KULeuven/SADL 2011a). While in this intersectoral INSPIRE project group especially data providers were represented, recent discussions with different stakeholders made clear that the focus should be shifted towards the inclusion of stakeholders who are not responsible for managing and collecting spatial data. It was proposed to create a new or strongly adapted common platform in which also private sector representatives and representatives from research and education in the field of geo-informatics are closely involved in decision-making (Government of the Republic of Slovenia 2013).

Several important changes towards making the Slovenian SDI more open took place between 2013 and 2015 (Petek 2016). These changes were driven by or related to the legal framework, strategic planning, the establishment of coordination bodies and awareness-raising. With regard to the legal framework, a new act amending the original Infrastructure for Spatial Information (ISI) Act, which transposed the INSPIRE Directive into national legislation, was passed in 2015, on the basis of an EU Pilot enquiry procedure of the European Commission (Government of the Republic of Slovenia 2016). To ensure the correct and complete transfer of the INSPIRE Directive, several changes and supplements had to be introduced into the original ISI Act. For instance, changes were needed to the provisions on restrictions for public access to spatial datasets and network services, and on data and service-sharing. In 2016, a decree on the criteria and conditions for determining costs for the use of network services and for determining charges for spatial datasets and services sharing was passed. This decree regulates the preparation of a bill of costs regarding use and sharing of network services and spatial data. While in previous years data sharing between public authorities was organised through mutual agreements among data providers and data users, because of the changes in the legislation, such agreements are no longer needed. Another major development in the legal framework was the Amendment of the Public Information Access Act (ZDIJZ-E), which transposed the new directive on the reuse of public sector information (2013/37/EU) into national legislation. As a result of the amendment, data gathered in the public administration during the execution of public tasks now have to be available for reuse without charging fees (Government of the Republic of Slovenia 2016).

Since 2009, the development and implementation of the Slovenian spatial data infrastructure was mentioned and included in several national strategic documents, such as the National e-Government Strategy, Slovenia's development strategy, and its strategy on e-commerce in public administration bodies (Petek 2014). In the latest phase of INSPIRE implementation, the activities to further develop and establish an SDI in Slovenia were embedded in a broader e-spatial strategy, which aims to improve processes in the field of spatial planning, construction and real estate management through reliable, interoperable and easily accessible spatial information (Government of the Republic of Slovenia 2016). The e-spatial strategy itself was considered to be part of the broader e-government strategy in Slovenia. In order to realise better alignment of spatial information activities and e-government activities in Slovenia, the proposal was launched to establish a strategic board for geo-informatics which would operate as a part of the strategic board for development of informatics and would be in charge of coordinating all strategic tasks in the development and management of the SDI in Slovenia. Another important evolution since 2013 was the increased effort and energy that has been invested in promotion and awareness-raising activities on the implementation of INSPIRE in Slovenia (Petek 2016). An example of such activities is the Slovene INSPIRE day, which brought together not only representatives from data providers but also from private firms and educational and research institutions.

Luxembourg

In the first years of INSPIRE implementation, public research centres and universities were considered to be stakeholders of the SDI in Luxembourg, in addition to several public administrations. It was argued that these research centres and universities could produce and maintain data that might become relevant for INSPIRE in the future (Konnen & Kaell 2010). This means that originally, private companies and citizens were not regarded as relevant stakeholders. Only the use of public sector data by engineering firms and architects in the scope of their projects was considered as a potential context in which private companies could take advantage of the SDI. In the second official INSPIRE report, private software producers were added to the list of stakeholders of the national SDI, although their precise role and how they would be involved in the SDI was not defined in detail (Kaell & Konnen 2013). Until 2013, the SDI in Luxembourg was mainly about facilitating and coordinating the exchange of spatial data among public sector organisations, and only public sector organisations were involved in decision-making processes on the SDI (KULeuven/SADL 2011b). This did not change in the latest phase of INSPIRE implementation. A recent development relevant in the light of realising a more open SDI was the establishment of a working group on spatial data policy, which aimed to develop a government-wide spatial data policy (Kaell et al. 2016). The main reason behind the establishment of this working group was the absence of a legal framework dealing with the (public) access and use of spatial data, while in reality public administrations were adopting several different technologies for making their data available. Also, the transposition of the PSI Directive into national legislation, and the commitment of the national government to develop and implement an open data policy, were important drivers behind the establishment of the working group on spatial data policy (Kaell et al. 2016).

Luxembourg law stipulated that spatial data could be shared free of charge between all the public authorities, which was done via a set of view and download services (Kaell & Konnen 2013). Spatial data were made available via spatial data services, but were only accessible from inside the official government network (UN-GGIM, 2016). Non-government actors could only view and query these data via viewer(s) on the national geoportal; downloading the data was not possible for them. An important change in opening the Luxembourg spatial data infrastructure took place recently, with the launch of the national open data portal (Kaell et al. 2016). The Administration du Cadastre et de la Topographie (ACT) who is leading and coordinating the development of the SDI in Luxembourg, also played a key role in the development of the open data portal. For ACT, this was an important change in its data policy, as before the launch of the portal most of the datasets of the ACT had a restricted access policy and were not available free of charge. With the launch of the open data portal, several key datasets such as the cadastral map, topography and addresses were released as 'open and free services'. However, not all the datasets behind these services are free of charge. For instance, access to datasets such as cadastral data and topographical data still require certain fees to be paid. Some datasets were made available as open data. These included old version of datasets and new datasets for which the price and use conditions are not determined by law, such as address data and street names. With the creation of a first list of datasets and services that could be considered as open and free data, the ACT aimed to stimulate other data providers to open their data. It is expected that in the near future all datasets that can be accessed via existing geoportals will be available as open data (Kaell et al. 2016).

An important barrier to opening spatial data in Luxembourg is the lack of an official government-wide license framework or model for the reuse of data (Kaell et al. 2016). Each public data provider still uses its own terms and conditions for declaring their data to be open, and no commonly known national or international licenses or declarations are being used. In recent months, the Luxembourg's Spatial Data Infrastructure seemed to be heading towards the adoption of CC zero as a general 'licence' for its spatial data, for all datasets that are not explicitly put under other rules. However, this still needed to be decided and implemented in the context of the working group on data policy (Kaell et al. 2016).

Flanders (Belgium)

Although in the first years of INSPIRE implementation, the SDI in Flanders mainly aimed to support governments in the execution of their public tasks and the commercial reuse of data was rather uncommon, from the beginning actors outside the public sector were considered and treated as important stakeholders of the SDI (Member State Contact Point Belgium 2009). This was especially reflected in the governance structure of the SDI, in which an advisory body was established, composed of representatives from civil society, the private sector and the academic sector. This body, the GDI Council, gave strategic advice to the responsible minister on issues related to the development of the Flemish spatial data infrastructure (Vancauwenberghe 2013). While the GDI Council rather had an advisory role, decision-making on the SDI mainly took place in the steering committee, in which experts from public authorities from the Flemish administration, the Flemish provinces and the Flemish towns and cities and municipalities are represented (KULeuven/SADL 2011c). One of the tasks of the steering committee was to determine the conditions under which government data are made available to third parties, in consultation with the public data provider. Private companies were involved in the Flemish SDI in the first years of the development as data providers of datasets that were made available to all partners of the Flemish SDI. This was organised by the AGIV, the coordinating body of the Flemish SDI, that concluded agreements with third parties regarding the dissemination of the geographical data of third parties to Flemish public authorities (Member State Contact Point Belgium 2009).

In the second phase of INSPIRE implementation (2010–2012), public authorities were still seen as the main users of the data and services of the SDI (Member State Contact Point Belgium 2013). By means of electronic 'viewers' public access to the data in the SDI was realised. However, making the SDI more accessible for commercial reuse was considered as a policy priority for the following years. Awareness-raising on the topics of open data and commercial reuse was considered to be essential, but an important development towards a more open SDI in Flanders was the creation of a license framework consisting of five licence models for the provision of open data by entities in Flanders (Flemish Government 2014). These included a creative commons zero deed, a free open data licence, an open data licence at a fair cost, a free open data licence for non-commercial reuse and an open data licence at a fair cost for commercial reuse.

After the introduction of an open data license framework, the Flemish government also implemented a monitoring approach for assessing and monitoring the availability, accessibility and reusability of its spatial datasets, as an extension of the official INSPIRE monitoring (Departement Informatie

Vlaanderen 2015). Also, information on the charges for data and the license model used was collected for all datasets. By the end of the 2012, 73% of the INSPIRE datasets were accessible to the public, which meant they could be viewed and downloaded. It was expected that by the end of 2013, 87% of the INSPIRE datasets would be accessible to the public. Commercial reuse was authorised for about 33% of the datasets. According to the latest information on the status of the SDI in Flanders, more than 80% of the approximately 140 identified datasets are currently made reusable, mainly through a Free and Open Data license. The most recent development in the SDI Flanders towards a more Open SDI is the establishment of the 'Information Flanders' agency, in which several departments and agencies dealing with information and information policies in Flanders are merged into one single agency (Member State Contact Point Belgium 2016). The aim of this agency is to support the Flemish government with its digitisation policies, acquisition, management and use of information, along with the integration of e-government services and management of public archives. Government information and e-government services will be made available in user-friendly ways, and public administrations, companies, organisations and citizens will be supported in making use of this information.

Findings and discussion

The aim of this chapter was to analyse how public administrations in Europe are dealing with the governance of their 'open' spatial data infrastructures. The analysis builds further on the instruments-based approach developed and used by Verhoest et al. (2007) for analysing coordination in the public sector. The analysis demonstrated that the instruments-based approach for analysing governance as introduced by Verhoest et al. is a relevant and useful approach for analysing governance of open data infrastructures, and open spatial data infrastructures in particular. Several of the instruments identified by Verhoest et al. are also used in the governance of open spatial data infrastructures. Strategic planning and evaluation, collective decision-making, reshuffling of competences and knowledge and information sharing all are commonly used instruments for the governance of open spatial data infrastructures. Also, regulation of the market, another instrument proposed by Verhoest et al. (2007), is relevant in the domain of open spatial data infrastructures. Both the development and use of license frameworks and the creation of data portals can be seen as instruments contributing to creating a market between data providers and data users. Based on our analysis of recent governance efforts and activities in the four cases, nine main governance instruments can be identified and used for the governance of open spatial data infrastructures in Europe. Table 2 gives an overview of these nine instruments and the way in which they have been implemented in the four cases.

Table 2 Governance instruments used for the governance of open spatial data infrastructures

Strategic planning: Design of SDI strategies and actions plans addressing open spatial data or linked to open data strategies	**Netherlands**: Private sector and academic sector strongly involved in SDI strategies, in which open data are considered to be essential and the user is central **Slovenia**: Inclusion of spatial data and SDI in the national e-government and e-commerce strategies
Strategic evaluation: Assessing and monitoring the openness of the infrastructure (readiness, data, use, benefits)	**Netherlands**: Costs-benefits analyses of INSPIRE and of open spatial datasets **Flanders**: Regular monitoring of the accessibility, availability and reusability of spatial data, also to non-government users **All**: Collection of user statistics of geoportals and open data portals
Collective decision-making: Governance structure in which non-government actors have an advisory or decision-making role	**Netherlands**: Non-government actors involved in SDI decision-making through the Top Team and Strategic Council **Flanders**: Non-government actors involved in SDI decision making through participation in SDI Council **Slovenia**: Decision-making on spatial data integrated in decision-making on e-government and informatics
Reshuffling of competences: Assignment of tasks and competences in developing the infrastructure for non-government actors	**Netherlands**: Research programme to stimulate the involvement of research institutions in the infrastructure **Flanders**: Private companies as data provider to SDI, under data-sharing agreement with coordinating body of the SDI **Luxembourg**: Especially research centre and universities seen as (potential) data providers
Establishment of coordinating functions/ entities: Creation of coordination bodies or functions responsible for open spatial data and/or the alignment between open data and spatial data	**Flanders**: Integration of SDI coordinating body and open data coordinating body into single Agency Information Flanders, responsible for all government data and information
Knowledge and information sharing: Awareness-raising and capacity-building on open data and SDI among different stakeholder groups	**Flanders**: Awareness-raising on SDI and open data through information sessions within public administration and yearly events with public sector, private sector, academic sector and others **Slovenia**: Promotion and awareness-raising on INSPIRE and SDI through the organisation of joint events for public data providers, private companies and research institutions
Licenses: Use of open licenses for spatial data	**Netherlands**: Development of harmonised licenses framework and government-wide use of international license framework **Flanders**: Creation and use of standard license framework for all government data, including spatial data
Access mechanisms: Making spatial data discoverable and accessible through different mechanisms	**All**: Spatial data discoverable and accessible via geoportal and national open data portal
Legal framework: Regulations and laws on open spatial data	**All**: Transposition of INSPIRE Directive and revised PSI Directive into national legislation

The analysis revealed some important similarities and differences in the approaches adopted and the instruments used to govern the relationships with non-government actors. In the Netherlands and Flanders, actors from outside the public sector such as private firms, research institutions but also citizens were seen as important stakeholders from the start of SDI/INSPIRE implementation. In Slovenia and Luxembourg, the focus for a long time was mainly or even solely on public sector bodies, and non-government actors were only recently recognised as relevant actors in the SDI. This is also reflected in the governance structures of the SDIs. A similar coordination structure was implemented in the Netherlands and Flanders, in which private companies and other actors outside the public sector were involved in decision-making on the SDI. Luxembourg and Slovenia only recently started to consider a more open governance and decision-making structure.

Another difference can be seen in terms of the development of a government-wide license framework for spatial data and services. In all four countries, several geoportals and thematic viewers to provide citizens and other stakeholders access to certain thematic datasets were developed in the first phase of INSPIRE implementation. However, with regard to the actual reuse of data, for commercial or non-commercial purposes, and the existence of a government-wide license framework or standard licenses, differences between the four cases were more pronounced. The Netherlands was the leading country in the development of such a common license framework, followed by Flanders a few years later. Both governance instruments clearly illustrate the differences in timing between the four countries in their move towards a more open spatial data infrastructure, and the development of an appropriate governance model for such an open infrastructure. In Flanders and the Netherlands, governance instruments to actively involve non-government actors in the development and implementation of the infrastructure have been implemented from the start of SDI/INSPIRE. In Slovenia and Luxembourg, businesses and other stakeholders outside the public sector were only recently recognised as relevant actors in the infrastructure, and the implementation of instruments for governing the infrastructure in a more open manner is less widespread.

In addition to the modification of governance structures and the development of license frameworks, the analysis revealed several other instruments that are used to govern relationships with actors and parties outside the public sector. An instrument that has been employed in several countries is the creation and adoption of strategic plans and vision documents on the spatial data infrastructure. Both the content of these plans and the way in which they are developed could contribute to the realisation of a more open spatial data infrastructure. Not only could actors not belonging to the public sector be closely involved in the preparation of the documents, the documents themselves could address the relevance of the spatial data infrastructures to citizens, businesses and society in general, and should provide guidance on how these non-government actors could contribute to the development of these infrastructures. While awareness-raising and promotional activities towards businesses, research institutions and other organisations are also often organised to promote the participation of these organisations in the infrastructure, another often used instrument to govern the relationships with these non-government actors is the establishment of an appropriate legal framework.

Conclusion

The aim of this chapter was to analyse how public administrations in Europe are dealing with the governance of their national spatial data infrastructures. The focus of this chapter was on the governance of open spatial data infrastructures in Europe. Three European countries (Netherlands, Luxembourg and Slovenia) and one region (Flanders) were included in the analysis. The analysis showed how all countries have taken certain measures to engage actors outside the public sector in the governance of the open spatial data infrastructure. Typical instruments used to govern the relationships between different stakeholders in the infrastructure, including businesses, research institutions, non-profit organisations and citizens, are the modification of decision-making structures, the development of strategic plans focused on the use of spatial data outside the public sector, the development and implementation of licensing frameworks and changes in the legal framework. The main differences between countries are both in the extent to which open governance instruments have been adopted and in the timing of the adoption of these instruments. While Flanders and especially the Netherlands have been aiming to implement governance instruments to make their spatial data infrastructure more open from the start of SDI/INSPIRE implementation, in Slovenia and Luxembourg the focus was for a long time mainly or even solely on public sector bodies, and non-government actors were only recently recognised as relevant actors in the SDI.

In its analysis of the shift towards more open spatial data infrastructures, the chapter also showed the impact of open data initiatives and policies on the establishment of these open SDIs. At European level, the revision of the PSI Directive clearly had an impact on open data policies, but also on spatial data policies in the different countries. At national and regional level, evidence was found of the impact of open data policies on the implementation of spatial data infrastructures and the opening of these infrastructures to non-government bodies. Open data license frameworks have been applied to spatial data, spatial data are made available through national open data portals and national SDI strategies were in line with the national open data strategies and policies. It can be concluded that some countries started with the implementation of an open spatial data infrastructure before the adoption of a national open data agenda, but in all countries in the analysis the national open data agenda clearly had an impact on the spatial data infrastructure. However, a more systematic and in-depth investigation of the links and interplay between open data and spatial data policies and infrastructures is required to better understand how both domains are influencing each other. Also, the impact of existing and ongoing spatial data initiatives and policies on the development of open data policies since 2010 should be included in this analysis.

As for other technological and organisational components of open spatial data infrastructures, it can be argued that the implementation of appropriate governance instruments should not be seen as an end in itself. Rather, effective governance of the infrastructure should lead to or contribute to an increased availability of spatial data and services, a better use of these data and services, and the realisation of different types of benefits. In this way, the analysis presented in this chapter should only be regarded as a very first step in the analysis of the governance of open spatial data infrastructures. Determining the importance and impact of different governance instruments and governance models also requires a correct and complete assessment of the performance of open spatial data infrastructures, but especially an investigation of the impact of different governance models on the performance of these infrastructures. Much work has been done on developing and applying different frameworks and methods for the assessment of spatial data infrastructures (e.g. Grus 2013, Giff & Crompvoets 2008, Kok & Van Loenen 2005, Rodriguez Pabon 2005) and open data initiatives (e.g. Caplan et al. 2014, World Wide Web Foundation 2015, Open Knowledge International 2014), leading to a better insight in the performance of these infrastructures and initiatives.

While this chapter provides a first explorative analysis of how European countries and public administrations have taken actions and implemented instruments to make their spatial data infrastructures more open, some important conclusions can be drawn on the current state of openness of these infrastructures. Our analysis showed how European public administrations in recent years have moved towards more open spatial data infrastructures, through the adoption of common governance instruments, such as decision-making and consultation structures, re-shuffling of competences, and strategic planning and evaluation. Despite these efforts and implemented instruments, the level of openness of these infrastructures, however, still remains limited. So far, the development of spatial data infrastructures was especially successful in opening the spatial data, by increasing and improving the availability, accessibility and reusability of spatial data. Nonetheless, the openness of the infrastructure itself still is restricted, since government remains dominant in the development and implementation of spatial data infrastructures in Europe, and participation of and collaboration with non-government actors such as businesses, research institutions and other stakeholders still remains relatively low. In the past, governments have mainly been working on making their traditionally closed infrastructures more open, but not on building a truly open spatial data infrastructure. An important and unsolved challenge in realising such an open spatial data infrastructure will be the governance of this infrastructure, which will require new and innovative governance approaches.

About the authors

GLENN VANCAUWENBERGHE is a postdoctoral researcher at the Knowledge Centre Open Data at Delft University of Technology. His main field of research is related to the governance and performance of inter-organisational information sharing. Glenn holds MSc degrees in Sociology and in the Management of Public Organisations, and obtained his PhD in Social Sciences on the topic of 'Coordination in the context of Spatial Data Infrastructures'. Since 2007, Glenn has been involved as the principal investigator in several projects in the domain of open data and spatial data in Europe, in which he mainly focused on data governance and data policies, the integration of spatial data in e-government and the performance of data policies. As a Marie Skłodowska-Curie Fellow, Glenn is currently doing research on the impact of different models for governing open spatial data on the performance of open spatial data policies in Europe.
E-mail: G.Vancauwenberghe@tudelft.nl

BASTIAAN VAN LOENEN is director of the Knowledge Centre Open Data and associate professor in the Faculty of Architecture and the Built Environment, Delft University of Technology. His main focus is on open data research, and the stimulation of re-use of public sector geo-information in particular. Other research interests include the development and assessment of spatial data infrastructures, the assessment of access and re-use policies and legal aspects of open data (e.g. location privacy, harmonising licenses and intellectual property rights). Bastiaan chairs the Geo-Information Infrastructure Committee of the Dutch Geodetic Commission, was chair of the Legal and Socio-economic Committee of the Global Spatial Data Infrastructure Association (GSDI) (2011–2015), and participated in various European research projects in the domain of geo-information and spatial data infrastructures.

REFERENCES

Algemene Rekenkamer (2014). Trendrapport open data. Den Haag: Algemene Rekenkamer

Andresani, G. & Ferlie, E. (2006). Studying governance within the British public sector and without: Theoretical and methodological issues. *Public Management Review* 8(3): 415-431

Dekkers, M., Polman, F., Te Velde, R. & De Vries, M. (2006). Measuring European public sector information resource. Final report of study on exploitation of public sector information — Benchmarking of EU framework conditions. https://ec.europa.eu/digital-single-market/en/news/mepsir-measuring-european-public-sector-information-resources-final-report-study-exploitation-0

Bevir, M., Rhodes, R. A. & Weller, P. (2003). Comparative governance: prospects and lessons. *Public Administration* 81(1): 191-210.

Bregt, A. K., Castelein, W., Grus, L. & Eertink, D. (2013). De effecten van een open basisregistratie topografie (BRT). Wageningen: Wageningen University and Research

Bregt, A., Nijpels, E. & Tijl, H. (2014). Partners in GEO: Shared vision of government, private sector and scientific community on the future of the geo-information sector. http://geosamen.nl/wp-content/uploads/2014/11/GeoSamen-UK.pdf

Bregt, A.K., Grus, L., Van Beuningen, T. & Van Meijeren, H. (2016). Wat zijn de effecten van een open Actueel Hoogtebestand Nederland (AHN)? Wageningen: Wageningen University & Research

Box, P. (2013). The Governance of Spatial Data Infrastructure: A Registry Based Model. Melbourne: University of Melbourne, Department of Infrastructure Engineering

Budhathoki, N.R., Bruce, B.C. & Nedovic-Budic, Z. (2008). Reconceptualizing the role of the us-er of spatial data infrastructure. *GeoJournal* 72(3): 149-160

Cabinet Office (2013). Policy paper: G8 open data charter and technical annex. 18 June 2013

Caplan, R., Davies, T., Wadud, A., Verhulst, S., Alonso, J.M. & Farhan, H. (2014). Towards common methods for assessing open data: workshop report & draft framework. Washington DC: World Wide Web Foundation

Coleman, D.J., Rajabifard, A. & Kolodziej, K.W. (2016). Expanding the SDI environment: comparing current spatial data infrastructure with emerging indoor location-based services. *International Journal of Digital Earth* 9(6): 1-19

Craglia, M. & Johnston, A. (2004). Assessing the impacts of spatial data infrastructures: Methods and gaps. 7th AGILE conference on Geographic Information Science. Heraklion, 29 April – 1 May 2004

De Kleijn, M., Van Manen, N., Kolen, J.C.A. & Scholten, H.J. (2014). Towards a user-centric SDI framework for historical and heritage European landscape research. *International Journal of Spatial Data Infrastructures Research* 9: 1-35

Departement Informatie Vlaanderen (2015). Toegankelijkheid geografische databanken. http://www.geopunt.be/actualiteit/2015/juni/toegankelijkheid-geografische-databanken

Dessers, E., Crompvoets, J., Janssen, K., Vancauwenberghe, G., Vandenbroucke, D. & Vanhaverbeke, L. (2011). *SDI at Work: The Spatial Zoning Plans Case.* Leuven: Spatialis

Ecorys & Grontmij (2009). Kosten-batenanalyse INSPIRE. Geonovum

Ecorys (2016). Actualisatie KBA INSPIRE. Geonovum

European Commission (2003). Directive 2003/98/EC of the European Parliament and of the council of 17 November 2003 on the re-use of public sector information. OJ L 345/90

European Commission (2007). Directive 2007/2/EC of the European Parliament and of the Council of 14 March 2007 Establishing an Infrastructure for Spatial Information in the European Community (INSPIRE). OJ L 108/1

European Commission (2010). Communication to the European Parliament, the Council, the European Economic and Social Committee, and the Committee for the Regions. A digital agenda for Europe, COM (2010) 245 final

European Commission (2013). Directive 2013/37/EU of the European Parliament and of the council of 26 June 2013 amending Directive 2003/98/EC on the reuse of public sector information. OJ L 175/1

European Commission (2014). Commission notice — Guidelines on recommended standard licences, datasets and charging for the reuse of documents. OJ C240/01

Flemish Government (2014). Open data license Models. Online accessible at https://overheid.vlaanderen.be/sites/default/files/Modellicenties_NL_20141119.pdf

Fornefeld, M. (2009). The value to industry of PSI: The business sector perspective. In: Uhlir, P. (2009). *The Socioeconomic Effects of Public Sector Information on Digital Networks: Toward a Better Understanding of Different Access and Reuse Policies: Workshop Summary.* Washington DC: National Academies Press

Georgiadou, Y., Puri, S.K. & Sahay, S. (2005). The rainbow metaphor: Spatial data infrastructure organization and implementation in India. *International Studies of Management & Organization* 35(4): 48-70. https://doi.org/10.1080/00208825.2005.11 043738

Giff, G. & Crompvoets, J. (2008). Performance indicators a tool to support spatial data infrastructures assessment. *Computers, Environment and Urban Systems* 32(5): 365-376

Government of the Republic of Slovenia (2013). INSPIRE Country Report Slovenia 2010-2012

Government of the Republic of Slovenia (2016). INSPIRE Country Report Slovenia 2013-2015

Gray, J. & Davies, T. (2015). Fighting phantom firms in the UK: From opening up datasets to reshaping data infrastructures? Paper presented at the Open Data Research Symposium, Ottawa, 27 May

Groot, R. & McLaughlin, J. (2000). Introduction. In: R. Groot & J. McLaughlin (eds), *Geospatial Data Infrastructure: Concepts, cases, and good practice.* New York: Oxford University Press. pp. 1-12

Grus, L. (2010). Assessing spatial data infrastructures. PhD dissertation, Wageningen University

GSDI (2012). *The GSDI Cookbook.* GSDI. Available online at http://www.gsdi.org/gsdicookbookindex/

Hendriks, P., Dessers, E. & Van Hootegem, G. (2012). Reconsidering the definition of a spatial data infrastructure. *International Journal of Geographical Information Science* 26(8): 1479-1494

I&M/Geonovum (2013). INSPIRE Country Report Nederland 2010–2012

I&M/Geonovum (2016). INSPIRE Country Report Nederland 2013–2015

Janssen, K. (2010). *The Availability of Spatial and Environmental Data in the EU at the Crossroads between Public and Economic Interests.* Dordrecht: Kluwer

Janssen, K. (2011). The influence of the PSI directive on open government data: An overview of recent developments. *Government Information Quarterly* 28(4): 446–456.

Jetzek, T. (2016). Managing complexity across multiple dimensions of liquid open data: The case of the Danish Basic Data Program. *Government Information Quarterly* 33(1): 89-104

Kabinet (2013a). Visie open overheid. *Kamerstukken* 2013–2014, 32 802, nr. 5, Toepassing van de wet openbaarheid van bestuur. https://data.overheid.nl/sites/data.overheid.nl/files/visie-open-overheid.pdf

Kabinet (2013b). Actieplan open overhead. https://data.overheid.nl/sites/data.overheid.nl/files/actieplan-open-overheid.pdf

Kabinet (2015). Nationale open data agenda. Toepassing van de wet openbaarheid van bestuur. *Kamerstukken* 2015/2016 32 802, Nr. 20

Kaell, F. & Konnen, J. (2013). INSPIRE Country Report Luxembourg 2010–2012.

Kaell, F., Konnen, J. & Weber, P. (2016). INSPIRE Country Report Luxembourg 2013–2015.

Kitchin, R. (2014). *The Data Revolution: Big data, open data, data infrastructures and their consequences.* Thousand Oaks: Sage

Kok, B. & Van Loenen, B. (2005). How to assess the success of national spatial data infrastructures? *Computers, Environment and Urban Systems* 29(6): 699-717

Konnen, J. & Kaell, F. (2010). INSPIRE Country Report Luxembourg 2009

KULeuven/SADL (2011a). Spatial Data Infrastructures in Slovenia: State of Play 2011. Leuven: KU Leuven

KULeuven/SADL (2011b). Spatial Data Infrastructures in Luxembourg: State of Play 2011. Leuven: KU Leuven

KULeuven/SADL (2011c). Spatial Data Infrastructures in Belgium: State of Play 2011. Leuven: KU Leuven

Lämmerhirt, D. (2017). Mapping open data governance models: Who makes decisions about government data and how? Blog post, Open Knowledge International Blog. https://blog.okfn.org/2017/02/16/mapping-open-data-governance-models-who-decides-and-how

Latre, M.A., Lopez-Pellicer, F.J., Nogueras-Iso, J., Bejar, R., Zarazaga-Soria, F.J. & Muro-Medrano, P.R. (2013). Spatial data infrastructures for environmental e-government services: The case of water abstractions authorisations. *Environmental Modelling & Software* 48: 81-92

Lee, G. & Kwak, Y. H. (2012). An open government maturity model for social media-based public engagement. *Government Information Quarterly* 29(4): 492-503

Lynn, L.E., Heinrich, C.J. & Hill, C.J. (2000). Studying governance and public management: Challenges and prospects. *Journal of Public Administration Research and Theory* 10(2): 233-262

Masser, I. (2009). Changing notions of a spatial data infrastructure. In B. Loenen, J.W.J. Besemer & J.A. Zevenbergen (eds), *SDI convergence*. Delft: Nederlandse Commissie voor Geodesie. pp. 219-228

Martin, S., Foulonneau, M., Turki, S. & Ihadjadene, M. (2013). Risk analysis to overcome barriers to open data. *Electronic Journal of E-Government* 11: 348-359

McLaughlin, J. & Nichols, S. (1994). Developing a national spatial data infrastructure. *Journal of Surveying Engineering* 120(2): 62-76

Member State Contact Point Belgium (2010). INSPIRE Country Report Belgium 2009

Member State Contact Point Belgium (2013). INSPIRE Country Report Belgium 2010–2012

Member State Contact Point Belgium (2016). INSPIRE Country Report Belgium 2013–2015

Nedović-Budić, Z., Crompvoets, J. & Georgiadou, Y. (eds) (2011). *Spatial Data Infrastructures in Context: North and South*. Boca Raton: CRC Press

Netherlands Ministry of Infrastructure and Environment (2012). *Open Data Roadmap*. Den Haag

Netherlands Ministry of Housing, Spatial Planning and the Environment (2008). *GIDEON – Key geo-information facility for the Netherlands. Approach and implementation strategy (2008-2011)*. The Hague: Ministry of Housing, Spatial Planning and the Environment

Obama, B. (2009). Transparency and Open Government: Memorandum for the Heads of Executive Departments and Agencies. Washington DC: The White House

OpenGovData (2016). Eight principles of open government data. http://www.opengovdata.org

Open Knowledge International (2014). Global Open Data Index. http://index.okfn.org.

Petek, T. et al. (2010). INSPIRE Country Report Slovenia 2009

Petek, T. (2014). State-of-play and organisational context of data infrastructure in Slovenia (Danube_Net D1). Ispra: EC Joint Research Centre

Petek, T. (2016). INSPIRE in the Republic of Slovenia. INSPIRE Webinar

Pira International, University of East Anglia, & KnowledgeView (2000). Commercial exploitation of Europe's public sector information. Final report for the European Commission Directorate General for the Information Society.

Rodriguez Pabon, O. (2005). Cadre théorique pour l'évaluation des infrastructures d'information géospatiale, PhD thesis, Département des Sciences Géomatiques, Faculté de Foresterie et de Géomatique, Laval University, Québec

Saxby, S. (2011). Three years in the life of UK national information policy–the politics and process of policy development. *International Journal of Private Law* 4(1): 1-31

Ubaldi, B. (2013). *Open Government Data*. Paris: OECD

UN-GGIM (2016). Luxembourg Legal Framework. UN-GGIM Knowledge Base. http://ggim.un.org/knowledgebase/Knowledgebase.aspx

Vancauwenberghe, G. (2013). SmeSpire Country Report Belgium. SmeSpire

Vancauwenberghe, G., Crompvoets, J. & Vandenbroucke, D. (2014). Location information strategies: Bringing location into e-government. In L.G. Anthopoulos & C.G. Reddick (eds), *Government e-Strategic Planning and Management: Practices, patterns and roadmaps*. New York: Springer. pp. 65–82

Vancauwenberghe, G., Dessers, E., Crompvoets, J. & Vandenbroucke, D. (2014). Realizing data sharing: The role of spatial data infrastructures. In Gascó-Hernández M. (ed.), *Open Government: Opportunities and challenges for public governance*. New York: Springer. pp. 155-169

Van Loenen, B. (2006). Developing geographic information infrastructures: The role of information policies. Delft: DUP Science

Van Loenen, B. & Van Barneveld, D.W. (2010). Implementing INSPIRE: the process towards the harmonization of licenses for public sector geographic information in the Netherlands. The 4th INSPIRE Conference, Krakow, 22–25 June

Van Loenen, B. & Grothe, M. (2014). INSPIRE empowers re-use of public sector information. *International Journal of Spatial Data Infrastructures Research* 9: 86-106

Verhoest, K., Bouckaert, G. & Peters, G. (2007). Janus-faced reorganization: Specialisation and coordination in four OECD countries in the period 1980–2005 *International Review of Administrative Sciences* 73(3): 325-348

Vickery, G. (2011). Review of recent studies on PSI re-use and related market developments. Paris: Information Economics

VROM/Geonovum (2010). INSPIRE Country Report Nederland 2009.

Wehn de Montalvo, U. (2001). Strategies for SDI implementation: A survey of national experiences. In *Proceedings of 5th Global Spatial Data Infrastructure Conference*. Cartagena de Indias, 21–25 May

Wirtz, B.W. & Birkmeyer, S. (2015). Open Government: Origin, Development, and Conceptual Perspectives. *International Journal of Public Administration* 38(5): 381-396

World Bank Group (2015). Open Data Readiness Assessment – Part B: Methodology. http://opendatatoolkit.worldbank.org

World Wide Web Foundation (2015). Open Data Barometer Global Report. 2nd edn. http://barometer.opendataresearch.org

5.

Beyond mere advocacy:
CSOs and the role of intermediaries
in Nigeria's open data ecosystem

Patrick Enaholo

Introduction

Since 2011, the open data community in Nigeria has developed organically from what was previously a fragmented gathering of activists and enthusiasts to what is now becoming a sophisticated and formidable pool of organised groups advocating for the government's adoption of open mechanisms to de-obfuscate its public processes. So far, the community can lay claim to a number of points scored in the struggle to bring about change in policy, the adoption of open standards and the proactive disclosure of government information for the benefit of citizens. Furthermore, while in previous years the strategies employed by various groups ranged from pure advocacy in the form of protests and strikes, current approaches include the use of online platforms and digital tools which, by way of transcending physical space, offer the community the opportunity to engage with a wider spectrum of citizens.

At the forefront of these engagements in Nigeria have been civil society organisations (CSOs) which, depending on the prevailing political, economic and socio-cultural climes at different epochs in the country's history, have employed an assorted range of strategies to attain their self-assigned goals (Fadakinte 2013, Ikelegbe 2013). Today, one of these strategies includes the use of open data. The aim of this chapter is to examine the roots of their adoption of this strategy by tracing the historical evolution of CSOs in Nigeria from their position as activists to their current status as open data advocates. Understanding this strategy requires an appreciation of the role of CSOs in Nigeria more generally and how they can optimally fulfil their burgeoning role as open data intermediaries. To this end, this chapter aims to provide answers to the following questions: How has the open data ecosystem evolved in Nigeria and what is its current structure? What role do CSOs, as open data intermediaries, play within it? And how can these roles be optimised to achieve greater citizen participation in the governance of Nigeria?

To answer these questions, I begin by proposing a definition of CSOs, drawing on existing definitions. Thereafter, I trace the history of CSO activity in Nigeria with emphasis on their role as representatives of the rest of society and as intermediaries between citizens and government. I then proceed to discuss how the evolution of CSOs has led to the adoption of open data as a key strategy which, going beyond mere advocacy (the supply side), aims to attain higher levels of citizen participation (the demand side) in government decision-making on the path towards greater accountability, transparency and good governance in Nigeria. Finally, I examine the structure of Nigeria's growing open data ecosystem and, using case studies of three Nigerian organisations, I propose ways by which open data intermediation among CSOs can be optimised.

What are CSOs?

In the literature, academic scholars and policy groups have proffered varied but complementary definitions of civil society organisations based on their understanding of what role they perform in society. For example, adopting a definition that focuses on 'civil society organisations as agents of change and development', CSOs have been defined to include 'all non-market and non-state organisations outside of the family in which people organise themselves to pursue shared interests in the public domain' (OECD 2009: 123). The focus of this definition lies in the notion that the role of CSOs is determined by the common societal goal that they strive for. A more elaborate view by the World Bank (2013: online) states that CSOs are:

> the wide array of non-governmental and not-for-profit organisations that have a presence in public life, expressing the interests and values of their members or others, based on ethical, cultural, political, scientific, religious or philanthropic considerations. Civil society organisations therefore refer to a wide array of organisations: community groups, NGOs, labour unions, indigenous groups, charitable organisations, faith-based organisations, professional associations, and foundations.

In the above, attention is drawn to three key ideas about CSOs: first, that they are non-profit which means that all of the money earned by or donated to them is used to pursue the organisation's objectives; second, that these objectives which are based on 'interests and values of their members and others' constitute the *raison d'être* of the organisation; third, they have a presence in public which implies that their activities involve offering a public service and therefore being known by the public. It also suggests that the interests and values that they share are promoted in the public domain on behalf of the public. This points to a dimension of 'representation' as a characteristic of CSOs. Indeed, CSOs have been understood as those organisations that 'operate on the basis of shared values, beliefs, and objectives with the people *they serve or represent*' (OECD 2009: 26, emphasis added). Thus, there exists an 'extensive diversity of CSOs in terms of values, goals, activities, and structure' (OECD 2009: 26). In this sense, the role of CSOs can be understood as one that goes beyond promoting or advocating for beliefs that are upheld by their members. The representational character of CSOs implies that the values they express are those which they believe to also be held by the wider public.[1]

For CSOs to represent the interests and values of the wider public suggests that they promote values which are relevant to a relatively large segment of people within a society. In many instances, one may argue that such widely-held values necessarily refer to fundamental principles on which sustainable societies are based such as the basic human needs of food, clothing and shelter; but also broader needs like jobs, livelihood and employment as well as food security and safety. As Sen (1999) suggests, the provision of such needs in a society is the hallmark of good governance. Therefore the pursuit of these fundamental human needs in any society can be translated as the pursuit of good governance. There are a plethora of definitions for good governance, but commentators generally agree that it is the manner in which power is exercised in the management of a country's economic and social resources for development in the service of and commitment to the public good (Diamond, cited in Fadakinte 2013). Thus, good governance refers to the exercise of authority in the name of the people in ways that respect their integrity and needs within a state (Odo 2015). It is therefore obvious that good governance is dependent on the establishment of frameworks which ensure that citizens (the public) are well served. According to Odo (2015: 3), it should have 'the basic ingredients that make a system (a state) acceptable to the generality of the people'. For this reason, good governance thrives in democratic settings and must be cultivated for democracy to mature further. Indeed, various scholarly writings and policy documents have linked good governance to the growth of democracy particularly in developing countries (Abdellatif 2003, Ogundiya 2010, Santiso 2001).

From the foregoing, it is clear that good governance is vital for achieving the basic human needs in society. It can therefore be said that good governance is one of the goals of CSO activity, especially in developing countries and those with less mature democracies where CSOs involve themselves in the struggle to promote the eradication of poverty and the advancement of human and economic development. As Annan (2001) suggests, attentiveness to these goals by leaders of any state is a distinctive feature of good governance. To ensure

---

1 Other roles of CSOs that have been put forward in other writings include: watchdog, service provider, capacity builder, expert, citizenship champion, solidarity supporter (World Economic Forum 2013).

that such attentiveness exists and is sustained, CSOs assume the role of being representative of groups of people when they engage with those who govern *on behalf of* those who are governed. Thus, CSOs occupy the gap between the government and the people. By definition, therefore, CSOs are intermediaries. In line with this reasoning, Fadakinte (2013:136) has defined civil society as the 'space that exists between the national government and the individual', and which 'consists of a variety of different groups and associations, each of which is dedicated to upholding certain values and to achieve particular ends'. Based on the discussion so far, I define CSOs as *those organisations that represent society as intermediaries between the government and citizens in the pursuit of good governance.* In the next section, I discuss how this definition of CSOs applies in the Nigerian context.

CSOs as intermediaries in the Nigerian context

In Nigeria, CSOs have historically served as intermediaries (Fadakinte 2013, Obadare 2015). However, the means and the effectiveness with which they have carried out this role vary according to the context and milieu within which they operated. In general terms, CSOs in Nigeria have been directly involved in the pursuit of good governance through the advocacy for more transparency in government decision-making, greater commitment to the rule of law within government processes, increased accountability in the use and expenditure of public funds, as well as justice, fairness and equity in conflict resolution (Ikelegbe 2013). Among the diverse ingredients of good governance put forward in various commentaries on the topic, I draw on three proposed by Sen (1990) – freedom, accountability and participation – because they align with the methods and strategies historically applied by CSOs in their role as intermediaries, namely, *activism* in the struggle for freedom from repressive rule, *advocacy*[2] in the pursuit of greater accountability from the government and *citizen participation* as a means of eliciting informed reaction from Nigerians. In what follows, I discuss each of these. I argue that, in progressive order, each strategy corresponds to a particular historical stage of CSO activity in Nigeria up to the present period. First, I discuss the activities of CSOs in Nigeria which portrays their activist role in the struggle against military leadership characterised by the suppression of freedom and the infringement of citizens' rights. Second, in the transition from a post-military era to an, albeit immature, democratic one, I discuss how CSO activity has been characterised by the pursuit of good governance through the advocacy for increased government accountability. Finally, I explain how

---

2   Here, I use the term activism to refer to the policy of taking direct action or intervention (such as a protest) to achieve a political or social change (Zeitz 2008) while the advocacy should be understood as milder form of action which may involve the act of pleading or arguing for a cause. Advocacy can also be seen as working 'within the system' whereas activism is seen as working 'outside the system' to generate change (Toope 2010).

CSOs are currently taking advantage of internet technology in the development of a burgeoning open data ecosystem as a way to achieve greater participation of citizens in government decision-making. Thereafter, I discuss the rise of open data engagement in the evolving strategy of CSOs amid the obstacles and pitfalls that characterise developing countries like Nigeria. Table 1 shows a summary of CSO activity and strategies in Nigeria.

Table 1 A historical overview of CSO activity in Nigeria

	Period of military and colonial rule (pre-1960; 1966–1979; 1983–1999)	Early democratic period (1979–1983)	Current democratic period (1999–present)
Societal causes	Basic freedoms and citizens' rights	Accountability and transparency in government	Citizen participation in government processes and decision-making
Primary strategy	Activism	Advocacy	Open data
Methods employed	Mass protests, boycotts, riots and strikes	Campaigns, lobby, town hall meetings etc.	Engagement through digital platforms

CSO activism and the pursuit of citizens' basic rights

Fadakinte (2013) periodises the activities of CSOs in Nigeria as follows: a post-independence period (1960–1965); two periods of military rule (1966–1979 and 1983–1999); and two periods of civilian democracy (1979–1983 and 1999 to the present). Of these, he notes that the second period (that is, military rule) was the one which witnessed a substantive rise of civil society activity in Nigeria due to a rapid increase in the number of CSOs. According to him, CSOs during this period acted as 'the main opposition to military (mis)rule and were in staunch defence of the citizens' rights' (Fadakinte (2013: 134). Since military rule was characterised by dictatorship, regardless of which individual assumed the role of head of state, civil society organisations took on the role of resisting repressive systems of governance, fighting against state abuses and curbing the excesses of those at the helm. Their strategies were actualised through the mobilisation of public protests and demonstrations, labour strikes and, when deemed necessary, riots (Ikelegbe 2013). According to Obadare (2005:84), it was not until the early 1990s with increasingly 'popular discontent against military rule and depression in the economic realm' that the concept of *civil society* came to the fore in popular vocabulary. During this time, 'individuals and groupings that were central to this open challenge to the state in Nigeria [...] began to refer to themselves as belonging to, and defending the values of, civil society' (Obadare 2005:85).

However, Ikelegbe (2013) suggests that the rise of activism as a means to confronting oppressive or discriminatory rule in Nigeria took its roots from the country's colonial era. According to him, colonialism brought with it 'new social exchanges, modernism and attendant social dislocations' that 'provided a new platform of consciousness and agitation which catalysed the formation of communal, traditional, cultural and other groups' (Ikelegbe 2013: 33). Here already, the struggle for freedom to self-rule, as a value perceived to be commonly held and accepted by the general populace (the public), led the nascent civil society to begin to fulfil the role of intermediary between the government and governed. In this case, it was between the British colonial masters and the colonised people. This struggle would lead civil society representatives to serve as activists in the campaign for the country to operate as a sovereign nation. Their campaigns, which eventually proved successful when the country gained independence in 1960, were arguably the prelude to subsequent confrontations between the government and civil society, including those that took place during the periods of military rule already discussed above.

CSOs advocacy for government transparency and accountability

Following what appears to have been the definitive end of military rule and the onset of a sustained period of democracy, the focus of civil society in Nigeria inevitably shifted from issues related to liberation from colonial and repressive systems to those centred on increased transparency and accountability within government. Just as previous leadership regimes during colonial and military eras demonstrated little regard for basic citizens' rights in a way that prompted the demand for freedom, self-determination and democracy, the ensuing democratic period also witnessed the mismanagement and embezzlement of public funds which led to calls for greater accountability among elected government officials. Thus, while CSO activity in the former period was characterised by the desire to bring about change through activism, the latter was characterised by the adoption of strategies based on advocacy. The difference is significant. While CSO activism relied primarily on open protests through mass mobilised rallies, riots and strikes (which were prevalent mostly during the colonial and military eras), advocacy serves more as a tool for engaging with the government on behalf of the people through 'milder' forms of action such as the lobbying for change in laws, policies and regulations, equity in resource distribution, and so on.

The inception of democracy in Nigeria ushered in a greater variety of issues advocated for by CSOs. Ikelegbe (2013) notes that civil and primary groups which articulated and expressed diverse interests blossomed during this period. However, the absence of good governance manifested by endemic corruption, infrastructure deficit and high unemployment rates was an abiding concern across the country. To tackle these, a new generation of CSOs began to evolve. Besides their deviation from strictly activist strategies, these CSOs were different from those of the past in their professional commitment and general approach to civil society work. While the activists of earlier years earned their living through diverse professions and engaged in civil society labour mostly on part-time basis, many of the leading advocates of the later period acquired formal training in professional disciplines closely aligned to civil society work. Among other reasons, it can be argued that the increased professional status of CSO work was to qualify for funding (mostly) from international donor agencies. As Anyanwu (n.d.: online) observes,

> Nigerian CSOs have come to be stymied in the quagmire of 'establishment mentality', whereby it becomes fashionable to merely pass through the motion of gaining recognition and visibility by performing form activities prescribed by donor agencies and 'international best practices' of: 'accountability', 'zero tolerance', 'transparency', 'anti-corruption', 'due process monitoring', 'capacity building', 'empowerment/skills acquisition', 'communiques', etc.

As a result, CSOs became mostly urban in their mentality. And 'being more of professionals and middle-class associations, [they] have been delinked from localities and the grassroots' (Ikelegbe 2013:38). This is in contrast to those CSOs of the military years whose successes depended greatly on their ability to rally masses at the grassroots level and even in rural areas. This is not to suggest that CSOs which focus solely on advocacy are ineffective. While an activist approach may expect to draw instant victories or losses, the desired results expected through strategies based on advocacy may be slower to realise – but, perhaps, more deep-rooted. Also, activist approaches to CSO work typically involve the organisation of public rallies, demonstrations, boycotts and strikes which, arguably, may not require high levels of cognitive activity; while those based on advocacy arguably demand more subtlety and sophistication. Among other instruments, advocacy approaches require the organisation of public meetings, debates, petitions and polls which potentially call for higher proficiencies and skills. Significantly, this level of sophistication has prepared CSOs to join the global trend towards utilising open data as a tool in the advocacy for greater transparency and accountability in government. In this way, moving beyond mere advocacy towards greater citizen participation, the adoption of open data serves as the next strategy for CSOs in the pursuit of good governance. In the following sections, I examine how CSOs are adopting open data and the challenges they encounter in doing so.

CSOs and the adoption of open data

For a few years now, it appears that civil society organisations in Nigeria have been metamorphosing into a community of open data enthusiasts, perhaps in the hope that, through open data, the effectiveness of their role as advocates for good governance would be enhanced. Indeed, as laid out thus far in this chapter, a growing number of CSOs in Nigeria have gradually and organically developed from a fragmented gathering of activists to a sophisticated pool of organised groups whose approach to civil society work has become closely associated with the uptake of open and publicly accessible data (Mejabi et al. 2014) as an instrument in the promotion of good governance. Indeed, this trend points to the gradual development of an open data ecosystem in which data is being used, re-used and redistributed more frequently and with greater ease among citizens. In Nigeria, this is arguably leading to a higher level of citizen awareness and participation in government processes than in the past, and is driven by the proliferation of CSOs with the skills and knowledge of web-based open data systems and tools.

However, this does not necessarily imply that the activities of these CSOs demonstrate the workings of an *effective* open data ecosystem. What is required is not simply the isolated use and advocacy for open data by individual groups, but the integrated and collaborative application of systems that facilitate the flow of data for the benefit of both government and citizens. For an ecosystem to work effectively, Heimstädt et al. (2014) propose that there should be the active intervention of three groups within the life cycle of data: suppliers, intermediaries and end users. While governments remain the primary suppliers and citizens the final consumers in the open data value chain, the role of intermediaries is known to be multifaceted and multileveled (Van Schalkwyk et al. 2016). Scholars point out that intermediaries consist of grassroot organisations, researchers (domain experts) and developers (data experts), as well as donors and funders along with other individuals and organisations that facilitate and support the development of data-driven products and services (Chattapadhyay 2014, Davies 2014, Khan & Foti 2015). In sum, intermediaries are those who operate within the open data ecosystem by means of their contribution, in one way or the other, to the supply of open data by governments as well as to the demand for such data by citizens.

A healthy open data ecosystem may therefore be described as one which comprises some or all these actors who actively perform roles that are essential to the effective flow of data among all the stakeholders. It becomes evident therefore that, for this constant flow of data to occur, intermediaries are indispensable (Van Schalkwyk et al. 2015, 2016). In the Nigerian context, I argue that those CSOs with the required skills need to assume a primary role of intermediation within the country's burgeoning open data ecosystem. However, in line with my definition of CSOs as intermediaries in society, I suggest that the effectiveness of the role of CSOs as open data intermediaries should equally be measured by two factors: first, the efficacy of their engagement with the government and, second, the active participation of citizens. On the side of the government (the supply side), the role of CSOs would be to ensure that there is disclosure of government data which can be accessed through online or offline means created by the CSOs themselves, or the government. This data which will be made available in open formats would allow citizens to engage with them and elicit reactions from citizens through official channels such as elections (the demand side). These reactions would in turn lead the government towards greater accountability and transparency and, among other things, sustain the desired culture of data disclosure by government – thus closing the loop. This cycle from government disclosure through citizen engagement and citizen reaction and back to government disclosure is illustrated in Figure 1. In the next section I discuss this cycle with focus on citizen participation and its challenges for CSOs in the Nigerian context.

Figure 1 A diagrammatic representation of the open data ecosystem in Nigeria

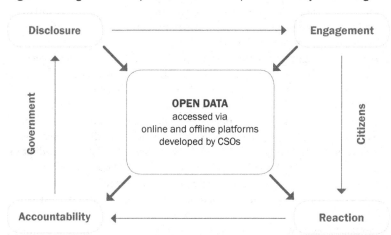

CSOs, open data and the challenges of citizen participation

Citizen participation is a key component of an open data ecosystem (Zuiderwijk et al. 2014). It is one end of the open data value chain which has government disclosure at its other end. Between these two are the intermediaries who try to ensure that data successfully passes from the latter to the former. Since not all data supplied by the government can be utilised in their raw formats by citizens, intermediaries help to fill the breach by translating the data into structures that can be more easily understood. In most cases, this translation is done through the use of web applications and digital tools deployed by the intermediaries. Thus, the internet plays a significant and increasingly indispensable role globally as an enabler in the open data value chain. In developing countries like Nigeria with limited internet penetration,[3] the reliance on web technology for the transmission of open data from its suppliers to potential users is likely to be fraught with challenges. It leads to an imbalance in the open data ecosystem whereby citizens without access to internet technology are excluded and marginalised. Gurstein

---

3   According to the Internet World Stats, internet penetration as at June 2015 was 51.1% which means that just over half of the population have access to the internet.

(2011) identifies access to internet and technology as the first stage in what he referred to as a three-step process towards the effective use of open data. He highlights the importance of access to telecommunications and internet services and infrastructure in making open data available to all users. According to Gurstein, this includes the affordability of internet access (which is a major issue for many, particularly in the developing world), the availability of sufficient bandwidth and the accessibility of the underlying networks on which internet technologies depend. Even more fundamental are the hardware and software required to access and process the data, along with tools that have the capacity to carry out various kinds of analyses with it.

This is not to suggest that the internet (and accompanying technologies) is the only channel through which citizens can gain access to open data. In order not to rely solely on the internet, a multi-faceted strategy can be employed by suppliers and intermediaries to reach users who are disadvantaged by the lack of access. The value and effectiveness of an open data strategy in countries where a significant percentage of potential users are without access to the internet would therefore be partly determined by the variety of methods intermediaries adopt to keep citizens in the loop. Still, beyond issues related to the lack of internet access and the availability of related technologies is the challenge of the availability of computer and software skills by potential users of open data. According to Gurstein, 'techies know how to do visualisation, university trained persons and professionals know how to use the analytical software but ordinary community people might not know how to do either and getting that expertise/support might be either difficult or expensive or both'. Related to this, Gurstein (2011) also highlights the challenge of data interpretation which can be the result of low levels of data literacy in some countries. For Nigeria, the current literacy rate is 59%[4] which is well below the world's average of 86.1%. For low percentage countries like Nigeria, it may be safely inferred that a reasonable number of citizens in the country lack sufficient knowledge required to make sense of open data due to a potential inability to identify the information that would be worthwhile to them and that could change their lives for the better – as is the expected goal of open data strategies.

A final step in Gurstein's process refers to the 'use' of open data. This step is based on the presumption that problems of access and interpretation have been resolved. Effective use of data points to the ability of users to combine datasets in such a way as to apply them in their engagement with the government and its processes. The ability to utilise open data effectively suggests that users are empowered to take action within their rights as citizens. Therefore, one indication that data is used effectively by citizens is when it helps them to make informed choices during democratic exercises such as plebiscites and general elections.

---

4   According to the *CIA World FactBook*, this refers to the number of people who can read and write at the age of 15 and above (2015 est.).

For effective CSO intermediation in the Nigerian open data ecosystem, I suggest that open data strategies should be developed in such a way as to attain balance between the provision of data by the government (supply side) and the implicit or explicit demand for data by users (demand side). This requires that, as open data intermediaries, CSOs may advocate for the disclosure of data by the government while also ensuring that such data is made available to ordinary citizens in formats that are accessible, interpretable and can be utilised effectively. For this to occur, it is clear they need to find solutions to the challenges of access and literacy prevalent among a significant cross-section of Nigerian citizens. In my view, this necessarily requires that CSOs *themselves* possess the means to access data and the literacy levels needed to interpret them in order to make it utilisable by the public, therefore warranting higher levels of commitment, knowledge and skills among those in their ranks. As I argue in this chapter, this appears to be the path taken by CSOs operating as in the open data ecosystem. However, since the reality is that individual CSOs typically operate along specific areas of the open data spectrum (that is, either the supply side or the demand side), I suggest, as argued by Van Schalkwyk et al. (2016), that effective open data intermediation in Nigeria necessarily involves a consolidated effort among various CSOs. In this way, the strengths and weaknesses of different agents in the open data value chain can be combined, complemented and compensated for. In the next section, I propose how this synergy may take place among selected CSOs.

CSOs in Nigeria: Three case studies

CSO activity in Nigeria has gradually become less reliant on activism and more on advocacy directed at the government. I also argued that there is currently a greater drive towards citizen participation by CSOs due in great part to the adoption of open data. I also suggested that, among other reasons, this uptake of open data appears to be leading CSOs in the present dispensation to become more skillful in the ability to interpret and analyse data (through the acquisition of higher levels of education and development of skills) and more sophisticated in the strategies they employ (through greater professionalisation of CSO work) – more than those in the past who adopted activism or simple advocacy as their primary approach. As further suggested, this sophistication is reflected in their full-time commitment to CSO work, their educational status and their adoption of arguably more cognitive ways of engaging with the government. Another reason for this recent trend is that, for CSOs, such a profile arguably improves their chances of obtaining funding from international donors (Anyanwu n.d.). In summary, these changes imply that, to serve more effectively as intermediaries within Nigeria's open data ecosystem, CSOs have to enhance their cultural capital in order to gain more economic capital (see Van Schalkwyk et al. 2016).

In their study of intermediaries in developing countries, Van Schalkwyk et al. (2016) adopted Bourdieu's theory of social fields and capital to investigate the role of multiple intermediaries within open data ecosystems. Acknowledging that 'intermediation does not only consist of a single agent facilitating the flow of data in an open data supply chain' (Van Schalkwyk et al. 2016: 19), they noted that the existence of diverse intermediaries has the potential effect of increasing the use and impact of open data since, according to them, 'no single intermediary is likely to possess all the types of capital required to unlock the full value of the transaction between the provider and the user' (Van Schalkwyk et al. 2016: 20). In their empirical analysis, they expanded Bourdieu's four species of capital (economic, social, cultural and symbolic) by including a 'technical' component. While technical competences can be grouped within individuals' cultural capital, the distinction is useful because, as they argue, technical skills often come after those of cultural or social capital in the order of acquisition by intermediaries. For the purpose of my study, the distinction helpfully buttresses my argument that technical skills are increasingly being acquired by CSOs in order to adequately fulfil their role as intermediaries of open data. While these skills were not a requirement for entry into CSO work, they are now becoming essential as CSOs gradually adopt open data strategies for their advocacy.

One manifestation of the growing reliance of technical skills can be seen in the adoption of online platforms and digital tools by CSOs as spaces for more effective open data engagement. These tools, since they transcend physical space and time, potentially offer CSOs the opportunity of reaching a wider spectrum of citizenry. The tools also facilitate the transmission of data and information from government to citizens, and vice versa, which greatly enhances their intermediatory role as CSOs but, more importantly, as intermediaries of open data. Some of these online tools have attained varying level of acclaim. However, since they remain restricted to those with access (as discussed above), they must be complemented by offline strategies for engagement with citizens without access. As I discuss below, this combination of online and offline methods (often through synergising efforts with other actors) offers some level of completeness to the role of CSOs as open data intermediaries.

In the next section, I explore the roles of three CSOs in Nigeria which serve as case studies to demonstrate how open data intermediation is taking place in the open data ecosystem. I then propose ways by which these CSOs, based on their individual competencies (whether technical, cultural or social), can form synergies with each other in the open data ecosystem. The CSOs are BudgIT, Public and Private Development Centre (PPDC) and Connected Development (CODE). One reason for the choice of these organisations for the study lay in the fact that they were easier to access within the timeframe available for the research. However, and more importantly, these CSOs were selected on the basis of their high level of activity and presence in civil society spheres in Nigeria, and by their having featured in other related open data studies (such as Mejabi et al. 2014 and Van Schalkwyk et al. 2015, 2015). The research methods adopted varied with each organisation. Information from PPDC was acquired through semi-structured interviews with key officials and complemented by participant observation. For BudgIT, data was obtained by means of semi-structured interviews with relevant personnel while CODE was unavailable for interviews. However, secondary data was obtained through textual analysis of information available on the websites of the three organisations. Admittedly, a more rigorous methodological and consistent approach may have been adopted for the research, but these were deemed sufficient for the purpose of giving support to the ideas presented in this chapter. Thus, the case studies are aimed at demonstrating what currently exists in Nigeria and at proposing a framework for optimising the effectiveness of open data intermediation within the Nigerian ecosystem.

BudgIT

Founded in 2011, BudgIT identifies itself as a civic organisation and a 'pioneer in the field of social advocacy melded with technology'. It thrives on using 'technology to intersect citizen engagement with institutional improvement' through a methodology that deploys 'data mining skill sets to creatively represent data and empower citizens to use the resulting information in demanding improved service delivery' (BudgIT 2011). BudgIT claims to use an array of technological and creative tools (such as infographics) to simplify Nigeria's budget in order to make it more comprehensible for citizens. It also claims to employ a specific methodology based on data mining skill sets to represent data in ways that can empower citizens to use the resulting information to demand improved service delivery from the government. According to them, this is done 'with the primary aim of raising [the] standard of transparency and accountability in government'. BudgIT's most notable tool is called *Tracka*[5] which 'allows Nigerians [to] post pictures of developmental projects in their communities [...] and demand completion of the government projects in their neighbourhoods' (Budgit 2014). According to the 2015 report on the Tracka tool, it is highlighted that:

> Tracka was created to assist active interested citizens in efficiently tracking budgets and public projects in their respective communities. The reoccurrence of capital projects listed and not executed in successive budget dampens the spirit of people whose sense of belonging comes from an inclusion in the State and Federal budgets. The platform is therefore layered on Open Data, bringing people aware of their civic duties together to share photos, videos, documents and also post comments on existing projects, and alert government and civil society to the non-implementation of any capital projects as well. (BudgIT 2015)

Based on the above, BudgIT is evidently aware of its position as a civil society

---

5   http://www.tracka.ng

organisations which serves as a bridge between the Nigerian government and its citizens. Therefore, within the open data ecosystem, it operates as an intermediary. BudgIT does not claim to carry out advocacy for the disclosure of open government data. Rather, it relies on data which is already made publicly available by government's budget office, a department of the Ministry of Finance (Mejabi et al. 2014).[6] Therefore it focuses less on the supply side of the open data ecosystem. Moreover, due to the unavailability of the contact details (emails and telephone numbers) of government representatives, they have encountered challenges in their attempts to reach the government using their open data platforms such as Tracka. In its various documentations, BudgIT positions itself as an advocate for greater citizen engagement. At the centre of their strategy is the Tracka platform which has covered over 450 projects in 15 local communities across the country. Furthermore, BudgIT claims to have reached more than 750 000 Nigerians through digital channels and physical spaces with 'over 2 000 unique data requests monthly from private, corporate and development entities/ individuals' (BudgIT 2015). However, they have also met with challenges caused by the lack of access to the internet on which their Tracka platform is based; and also the apparent reluctance of users to engage with it as a result of the costs associated with using the internet. To deal with these issues, BudgIT organises town hall meetings as a means to educate local communities who cannot access the data available on their digital platforms. During these meetings, they work with the local communities by means of letter-writing sessions. In this way, they give them the opportunity to react to the data that BudgIT makes available.

Connected Development (CODE)

Connected Development is a civil society group founded in 2012 with the aim of improving access to information in order to empower local communities. It claims to support local communities by 'creating platforms for dialogue, enabling informed debate, and building capacities of marginalised communities'. According to them, a key strategy to achieve their aims is the development of platforms that help to 'close the feedback loop between citizens and the government'. Their flagship platform is called *Follow the Money*[7] which is built for the promotion of 'transparency and accountability in the implementation of funds intended for local communities' (CODE 2013). Follow the Money serves as a digital space to showcase results of the investigations carried out by in-house and external researchers and journalists and presented in formats that include narratives, infographics, video and audio. They also organise training sessions

---

6   However, BudgIT has previously collaborated with other CSOs directly involved in the advocacy for the disclosure of government data in order to obtain specific contract information for capital projects that it monitors using its Tracka tool. I discuss this collaboration in the next section.

7   http://www.followthemoneyng.org

and workshops for journalists and individuals on diverse aspects of using and engaging with publicly available data.

As a CSO, CODE situates itself within the open data ecosystem as an intermediary since they claim to operate in the space between citizens and the government. However, their primary strategy is to source open and publicly available data for advocacy directed at the government. They also claim to provide access to information related to key development areas that affect the lives of citizens, such as health and education. They do this by reinterpreting complex budget data for citizens. The main strategy of CODE is to utilise this data in the process of conducting research and investigations aimed at unearthing and drawing attention to issues that raise questions about transparency and accountability within government processes. The results of these investigations are then published on their website, Follow the Money. Although the intention is for the platform to reach a wider audience, it is not clear whether this strategy achieves its purpose. On one hand, the website does not proactively elicit user feedback (beyond the basic comment feature that is emblematic of blogs); therefore, one could argue that the platform does not promote citizen participation effectively enough. On the other hand, there is no clear indication that alternative means are adopted to reach users who are without internet access. However, CODE can be described as a CSO that fulfils its role of representing the rest of society. This is achieved specifically through their own use of open data for advocacy to government for improved transparency, accountability and, ultimately, good governance.

Public and Private Development Centre (PPDC)

PPDC is a CSO which does not consider itself as an organisation that works directly with open data. This is based on their own unique understanding of what makes data open. However, one of their primary goals is 'to increase citizens' participation in governance processes' by enabling access to public contracting information as well as 'empowering and mobilising more citizens to participate in government processes' through radio programmes in which they share their data and experiences of project monitoring. Like BudgIT, they carry out monitoring and evaluation of capital projects initiated by the government. However, unlike BudgIT, they do not rely on crowdsourcing to report on these projects. Rather, they hire the services of project monitors who observe the progress of projects and send in reports which are then disseminated to the public through various media channels. Their online strategy is centred around *Budeshi*,[8] a web platform 'that seeks to link budget and procurement data to public services' (PPDC 2015). The data made available on the platform is derived from government sources that are publicly available or directly requested for by

---

8 http://www.budeshi.ng

PPDC. Thus, a key strategy for them is advocacy for the sustained and proactive disclosure of government data.

Although PPDC has existed longer than both BudgIT and CODE, it is a relatively newer entrant in the open data ecosystem. However, PPDC can be considered as an intermediary because of its role in the dissemination of public data from government to citizens. While PPDC does not interface directly with the latter (which therefore, in my view, limits their claims as promoters of citizen participation), it is specialised in advocacy for the proactive disclosure of data by the government and its agencies. One of PPDC's key strategies in this regard has been to develop and publish rankings of government institutions based on the proactive disclosure of data to the public.

In Table 2, I summarise the findings on the activities of these three CSOs within the Nigerian open data ecosystem. On the basis of their advocacy for disclosure of data, fostering citizen engagement and facilitating citizen reaction to openly accessible data, I classify the CSOs as either *very active*, *mildly active* or *not active*.

In a bid to consolidate their reputations as key actors within the open data ecosystem, along with the desire to gain further ground in their advocacy work, the above CSOs (along with others) have established an alliance that includes those civil society organisations at the forefront of the campaign for the provision and utilisation of government data in open formats. Having worked individually to promote open government, the aim of the alliance is to join forces in a coalition to engage government further on issues of openness and transparency. The overall objective of the alliance is to develop strategies that would enable member groups to synergise and, whenever possible, form a single frontier in negotiations with the government. However, since each group organises its own events and builds its own digital platforms, the alliance's strategy for consolidating the open data digital platforms of its members as a way to enhance their effectiveness as intermediaries in the ecosystem, remains, at best, fragmented and therefore less effective than its advocacy programme. I suggest that in order to grow the ecosystem and achieve the broader aims of open data in Nigeria, there is a need for CSOs to base their alliance on strategies that focus on their weaknesses and deficits in the promotion of greater citizen participation. Table 2 offers some direction on how this may be achieved.

As the table shows, BudgIT's appears to be the most active of the three CSOs that have been researched. However, its advocacy for the disclosure of open data from the government (the supply side) is limited or non-existent. To overcome this deficit, BudgIT could collaborate with PPDC which is reputed for its role as an advocate for the release of government data. Conversely, BudgIT could assist PPDC in tackling its deficit in the task of facilitating public reaction to the data it makes available. Similarly, CODE may choose to cooperate with PPDC in the dissemination of findings from its investigative work through the radio

Table 2 Classification of CSOs according to the level of their activity as intermediaries in the open data ecosystem

Civil Society Organisation (CSO)	Advocacy for the disclosure of government data in open formats	Fostering citizen engagement with open data made available on digital platforms	Eliciting and facilitating citizen reaction to open data
BudgIT	Not active	Very active Through its Tracka tool, digital infographics and other platforms, BudgIT actively tries to engage citizens using open data	Very active BudgIT adopts other means outside the internet and digital technology to ensure the effective use of open data among citizens.
Connected Development (CODE)	Not active	Mildly active On its Follow the Money platform, CODE publishes the results of its engage with open data; however, the platform does not offer enough opportunities for active citizen engagement	Mildly active By organising workshops and training sessions for journalists and other individuals in the use of open data; however, these sessions are directed at specialised groups
Public and Private Development Centre (PPDC)	Very active PPDC's specialises in advocating for government agencies to proactively disclose procurement data	Mildly active Through its engagement with citizens by means of radio programmes; however, at the time of writing, its new digital platform, Budeshi, was not fully utilised by citizens	Not active

programmes that the former organises. In the same vein, PPDC could benefit from the rigour of CODE's research in order to make better use of the data it publishes on its digital platforms. Also, BudgIT can support CODE in its outreach to citizens at the grassroots level in order to better disseminate results of the investigative research carried out by the latter.

Conclusion

Over the years, civil society in Nigeria has evolved alongside the economic, political and social milieu of the country. For a fledgling democracy like Nigeria's, the effort exerted to attain some of the basic needs of society (that is, basic rights of citizens; accountability and transparency in government; participation of citizens in government processes and decision-making) can be summarised as the pursuit of good governance. Civil society organisations have historically been identified as institutions at the forefront of this quest by serving as intermediaries between the

Fig. 2: A framework for open data synergy among selected CSOs in Nigeria

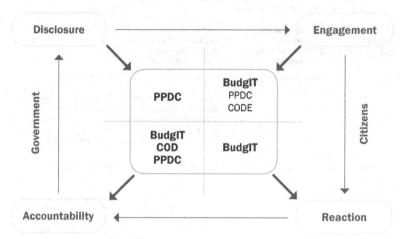

government and the rest of society through activism, advocacy and, more recently, through the engagement of citizens using open data.

In this chapter, I have attempted to trace the history of CSO activity in Nigeria and how their evolution is growthing the open data ecosystem in the country. I also discussed the structure of this ecosystem which is based on the primary role of CSOs within it, namely: as intermediaries between citizens and government. While the new generation of CSOs are equipping themselves with the knowledge and tools required to effectively utilise open data (and, thus, fulfil their role as open data intermediaries), they are also developing strategies that go beyond activism and mere advocacy (which were characteristic of previous eras in Nigerian history) towards higher citizen participation through open data. For most of them, formulating open data strategies translates to the deployment of online digital platforms and tools to reach a wider range of citizenry. However, I also discussed how strategies that rely on online platforms are accompanied by challenges (such as lack of access to technology and the low levels of literacy required to interpret open data) which are characteristic of less developed countries like Nigeria. For this reason, CSOs such as BudgIT have adopted both online and offline strategies to achieve greater citizen participation. Others like CODE and PPDC are also active at various levels of the open data ecosystem. However, since each one is deficient in one or more areas of the ecosystem, I have argued for a more cohesive alliance of CSOs which takes these deficits into account. By clearly identifying their points of weakness and inactivity within the open data ecosystem, it becomes possible to determine the most suitable ways by which CSOs can synergise their pursuit of a more active and vibrant participation of citizens on the path towards good governance in Nigeria. Finally, although the usefulness of my findings are limited by the scope of the study, they offer a helpful route to further research on civil society organisations and their role as intermediaries within open data ecosystems in Nigeria and elsewhere.

About the author

PATRICK ENAHOLO holds a doctoral degree in media and communication from the University of Leeds. In addition to conducting research and projects related to open data, he actively contributes to discourses around the growth of the Nigerian creative industries through the promotion of film, digital media and animation. He is currently a member of faculty at the Pan-Atlantic University in Lagos, Nigeria, where he also heads the Open Data Research Centre, a research unit focusing on developmental issues in Nigeria and across Africa.
E-mail: penaholo@smc.edu.ng

REFERENCES

Abdellatif, A.M. (2003). Good governance and its relationship to democracy and economic development. Paper presented at the Global Forum III on Fighting Corruption and Safeguarding Integrity, Seoul 20-31 May. http://pogar.org/publications/governance/goodgov.pdf

Advisory Group on Civil Society and Aid Effectiveness (2008). Civil society and aid effectiveness: Synthesis of findings and recommendations. Unpublished paper. http://siteresources.worldbank.org/ACCRAEXT/Resources/4700790-1208545462880/AG-CS-Synthesis-of-Findings-and-Recommendations.pdf

Anyanwu, V.T.C. (n.d.) Nigeria: A pradigm shift for the effectiveness of Nigerian CSOs. https://lawyersalert.wordpress.com/2014/01/07/nigeria-paradigm-shift-for-the-effectiveness-of-nigerian-csos-2/

BudgIT (2015). 2015 Annual Report. http://yourbudgit.com/wp-content/uploads/2016/06/annual-report-2015.pdf

BudgIT (2015). 2015 Federal Constituency Projects. http://yourbudgit.com/wp-content/uploads/2016/07/TRACKA-2015-Federal-Constituency-Project-Report.pdf

BudgIT (2016). About Us. http://yourbudgit.com/about/

Connected Development (2016). About Us. http://connecteddevelopment.org/about-us/

Fadakinte, M.M. (2013). Civil Society, Democracy and Good Governance in Nigeria: 1999-2012. *International Journal of Modern Social Sciences* 2(2): 133–154

Gurstein, M. (2011). Open data: Empowering the empowered or effective data use for everyone? *First Monday* 16:2. http://journals.uic.edu/ojs/index.php/fm/article/view/3316. DOI: 10.5210/fm.v16i2.3316

Ikelegbe, A.O. (2013). *The State and Civil Society in Nigeria: Towards a partnership for sustainable development*. Centre for Population and Environmental Development (CPED). http://dspace.africaportal.org/jspui/bitstream/123456789/35951/1/CPED%20Monograph%20Series%20No.%207-The%20State%20and%20Civil%20Society.pdf?1

Krishna, A. (n.d). *How are Civil Society Organizations Important for Development?* Washington DC: World Bank. http://info.worldbank.org/etools/docs/library/5683/civil_society_krishna.htm

Lukman, S.M. (n.d). Nigerian civil society organisations: How well and how right. *GAMJI*. http://www.gamji.com/article9000/NEWS9717.htm

Mejabi O.V., Azeez A.A., Adedoyin A. & Oloyede M.O. (2014). Case study report on investigation of the use of the online National Budget of Nigeria. Open Data Research Network. www.opendataresearch.org/sites/default/files/ publications/ Investigation%20of%20Open%20 Budget%20Data%20in%20Nigeria-print.pdf

Mohammed, A. (2016). CODE: The future we see through Follow the Money Newsroom. Connected Development. http://connecteddevelopment.org/2016/07/19/code-the-future-we-see-through-follow-the-money-newsroom/

Odo, L.U. (2015). Democracy and good governance in Nigeria: Challenges and prospects. *Global Journal of Human–Social Science Research* 15(3)

OECD (2009). *Civil Society and Aid Effectiveness: Findings, recommendations and good practice*. Paris: OECD

Obadare, E.B. (2005). The theory and practice of civil society in Nigeria. Unpublished PhD thesis, London School of Economics and Political Science. http://etheses.lse. ac.uk/1768/1/U194707.pdf

Ogundiya, I.S. (2010). Democracy and good governance: Nigeria's dilemma. *African Journal of Political Science and International Relations* 4(6): 201-208.

Public and Private Development Centre (2016). Quick Facts About PPDC. http:// procurementmonitor.org/ppdc/quick-facts-about-ppdc/

Santiso, C. (2001). International co-operation for democracy and good governance: Moving towards a second generation? *The European Journal of Development Research* 13(1): 154-180

Sen, A. (2001). *Development as Freedom*. Oxford: Oxford University Press.

Tomlinson, B. (2013). *Working with Civil Society in Foreign Aid: Possibilities for South–South Cooperation?* Beijing: United Nations Development Programme (UNDP)

Uadiale, M. (2011). The role of civil society organisations in democratic consolidation in Nigeria: The birth of a new order. *International Journal of Advanced Legal Studies and Governance* 2(1): 152-162

Toope, S., Kennelly, J. & Deibert., R. (2010, October 5). Advocacy oractivist: What is the best way to effect change? [Podcast]. https://www.alumni.ubc.ca/event/toronto-advocate-or-activist-what-is-the-best-way-to-effect-change/

Van Schalkwyk, F., Cañares, M., Chattapadhyay, S. & Andrason, A. (2016). Open data intermediaries in developing countries. *Journal of Community Informatics* 12(2): 9-25. http://ci-journal.net/index.php/ciej/article/view/1146/1205

Van Schalkwyk, F., Willmers, M. & Schonwetter, T. (2015) Viscous open data: The roles of intermediaries in an open data ecosystem. *Information Technology for Development*. http://dx.doi.org/10.1080/02681102.2015.1081868

World Bank (2013). Difining civil society. http://go.worldbank.org/4CE7W046K0

World Economic Forum (2013). The Future Role of Civil Society. *World Scenario Series*. Geneva: World Economic Forum. http://www3.weforum.org/docs/WEF_ FutureRoleCivilSociety_Report_2013.pdf

Zeitz, P. (2008). What is advocacy? What is activism? Presentation at Global Health Advocacy and Activism. 16 January, George Washington University. http://www. ccaba.org/wp-content/uploads/Paul-Zeitz-What-is-Advocacy-and-What-is-Activism-Compatibility-Mode1.pdf

Zuiderwijk, A. (2015). Open data infrastructures: The design of an infrastructure to enhance the coordination of open data use. Unpublished PhD thesis, Delft University of Technology. doi:10.4233/uuid:9b9e60bc-1edd-449a-84c6-7485d9bde012

Zuiderwijk, A., Janssen, M., & Davis, C. (2014). Innovation with open data: Essential elements of open data ecosystems. *Information Polity* 19(1, 2): 17-33

6.

Rethinking civil society organisations working in the freedom of information and open government data fields

Silvana Fumega

Introduction

This research has been developed within a rapidly changing international context. The research commenced with the supposition that there was a large gap in terms of understanding the relationship between freedom of information (FOI) and open government data (OGD) policies and, in particular, those advocating for FOI and OGD policies. The preliminary view was that despite the main actors being international non-government organisations (INGOs) working in the similar area of public sector information, there are a number of differences between FOI and OGD organisations that are not addressed in the literature.

In other words, there is an analytical vacuum in the academic literature related to FOI and OGD. And not only there is a void[1] in terms of literature on the linkages between the FOI and OGD fields, but the current literature on FOI and OGD does not reflect the varied and growing influence of civil society on FOI/OGD developments, the emergence of key international actors or the effects of the changes in ICT within both fields in the past two decades. This gap is a consequence of a predominantly one-dimensional approach to the analysis of FOI as pointed out by Darch and Underwood (2010 in Stubbs 2012: 49), as well as the recent emergence of OGD as an area of study. Thus, the dominant legal orientation found in FOI studies has, until recently, neglected the role of international civil society organisations. On the other hand, in relation to OGD, the dynamic of the field has outpaced the capacity of scholars to undertake rigorous analysis on many of its aspects and, in particular, civil

---

1 The literature on the overlap between FOI and OGD is very limited and has mostly has been produced by joint initiatives between scholars and civil society actors such as Access Info and Open Knowledge Foundation (2010), Hogge (2010) and some scholarly work such as that of Janssen (2012).

society actors. Thus, in both cases, the role played by organised civil society is neglected.

Despite the general uniformity of treatment and minimal coverage within the academic literature, civil society organisations working in the areas of FOI and OGD have been key actors in the development of both fields. However, they present not only different backgrounds but also a diverse set of goals and drivers. The influence exerted by information and communication technology (ICT) is a major factor that allows for a better understanding of those differences.

In the past decade, ICT-driven changes have dramatically influenced the way citizens and governments interact with information. Citizens and governments now have direct channels through which to interact: from feedback mechanisms, to information and data request platforms, to formal and informal channels. For example, citizens demand information and governments use social media tools to inform the public about their performance (Davies & Fumega 2014: 2). However, ICT has influenced not only the activities but also the way in which FOI and OGD civil society organisations are structured.

In this context, this chapter addresses the two-fold influence of ICT developments on the transformation of key FOI and OGD international advocacy actors. Scholars in both FOI and OGD have neglected international civil society organisations and this chapter aims to contribute to narrowing the gap regarding these crucial stakeholders in the governmental informational resources ecosystem. This chapter, in particular, explores the idea that differences between these organisations in these two information-related fields are not only heightened by the diverse professional and academic backgrounds of the key members of INGOs, but are also influenced by ICT and by the information environments in which these organisations were created.

This study of non-governmental organisations allows for a better understanding of the key features of the FOI and OGD fields while also aiming to provide researchers with new material and new areas to explore.

International NGOs[2]

There are no clear definitions of the non-governmental organisation (NGO). In general terms, it can be said that the term NGO refers to legally constituted organisations operating independently from any government and that are not conventional for-profit businesses (Stankowska 2014: 43). As the boundaries of the classic definitions are broad and sometimes do not reflect the changes that these organisations have experienced in the past years, new approaches to

---

2   This study does not claim to be universally applicable; it only applies to some transnational/international actors, mainly institutionalised non-for-profit organisations advocating for greater access to and use of government information and data. However, the limited progress in the study of non-governmental organisations means that this study contributes to a better understanding of key features of FOI and OGD as fields of study.

defining and analysing the subjects have to be explored. Multiple variables play a role when trying to define and delimit international civil society actors. Even defining the concept of civil society presents difficulties. And this is particularly relevant in a rapidly changing operational environment.

International, transnational and global[3] organisations are understood within this research as the main nodes to analyse the actors advocating for access to government information and data at a global level. They are, together with other civil society actors, vital in policy diffusion processes (Stone 2004). However, their role remains understudied and more often than not their features have been simplified and classified under static and broad categories. Instead of forcing a definition, some key common factors need to be analysed to delimit and clarify the universe comprised by international groups working on FOI and OGD.

What are the main variables that should be considered to better understand the common characteristics of civil society groups working on FOI and OGD? NGOs can be classified on the basis of different factors, such as what they do, how they approach their work, who they work for, and where they work. All these features, and more, can be grouped in three main areas to better understand this heterogeneous universe: content, engagement and structure. Thus, even though this study focuses on a heterogeneous universe, the organisations working on access to and the use of government information, do share some common features. These organisations, as with many modern professional civil society groups, do not focus their work on their own members and they do not rely on individual fees. At the same time, there is plenty of divergence in terms of their content, approach and their strategies of engagement.

Review of freedom and information (FOI) and open government data (OGD) international non-government organisations

Although occurring at different rates, the development of FOI and OGD fields in the literature present some significant similarities, as shown in the section below.

FOI

The FOI movement

In the first stage of the FOI movement, individual advocates, such as Frankel in the UK, Riley in Canada and McMillan in Australia, focus on the domestic arena. The topic starts to gain traction during the last part of the first stage and the beginning of the second period, with FOI advocates in most cases coming

---

3   Even though international, transnational and global are generally used as interchangeable terms (as it will be in this chapter), it is necessary to clarify that they are not always used as synonyms. For more information on the differences between these organisations, refer to Hines (2007).

from some of the newly created organisations, and some experts in this new field, start to be recognised as referents within the FOI movement and begin to cross borders to promote the passage of FOI legislation in other territories. Thus, while the organisations are being established, the topic becomes popular and the actors gain recognition among their peers and followers.

Not only the do the principles surrounding the FOI movement experience changes from FOI as administrative reform to the internationalisation process and thus the human rights discourse, but the actors (individuals as well as organisations) within this group change.[4] In this changing context, the identification of the actors from the FOI field proves to be a challenging task. (Similar difficulties are experienced in the identification of the actors in the OGD field.) A large number of organisations belong to the FOI advocacy group but only a very small number of them work on an international or transnational level. Most of the organisations surveyed by Kasuya (2013) as well as those included in different transparency emailing lists (e.g. Foianet[5] and Sunlight Foundation[6]) focus their main activities on the domestic and/or regional sphere.

Adding to this geographical delimitation, not all of the actors fit into the concept or groups that are actively working on the promotion/diffusion of FOI principles and legislation. Many of the organisations work on other aspects of government transparency. In addition to the large variety of particular sectors within the transparency field, it is also important to highlight that the abovementioned transparency-oriented lists present a self-identification policy. Thus, any organisation can include and define themselves as members of these lists in order to participate in discussions and activities.

Analysing variables such as approach, engagement and structure allows not only for a better understanding of these international groups and the field; but exploring these variables provides a better understanding of the reasons and rationale behind the main features of both FOI and OGD, and allows for distinctions to be made not only between fields but also within each of them.

Despite all their particularities, FOI-related INGOs have mainly focused on the construction, enactment and operation of access to information worldwide. In general terms, it can be said that these group focus on access to government-held and/or produced information while OGD groups emphasise the reuse of the information resources.

All these elements influence the way in which these organisations relate to governments. Most FOI advocates, who generally come from the transparency

---

4   Despite the growth in the importance of the topic as well as in the recognition of the actors, the number of international civil society organisations working on the diffusion/promotion of those FOI principles is clearly not numerous. The main examples are based on the analysis of five organisations. Some common features will be explored to understand not only these five actors but also to present a baseline to better understand international civil society organisations working on the OGD field.

5   Foianet: http://foiadvocates.net/

6   Sunlight Foundation: http://sunlightfoundation.com/

and accountability fields, present a more confrontational attitude towards governments than do OGD advocates, as the FOI approach is based on non-compliance. This analysis provides the basis on which to compare and contrast the roles played by INGOs in the diffusion and advocacy of OGD.[7]

FOI: A brief overview of the literature

There is an extensive body of literature on FOI legislation, its implementation and management. However, as Darch and Underwood note, the 'literature on freedom of information and its spread to countries around the world […] consists largely either of descriptive case studies or of normative commentaries on the adequacy of particular pieces of national legislation [...] There is relatively little in the way of comparative or theoretical analysis' (Darch & Underwood 2010: 50).

FOI legislation has attracted considerable interest over the past three decades among scholars (Stubbs 2012: 42). The speed and focus of the literature on the topic has largely followed the patterns of FOI adoption. While both experienced a slow pace at first, the number of FOI laws as well as the volume of studies have increased since the mid-2000s. The acceleration in the number of scholars, as well as in the diversity of approaches to the critiques of FOI, present a correlation in the diffusion process of the legislation on the topic (Darch & Underwood 2010, Michener 2010, Berliner 2012, Stubbs 2012, Berliner 2014).

The development of the literature on FOI parallels the geographic diffusion of access legislation around the world. Many case studies of the first adopters during the 20th century are focused on the development of these ideas in the Global North or Lockean[8] States as labelled by Stubbs (2012: 28), between the 1960s and mid-1990s, with examples from the US,[9] Canada, Australia[10] and NZ,[11] together with some early comparative work within the small number of cases in the western liberal established democracies (Hazell 1991, for example). This shows a similar path and convergence in terms of the work performed by advocates and academics in the area.

During the 1990s, FOI, which until then had predominantly been driven by domestic factors, gained traction globally. The explosion of global demands

---

7 For more details on the differences between FOI and OGD organisations, see Fumega (2015).
8 As clarified by Stubbs (2012: 4): 'Lockean' states because the relationship between state apparatuses and societies within those states developed as a consensual social contract facilitating a 'right to know'. Outside these 'Lockean' states and throughout much of modern history, so-called 'Hobbesian' states prevented the further diffusion of the law. Within 'Hobbesian' states, the authority of the state apparatus overshadowed weak civil societies and prevented the development of a 'right to know'. However, towards the end of the 20th century the 'Lockean'/'Hobbesian' dichotomy of modern states began to break down and FOI law proliferated widely. 'Hobbesian' structures underwent a process of transformation in the context of an emergent global political economy that facilitated the further diffusion of the law, and public sector transparency.
9 Davis (1998), Janssen (2012), Mendel (2003), Rees (1995)
10 Foerstel (1999), Snell (2001)
11 Fraser (2001), Eagles (1992)

for the disclosure of government-held information (commonly referred to as the 'Golden Period'[12] for FOI advocates) coincides with its emergence in the academic literature. Studies, sometimes advocacy-driven, start to focus on the need to establish international models and standards on government transparency (Article 19 1999, Coronel 2001, Mendel 2003, Neuman 2004, Kranenborg & Voermans 2005, Banisar 2006).

Following these initial studies, a few years later, a group of scholars, including Darch and Underwood (2010), start to break free from a largely legal-centric approach (Stubbs 2012: 50, Michener 2010: 5). While most of the FOI literature is still embedded within a legalistic perspective, more recent studies emerge that focus their research on a wider range of issues. These more recent FOI studies pay attention to the social and political context as being necessary for a comprehensive understanding of the logic of enactment and implementation of FOI legislation (Darch & Underwood 2010, Hazell & Worthy 2010, Berliner 2011, Stubbs 2012). This literature has begun to consider the institutional social and political contexts in which FOI regulations are enacted, in addition to studying the FOI diffusion process. Scholars, such as Michener, Berliner and Stubbs, have provided an extra dimension to FOI studies by adding political science and public policy elements to their analysis, as well as geographies outside the traditional liberal established western democracies.

This wider and more diverse approach to FOI analysis often adopted a critical and less idealistic or celebratory analysis of FOI. Advocacy-driven reports have a positive and at times naïve approach to FOI legislation. During this period, academia starts to shift the focus from a simple account of the legislative journey and a focus on the content of FOI legislation to more critical questioning of outcomes. Articles start to include less optimistic titles such as Roberts (2006) 'Dashed Expectations: Governmental Adaptation to Transparency Rules', Snell (2002) 'FOI and the Delivery of Diminishing Returns' and Worthy (2010) 'More Open but not more trusted?', to name a few. These studies acknowledge the increased gains in transparency but start to evaluate critically the performance post-implementation against predicted or hoped-for outcomes, as evident in the cases of Hazell and Worthy (2010).

These authors open up new lines of analysis and areas of research. The redirected focus on the conditions and context of the passage of FOI laws and/ or implementation start to identify a range of actors, including civil society organisations, formerly ignored or, at most, only briefly recognised.

FOI and INGOs

Some advocacy-driven studies have delineated the role of civil society advocates during the period of international diffusion (Neuman 2004, Puddephatt 2009,

---

12 As named in Darch and Underwood (2010).

One World Foundation India 2011). The limitations of funding, personnel and often very restrictive governmental regulations or control has meant that INGOs, directly or indirectly, have been the key drivers. Organised civil society mobilises pressure to enact FOI legislation and contributes to the drafting of the legislation. They also provide technical expertise during the implementation phase while making alliances with champions inside the public bureaucracy. In terms of the use of the information, they often act as 'infomediaries'[13] and can also build citizen capacity (One World Foundation India 2011). Additionally, NGOs can play a key role in monitoring the implementation and enforcement of the law. At the international level, INGOs also promote the application of lessons learned in one country to the specific situation of another (Neuman 2004, Puddephatt 2009).

Within the academic field, a handful of more recent studies including Darch and Underwood (2010), Berliner (2012), Stubbs (2012) and Kasuya (2013), and to some extent Snell (2000), Michener (2010) and Xiao (2011), provide some recognition or coverage of the role of NGOs in the diffusion of FOI, in some cases in terms of the international NGOs and in some cases their local partners. The coverage of NGOs in these studies is generally descriptive, often mentioning NGOs in passing while focussing on other elements. In particular, the role and importance of international NGOs seems to be downplayed or simply accepted as having little import or given a secondary importance in contrast to other actors such as the domestic news media or individual champions for FOI.

In the pool of political science-oriented studies, the literature in terms of the role of civil society organisations can be divided into three categories: (1) a group of authors such as Darch and Underwood (2010), Stubbs (2012), and Berliner (2014) who acknowledge the importance of organised civil society in the diffusion of FOI legislation but approach these actors as a monolithic group; (2) a second group, including for example McClean (2011) and Xiao (2011), who ignore their role, mainly due to the context of their research; and (3) a developing third group, including Kasuya (2013) and Kasuya and Takahashi (2013), who focus on civil society organisations as key actors in this FOI ecosystem. This chapter aims to make a contribution to this last group.

OGD

The OGD movement
After the preliminary observations of existing organisations working on the topic, it was necessary to draw some lines of exclusion in order to present a more accurate analysis, as previously stated in relation to FOI organisations. The geographic variable is one of the clearest delimitations of the OGD universe

---

13 'The term 'infomediaries' is widely used to refer to actors who stand between data originating from government and the intended users of the data, facilitating wider dissemination' (Davies & Fumega 2014: 21).

included in this research. However, one of the most relevant distinctions to be made relates to the ambiguity of the topic itself.[14] This ambiguity is the source of the problem to clearly identify the actors to be included in this analysis. These difficulties are closely connected to the myriad goals and approaches pursued by OGD organisations. These groups identify digital data in reusable formats as the primary output to achieve a large number of goals from greater transparency, development, business innovation and economic growth. The latter is associated with the idea that OGD has not only been defined as a policy or derived from the right to access government information, but also as an opportunity for entrepreneurs and companies interested in the liberalisation of markets for public sector information (Davies & Edwards 2012) to improve the profitability of their businesses (Pollock 2008, Fioretti 2010, Deloitte Analytics 2012). Corporations, academics and programmers are all part of the movement, unlike the recent FOI global movement, which has been a mostly transparency-advocates-only field from the outset.

OGD: A brief overview of the literature

There are several similarities and also some key differences in the development of the OGD literature compared to FOI. In addition to being a more recent development, largely post-2005,[15] OGD occurs at the intersection between technology and policy processes (Udell 2006). This intersection has required different types of stakeholders and skills than those found in the FOI process. A consequence has been more varied range of actors utilising different structures and techniques driven by a greater variety of motivations.

The academic literature on OGD has not kept pace with both ICT developments and the popular and variable use of this concept among practitioners, advocates from ICT and policy domains, public officials and politicians. Most of the ideas and insights in this emerging field are still in the early stages of development and articulation. Until recently, most of the attempts at analysis and understanding in the OGD field were to be found in blogs, social media, conference proceedings, government or international organisations' reports, and in a small number of journal articles, mostly in technology-oriented journals,[16] with a few exceptions.[17]

---

14 Morozov (2013) observes that 'Few words in the English language pack as much ambiguity and sexiness as open.' In a similar vein, Tkacz (2012: 387) notes that, 'open has become a master category of contemporary political thought. Such is the attraction, but also the ambiguity of openness, that it appears seemingly without tension, without need of clarification or qualification, in writers as diverse as the liberal legal scholar, Lawrence Lessig, and the post-Marxian duo Michael Hardt and Antonio Negri.'

15 Despite the fact that the main developments did not arise until the second half of 2000s, there were earlier mentions in the literature of the reutilisation of government information and data (Lewis 1995, Perritt 1997). The increasing automatisation of government functions and transactions, together with concerns related to the commercial use of government information (Perritt 1994) and to privacy risks (Paterson 1998) provided material for scholarly research.

16 Some examples are the *Journal of Community Informatics* and *Information System Management*.

17 For example, the *E-Journal of e-Democracy and Open Government*.

As with FOI, some scholars and, increasingly, advocacy groups,[18] have started to provide models and standards to develop definitions of OGD and related concepts. However, as with the first group of FOI academic studies, early reports are mostly based on case studies, at country or city level, of different OGD initiatives, such as the open data policies in the US, UK and Australia. The difference between the two fields is the origin of those reports. While in the first stages of FOI diffusion, the reports (aside from academia) were mostly from civil society advocates, in the case of OGD, the reports were developed or commissioned by governments implementing those policies (Mayo & Steinberg 2007, Government 2.0 Taskforce 2009, Power of Information Taskforce 2009, Davies & Lithwick 2010) and by different civil society and academic actors (Napoli & Karaganis 2007, Access Info and Open Knowledge Foundation 2010, Hogge 2010).

Similar to the material found in the FOI movement, most of the first reports on OGD provide a simplistic and optimistic view of its benefits (Maali et al. 2010, DiFranzo et al. 2011, Hoxha & Brahaj 2011, Villazón-Terrazas et al. 2011, Wang et al. 2011) but lack analysis of the barriers, risks, disclosure and use of open government data (Janssen et al. 2012). This largely relates to the work of advocacy and evangelists in both groups of initiatives (FOI and OGD). These actors initially emphasise the benefits and value of the access in the case of FOI, and data use in the case of OGD. As the academy usually enters later in the development, academics are only just beginning to analyse these issues as they relate to OGD.

A similar path to the first stages of the FOI literature can also be found in the incipient OGD-related documents. Most of those early case studies are based on the developed world or Global North. Even though some of them show a broader range of interests and only the description of the initiatives and their benefits, they are still primarily focused on country studies in the developed world. In this sense, some work has been done in the EU, focusing on open data and its relation to public sector information directives (Sheridan & Tennison 2010, Kalampokis et al. 2011, Bates 2012) and on the implementation and potential impact of OGD (Janssen 2011, De Chiara 2013). There are also some other studies focusing on the underlying political economic context, focusing on the case of the UK (Ubaldi 2013).

There has been a recent change in emphasis and coverage, including reports on the Kenya Open Data Portal (Rahemtulla et al. 2012), a variety of countries in Latin America (Fumega & Scrollini 2014, Gonzalez-Zapata & Heeks 2015) as well as the outputs of a research project funded by the Web Foundation and

---

18 In December 2007, 30 open-government advocates met in Sebastopol, California, to develop a more robust understanding of why open government data is essential to democracy. They spelled out key requirements for government data, which emphasised the need for easily accessible, machine-processable and reusable data. More details of the meeting can be found at https://public.resource.org/open_government_meeting.html

IDRC on the Emerging Impacts of Open Data in Developing Countries,[19] which included reports on cases in the Philippines (Canares 2014), India (Agrawal et al. 2013, Srivastava et al. 2014), Nigeria (Mejabi et al. 2014), South Africa (Van Schalkwyk 2013) and several Latin American countries (Fumega 2014b, Matheus & Ribeiro 2014, Scrollini 2014), to name a few. The current Latin American Open Data Initiative (ILDA)[20] has also contributed to this recent trend in the OGD literature. ILDA has provided exploratory studies on different aspects and sectors related to open data in Latin American countries, e.g. open data in local governments (Bonina 2015), parliaments (Belbis 2015), education (Khelladi 2015) and health (Pane et al. 2015).

These recent studies clearly demonstrate the rapid pace with which the OGD field of study is moving. In this sense, the OGD field, due to rapid developments in ICT, has moved through similar stages to FOI research, but at a much faster pace. While in the FOI field the passage from the domestic to the international realm took decades, in the OGD arena a similar process has taken only a few years. The result is an overlap of stages in a short period of time, leading to the present stage, similar to the FOI field, where studies are starting to focus not only on definitions and models to better understand OGD policies in the developed world, but are also exploring the context and outcomes in the developing world.

OGD and INGOs

Apart from a limited range of studies and more anecdotal information about the process of the implementation of open data initiatives, there is a lack of analysis and understanding of the role of not only civil society organisations but also all the actors involved in the area of OGD, from policy to social entrepreneurs to domestic and international NGOs. In terms of the role of NGOs in these initiatives, as consumers of information, or as advocates of OGD policies, the only studies that mention their role are advocacy-driven reports. One such report was produced by Access Info and OKFN (Access Info and Open Knowledge Foundation 2010), while Hogge produced another for the Open Society Foundation (Hogge 2010). The first report was developed as a document for practitioners' consultation on the main topics regarding the new OGD agenda. The second study focuses on the US and UK governments' OGD initiatives to understand how to transfer policy to developing countries, while including some quotes from civil society actors from transparency NGOs.

As with the experience in the FOI field, there is some acknowledgment of the potential role of international civil society actors (see, for example, Rubinstein 2014, Janssen 2012 and, to some extent, Pyrozhenko 2011). But, to date, there is a lack of a body of work that explores the roles of international civil society actors in a more systematic manner.

---

19 http://www.opendataresearch.org
20 http://idatosabiertos.org/about-ilda/

The professional backgrounds of the members of international FOI and OGD groups not only shapes their approach to information and data, but also their advocacy tools and strategies. The strong legal background of the main FOI organisations, as well as within individual advocates, influenced the approach to the advocacy and the tools to reach new countries and regions. On the other hand, the ICT component of OGD main organisations comes with a whole set of values that, at first sight, are distant from the ones promoted by traditional human rights organisations (Levy 1984, Coleman 2011, Coleman 2013).

Most FOI advocates have come either from the freedom of expression or public law fields and have used rights-based arguments to promote the enactment of FOI laws that are driven by a belief in the value of governments being publicly accountable for their action and inaction. The area has largely been a lawyer's domain.[21] This laid the foundations for a legalistic approach to the initiatives and adversarial relationships with government, since FOI laws are fundamentally about testing the strength of competing claims to where the public interest lies, in disclosure or secrecy. In contrast, the OGD community tends to attract professionals with strong IT knowledge, or technocratic policy backgrounds. These OGD actors look for more cooperative relationships with governments. The difference partially resides in the fact that the latest groups of actors mostly work with the data the governments are willing to disclose (Fumega 2013). The proactive disclosure of the data in the case of the OGD field generates a different dynamic between civil society organisations and governments than the one shaped by the duty to answer to the requests for information, called reactive transparency.

Thus, even though both movements present close ties with liberal principles, the particular professional background in each of the fields differentiates not only their leadership and main activities and goals[22] but also their relationship with other stakeholders in their respective fields.

The literature reveals that ICT has had a profound influence on the structure of a large variety of organisations, from businesses (Molone et al. 1987, Gurbaxani & Whang 1991, Fulk & DeSanctis 1995, Den Hengst & Sol 2001, Gustafsson et al. 2008) to the military (McChrystal et al. 2015). In this research, the influence of ICT is key to understanding the differences in the operating methods, goals, and activities of organisations engaged in the fields of FOI and OGD. Furthermore, within the complex sets of actors

---

21 Some human rights and administrative lawyers started to become popular names in the field (as important or even more important than the organisations they represented. In general, they later created their own organisations on the topic).

22 FOI, until recently, was characterised by a paper-based informational environment with a concern about the access to the information more than the actual use and reuse of it (the use of information has been more related to the work of investigative journalists and other infomediaries). That void was filled by open government data organisations (together with some media outlets), which are strongly focused on the use and reuse of the data, which became relevant actors in the governmental information ecosystem during this last decade (Fumega 2013).

included in this research, there are key differences between those organically and intellectually shaped to operate in a digitally-dominated environment and those more traditional organisations that are just starting to adapt themselves to operating in a digital environment.

Developments in ICT, in terms of daily communications and connective capacity, have had an important but variable influence over definitions of, and approaches to, civil society organisations. This influence has extended to both the means of communication and organisational structure. There is an additional type of impact on OGD organisations that arises from ICT developments in which the philosophical background associated with civic hackers permeated their activities, their organisational structures and their engagement with peers and with governments. In this changing environment, a more effective and dynamic analysis is required to better understand the complexity of these international civil society organisations.

Conceptual framework

The above review of the literature has demonstrated that there are significant differences between the operations of FOI and OGD international civil society organisations. These differences are important and complex, and can only be partially explained by the differences presented between the fields in terms of background, vision and mission. The role of ICT, intrinsically connected to OGD, has permeated other fields including FOI, and thus these technological tools, in particular their adoption by FOI organisations, provides some evidence for a greater explanation of similarities and divergences between the organisations.

In spite of the powerful influence of ICT across all the fields related to informational resources, the FOI, OGD and NGO literature has been relatively silent on how organisations have reacted and/or responded to these ICT developments. Thus, these fields offer almost no assistance in relation to analysing the impact of ICT. The more general not-for-profit literature is just as limited. In the face of these limitations, there are some significant insights and potential analytical approaches that can be drawn on from a wider pool of literature, especially in the area of management studies.

Management studies literature offers a model of analysis that provides a solution to this conceptual lacuna. The concept of post-bureaucratic organisations provides a useful conceptual framework to observe and explain the divergences between the organisations and, in particular, is able to capture or follow changes over time.

Bureaucratic and post-bureaucratic organisations

Since the late 1980s, from the end of the Cold War to the beginnings of a globalised world, management literature has strongly focused on the impact and influence of changes in ICT. This literature (Drucker 1988, Powell 1990, Heckscher & Donnellon 1994, Symon 2000, Grey & Garsten 2001) provides a key concept, post-bureaucratic organisations, that can assist in the analysis of the FOI and OGD groups included in this research. The key value of this concept is not only that it provides concepts to better understand the differences between FOI and OGD organisations, but it also allows for a more detailed and nuanced understanding of the differences over time and within each of these two fields.

The passage from bureaucratic to post-bureaucratic organisation types, derived from the adaptation of the Weberian concept of bureaucracy (Weber 1954) to a new technology-dominated environment, sheds some light on the organisational changes since the late 1980s. It provides further approaches to analyse the international groups included in this research. Whilst management literature has deployed the concepts of bureaucratic to post-bureaucratic organisations largely in the context of business and marketplaces, the concepts can be applied to understanding international civil society groups as well.

The literature on business management places emphasis on the idea that these new types of organisations are not only a product of ICTs, but that they need to adapt to survive in a competitive market. It also suggests, in some cases, the necessity to fight against a networked enemy (McChrystal et al. 2015). International and domestic NGOs, even though non-profit by definition, as they generally pursue philanthropic goals, also need to compete in their own specialised market. There is competition for funding, grants, wider donor support and backing, prestige and recognition from donors, intergovernmental organisations, as well as country partners.

These organisations compete in the 'transparency market' not only for material resources but also for influence. Together with these material constraints and the need to adapt in order to survive,[23] these international NGOs, in particular, need to be part of regional or international clusters of independent organisations to exert greater pressure and produce better results. Thus, in many cases, they not only need to adapt to a more flexible structure because of budget constraints but also because of communication and engagement needs. Therefore, the use of models largely derived from a business or market environment is not necessarily problematic.

The use of the bureaucratic/post-bureaucratic categories, and especially the post-bureaucratic concept, allows for a clearer understanding of the differences between organisations, in particular FOI, because of the greater differential influence of ICT in this field in contrast to the far more pervasive influence of ICT on all OGD groups. This differential influence provides some key insights into better understanding the differences between organisations in the areas of FOI and OGD, but in particular the differences among the organisations inside each field.

---

23 In particular, when the number of civil society advocates increase and diversify as it is the case with the new OGD actors entering the transparency field.

Structure

The concept of bureaucratic organisations, in relation to the well-known Weberian concept, describes hierarchical centralised organisations as those focused on rules, procedures and maintenance of the status quo (Kernaghan 2000). A hierarchical organisation can be defined as a structure where every unit in the organisation, except one, is subordinated to another unit (Ariza-Montes & Lucia-Casademunt 2014). Thus, these organisations tend to have little room for innovation (McChrystal et al. 2015). Therefore, it is not surprising that international FOI groups have largely adopted this bureaucratic model. Dominated by personnel who were legally trained and focused on direct legislative law reform, they worked to deliver a fairly uniform product (Snell & Macdonald 2015: 687). In contrast, one of the main goals and drivers of the OGD groups is the pursuit of innovation and the achievement of a wide variety of outcomes. In this regard, the concept of post-bureaucracy has greater utility to analyse OGD groups in general and the capacity to differentiate and deal with more recent FOI organisations that are more affected by ICT.

Post-bureaucracy is a very broad term (Grey & Garsten 2001). As Grey and Garsten (2001) note, this term conceals a great diversity of practices. Some authors define post-bureaucratic organisations as hybrids because the term is used to describe a range of organisational changes, which are mainly a product of the influence of new channels of communication, as a refurbishment of bureaucracy (Josserand et al. 2006). However, the amount and importance of the changes allow it to be referred as a new organisational form (Drucker 1988, Powell 1990, Heckscher & Donnellon 1994) and not merely a hybrid.

Post-bureaucratic organisations present a more horizontal and distributed structure in comparison to the bureaucratic ideal (Drucker 1988, Powell 1990, Heckscher & Donnellon 1994). These organisations present a more flexible and adaptable structure to face a society with increasing levels of uncertainty and change, as defined by postmodern scholars such as Harvey (1989), Giddens (1991), Beck (1992) and Castells (1996), among others.

Unlike bureaucratic organisations, the main features of post-bureaucratic forms include the reduction of formal levels of hierarchy, an emphasis on flexibility and an increase in the use of sub-contracting, temporary work and consultants rather than permanent and/or in-house expertise (Grey & Garsten 2001). All these aspects are closely tied to the development of ICTs and, in particular, the influence ICTs have in developing new forms of communication (Symon 2000).

Collaboration and networking

Another feature of post-bureaucratic organisations is that of collaboration between members (Mintzberg 1980, Hedlund 1994, Gooderham & Ulset 2002, Josserand 2004). Changes allow organisational learning to increase (Starbuck

1992, Nonaka 1994, Foss 2002) and, thus, lead to more innovative and flexible structures. Thus, some authors (Powell 1990, Nohria 1992, Contractor et al. 2006) put the emphasis on this particular characteristic of post-bureaucratic organisations and refer to them as 'network organisations'. The availability of easier and faster channels of communications between and within organisations is one of the main explanatory elements to better understand the diverse group of organisations included in this research.

From the 1980s to the present, ICT and these new structures have grown in parallel. Developments in ICT have allowed the extension of the scale and scope of communications between organisations and individuals 'into new entities that can create products or services' (Contractor, et al. 2006: 682). Thus, organisations since then have slowly started to structure themselves in flatter and leaner forms. These new structures also have allowed for more innovation and adaptability to the environment (Symon 2000, McChrystal et al. 2015). All these features are defined in contrast with the vertically oriented bureaucratic organisations (Powell 1990, Nohria 1992) characteristic of most FOI organisations. Bureaucratic organisations are aimed to achieve efficiency, however, in these new ICT environments, fast-pace changes are required not only for efficiency but also adaptability (McChrystal et al. 2015).

This concept of the network organisation emphasises intra- and inter-organisational interrelation and collaboration. One of the main characteristics of collaboration in the OGD community is that it has been strengthened by the developments in ICTs. These technologies have allowed for quicker and easier communication channels and options, changing the way in which some organisations structure their daily routines. This emphasis on information and communication technology allows for a better explanation of the relationship between this concept and the main features of organisations working with informational resources, such as FOI and OGD groups.

This idea of a post-bureaucratic network organisation is also closely associated with the concept of virtual teams; unthinkable a couple of decades ago. Lipnack and Stamps have defined these 'teams' (organisations) as independent nodes, people and groups, working together for a common purpose (Lipnack & Stamps 1994). Currently, these nodes, or teams, could be located in different places and time zones. They can communicate and interact with other groups as well as within themselves, in most cases by virtual channels.

These new organisational structures are variously described (Heinz 2006), including, for example, as virtual organisations (Markus et al. 2000), horizontal organisations (Castells 1996), hybrid organisations (Powell 1987), dynamic networks (Miles & Snow 1986) and post-industrial organisations (Huber 1984). However, the main features that prevail in all these concepts are the relationships between nodes and the autonomy of the parts of the organisation and/or network. By enhancing these relationships, ICT developments play a key role.

The independence of those nodes and individuals is a key characteristic of these post-bureaucratic/network organisations. In addition to formal arrangements, these nodes are sometimes connected together by informal networks and the demands of the task, rather than by a formal organisational structure. To sum up, the post-bureaucratic/network organisations prioritise a soft structure of relationships rather than strict reporting lines and structures (Hall 2013).

Applying the conceptual framework

The international FOI organisations selected for inclusion in this analysis were as follows: Article 19, Transparency International, Commonwealth Human Rights Initiative, the Carter Center, and the newly-created Canada-based Centre for Law and Democracy.

The OGD movement is difficult to define. Therefore, to identify its main international actors recognised by other organisations working on related topics, the responses to an international survey, the Global Open Data Initiative (GODI),[24] was used as one of the parameters, together with the organisation and participation in the main events of the community, and presence in the main mailing lists. Following these parameters, the most well-known international organisations are all members of the Global Open Data Initiative. In the OGD group are Open Knowledge (OKFN), the World Wide Web Foundation ('Web Foundation'), Sunlight Foundation and MySociety.

International NGOs working on FOI and OGD share many elements and interests. There are also many divergences, mostly based on the main professional background of their staff, their type of engagement, and their main activities. However, these differences in the organisational structures and performance can also be explained by their similarities to the two ideal types, bureaucratic and post-bureaucratic organisations.

These ideal types as analytical conceptual constructs allow for a better understanding of some of the changes that FOI and OGD organisations have experienced in the past few years. Even though as organisations function in the real world they do not fit all the criteria of the ideal types, there are several elements from these abstract constructions that are recognisable in FOI and OGD organisations. Hierarchically organised structures versus the predominance of networks, and complex organised procedures versus organisations that need to adapt to a rapidly changing environment are both features that are linked to the bureaucratic and post-bureaucratic ideal types.

A large organisation such as Transparency International (TI), one of the FOI-oriented groups included in this research, can easily be placed close to the ideal type of a bureaucratic organisation. TI is large, in comparison to other civil society organisations, and a highly structured organisation. The

---

24 See http://globalopendatainitiative.org for more information. This initiative has not presented any substantial activity since April 2014.

size and complexity of tasks clearly correspond with the structure of a highly bureaucratised organisation. The number of permanent staff, its permanent headquarters in Berlin, the amount of administrative procedures attached to four separate director's offices, as well as more than 20 units within those four offices, all correspond to the main features of a bureaucratic/hierarchical organisation.

In contrast, Open Knowledge (OKFN) presents strong leadership and a more decentralised structure, including remote work without central headquarters. The organisational structure of these two organisations reflects the way the staff of each organisation relates to each other, in some cases remotely. It also demonstrates the way the organisations relate to their beneficiaries/clients. Despite some of the clear references to the ideal types, bureaucratic and post-bureaucratic, neither organisation fits perfectly into the description of the ideal types. Thus, FOI and OGD organisations, included in this research, present shades of those ideal types extrapolated from the business world.

One of the main features that slightly differentiates TI from the typical bureaucratic organisation is its engagement structure with many independent organisations in the world. Unlike TI, Article 19 has, since 2007, developed a small number of branches to cover regional programmes. Employees in each of those regional programmes work closely with the staff in its headquarters in London. Despite the bureaucratic structure adopted by Article 19, the regionalisation of their work can be interpreted as being closer to post-bureaucratic forms, even though they are still far from the post-bureaucratic end of the spectrum. The small number of employees, in comparison to larger organisations, also implies less structural complexity than at, for example, TI. In comparison, the Commonwealth Human Rights Initiative (CHRI) presents an even smaller size and number of branches. Despite its small size, it still presents a structure that can be closely associated with bureaucratic organisations, an HQ based in India, two dependent branches and permanent staff. These organisations that are supposedly working in the same field with similar approaches differ in their visions and acknowledge the differential influence of ICT developments in apparently similar organisations.

The Carter Center Access to Information Program and the Centre for Law and Democracy, despite their importance and undeniable influence in the field, are too small to be classified in the same way as the previous organisations. The first one is a programme within a larger organisation and the latter organisation is without branches or other affiliated groups.

These two groups could be placed closer to the OGD groups. There are, however, some reasons for refraining from doing so. In the case of the Carter Center, its ATI programme is just a unit; however, it is located within a large organisation, with headquarters in Atlanta, which can be clearly defined as closer to the bureaucratic model. The Centre for Law and Democracy, on the other hand, is a very small organisation but despite that smallness, its staff are located at a permanent office in Halifax, Canada. It is also important to note that, in some cases, they collaborate with other organisations and groups on a project basis. Because of these characteristics this organisation is located further from the ideal bureaucratic type on the spectrum; it is closer to a post-bureaucratic type than an organisation working with ICT in most of their activities such as Sunlight Foundation. Thus, these organisations, from TI to the Centre for Law and Democracy, all differ according to size and complexity.

The OGD movement, as in the FOI field, also presents differences between the structures of their organisations. This complexity is a product of the varied influences of ICT, the diverse approaches to OGD, as well as their relatively short organisational life. Some of these organisations such as the OFKN are located closer to the post-bureaucratic/network type. Next to OKFN, but not so close on the spectrum to the ideal post-bureaucratic type, is the Web Foundation because it has central offices and a permanent lab in Asia, even though some of its staff also work remotely.

Life span is a key component to consider not only for OGD but also for FOI organisations. Most OGD organisations have existed for less than ten years and are still evolving.[25] The Web Foundation opened a lab in Asia during 2014, after the 'Exploring the Emerging Impacts of Open Data in Developing Countries' research project which provided the organisation with vital information on the region. My Society, at the time of this research, was also going through a process of transition with the change of Executive Director, after its founder, Tom Steinberg, stepped down from the position in early 2015 (Steinberg 2015). OKFN also has gone through some organisational changes with a new CEO, Pavel Richter, being appointed in early 2015, as well as some other changes in their staff (Open Knowledge 2014, 2015). The Sunlight Foundation was also experiencing changes in their leadership with John Wonderlich, who had long led Sunlight's Policy Group, acting as interim Executive Director (Klein 2016).[26]

Despite their short existence, the OGD organisations seem very responsive to changing operating environments. In contrast, FOI international civil society organisations are still relatively stable and predictable. The relationship between these changes and the pursuit of funds, competition over missions/work areas, the impact of new leadership, are unknown. It is still too early to visualise long-term trends and these topics might need further research.

ICT as the factor of change

Some of the organisations included in this analysis correspond with the idea that there are connections between the background, mission and vision of the organisations, and the way in which they are structured and how they engage

---

25 The research behind this article ended by late 2015.
26 Ellen Miller served as executive director for eight years. In September 2014, she announced her retirement from that role. Chris Gate succeeded her and served for fewer than two years.

with other organisations and governments. However, some groups do not entirely match this assumption, as explained above. Therefore, rather than using a simple categorisation of lying somewhere on the bureaucratic or post-bureaucratic continuum, alternative methods should be used.

Differences in professional backgrounds and philosophical backgrounds fail to provide a full explanation of the heterogeneous array of international organisations working with governmental information resources. The difference in terms of legal backgrounds between FOI and OGD groups is a useful initial generalisation but also fails to adequately or completely unpack the differences and changes over time between these two organisations.

Of the many reasons for the differences between the two groups of organisations, their year of establishment and the level and type of ICT capacity in their formative years are key factors. The next section demonstrates the insights that can be gained by using the lens of ICT developments to examine many of the key differences between FOI and OGD organisations, and the organisation of each of these two fields.

ICT in the FOI field

Rapid changes in the available technology, in particular regarding the information management field, have permeated the agenda of newly created FOI organisations. These groups were formed in recent years. The Center for Law and Democracy has a legally dominated imprint and they found themselves needing to operate in a digital and dynamic information environment. These groups have been created in the light of the mass diffusion of ICT tools and thus the penetration of ICT related changes is more evident than in the other FOI groups that have a longer history, and larger and more bureaucratic structures. The twofold impact of ICT has permeated these organisations in one sphere: the tools these organisations now use to communicate and engage with their constituencies have experienced changes. However, the philosophy behind developers and many OGD organisations has not influenced these FOI groups.

The assumptions about the nature of legal oriented groups are challenged by some of the groups working on FOI that were created less than a decade ago. The ICT influence over these newly created FOI organisations was too difficult to ignore, resulting in organisations with a more flexible structure. Thus, the Center for Law and Democracy presents a strong legal background informed by the professional background of its founder; however, it presents a much more adaptable and flexible structure.

There is a clear difference between the weak and strong influence of ICT in how these organisations structure the internal and external dissemination of knowledge. In particular, these different levels of influence are clearly associated with the year these organisations were created.

In the FOI field, where most of the organisations were created in the late

1980s and early 1990s, the rights-based approach within a bureaucratic style of organisation has dominated. The exception to that rule seems to be embodied by those organisations created during the new century when the ICT influence become much more difficult to ignore and where, for an organisation, adaptability is as necessary as efficiency (McChrystal et al. 2015).

Looking at the examples, FOI organisations created recently tend to adopt a more flexible structure. An example is the Centre for Law and Democracy. This organisation is composed of a small number of professionals and they are involved in different collaborative projects with other organisations including the domain of FOI expanded to other rights-based and ICT areas such as the digital rights agenda. Technological developments have permeated all forms of communication and information management but they have not altered, so far, the philosophical and professional background of FOI organisations. The strong rights-based focus remains unalterable.

Access Info Europe, although a regional organisation, presents a clear example of one organisation that it is still focused on the rights-based approach to Freedom of Information but it has also understood the key influence of ICT in all the initiatives and policies related to the disclosure of information. They have been one of the organisations more connected to the OGD movement.[27] In 2011, the collaboration between organisations in these two fields was unusual.

ICT in OGD organisations

In contrast to the more traditionally structured FOI organisations from the 1980s and 1990s, most OGD groups were created post-2005. In this group, the main factor of differentiation is the approach to the topic. In all cases, from OKFN to Sunlight Foundation, the technological component is inherent in their daily routines and projects. The Sunlight's approach is closer to a traditional transparency and accountability focus to the broader OKFN's interest on issues related to openness in all areas. As previously established, this centrality of ICT clearly affects not only their projects and activities but also their structure.

Organisations such as Sunlight focus on the demand for government accountability. They tend to structure their approach in a similar fashion to the traditional FOI organisations. A rights-based approach, mixed with the work with data in digital formats, positions them closer to a watchdog of governments, rather than as a collaborative partner. The latter has been the case of a more classic networked organisation such as OKFN.

The transformational influence of ICT in terms of organisational structures is still more marked than in most FOI organisations. Thus, in terms of structure, all these OGD organisations tend to be more flexible. Sunlight Foundation

---

27 As already mentioned, they have prepared a report back in 2011, together with OKFN, to clarify some concepts on the similarities and divergences of FOI and OGD.

is the organisation that not only continues a more traditional approach to its activities but also maintains a more traditional hierarchical structure. In contrast, organisations such as OKFN operate not only with a flatter and more flexible structure, but also works with a remote system of work. Thus, they present more flexibility in terms of geographical location and schedules. This flexible structure is a product of the possibility that new ICT tools provide in terms of remote work and the influence of the hackers culture.

Summing up, ICT technology is a key enabler of new ways of communication. However, the philosophy behind the mission and vision of these organisations are as relevant as key elements to new organisational forms. This relates to the ICT twofold developments, which have supported and facilitated new organisational practices, by providing new ways and channels of communication and information management. However, in some cases, these practices go further than providing the tools, and they imply philosophical and culture elements, such as in the examples provided by OGD organisations.

Conclusion

This chapter has demonstrated that ICT has affected information management-related fields included in this research as well as permeating most channels of communications. ICT has proved to be the facilitator for major changes in communication and information management. Thus, despite the fact that organisational changes are particularly noticeable in FOI and OGD fields, they are intrinsically connected to the changes in how information and data is handled, including by governments and civil society organisations.

FOI groups were formed in the context of low levels of social engagement, idea flows and were largely responders to their information environment.[28] Early FOI advocates were mostly operating in a paper based-era (pre-digital operations) where the disclosure was based on the governmental response to a particular request, and thus the benefits of that disclosure were at the individual level. The end-product was generally envisaged for a single user for a single use. In particular, the members of these organisations, as well as individual advocates and academics, especially during the first and second stage of FOI's development, relied heavily on slow postal communication that restricted the pace, volume, reaction and feedback on ideas about accessing and using government information. Furthermore, adding to restricted global communication channels, these early advocates had limited opportunities for face-to-face collaboration. Conferences, seminars and workshops for FOI specialists became usual forums to exchange ideas at the end of the third stage of FOI, when international organisations started to become popular actors within the FOI scene.

In contrast, OGD groups started their organisational life in a digital

---

28 This is a key point of Xiao's (2011) work on FOI in China.

environment where the information was proactively disclosed (sometimes not in the expected formats) and where the information was available for all users. Despite this more widespread availability, the particular skills to interpret and reuse the published data made it necessary for technical intermediaries to produce applications. However, those applications are, in many cases, those which enable access and use by a large and not so technology-savvy population.

Because of the impact of the hacker ethos on OGD groups, they consider collaboration and engagement as a central feature for the success of their work, either digitally or face-to-face (the number of offline and online events, forums, workshops is very high, in particular in comparison to their FOI counterparts). These actors form a digitally connected, highly collaborative community. For example, the Latin American OGD community has created mobile instant messaging groups to constantly communicate with each other. This type of interaction has created professional and personal bonds that enhance the interaction, feedback and mobility between OGD advocates from different areas and countries of this particular region.

Furthermore, in terms of engagement and the ideas emerging from it, OGD INGOs are sources of, and major contributors to, idea flows and creativity in the access to, (re)use of and further creation/collection of government information. Their counterparts in governments acknowledge this contribution, for example many spaces for co-creation, engagement and innovation are created within public institutions (from events to collaborative problem-solving to permanent spaces such as innovation labs). In contrast, FOI INGOs have been slower to adapt in the areas of idea flows and creativity. This, again, relates to the information environment in which the field started to be developed. For a significant period, they needed to focus on developing universal standards of accessing government information. Innovations in legislation, policy design or administrative practice were resisted or restricted to a minimal role. Indeed, it is only in recent years that FOI groups have moved towards other outputs involving implementation, improved government information delivery and concepts such as FOI 2.0. Nevertheless, FOI INGOs are still far less receptive to common practices or reforms pushed by OGD groups.

The passage from one type of environment to the other produces not only quantitative (more information and data available) but also transformative and qualitative changes. This research confirms this idea. INGOs (largely OGD but not exclusively) that were created in a very different information environment have in terms of creativity, innovation, and variety of outputs outperformed the more legalistic and less pluralistic FOI INGOs.

Furthermore, applying Pentland's (2014) concept of 'ideas factories', FOI organisations can be described as traditional, large-scale, uniform, single-product-focused and stand-alone entities while their OGD counterparts can be characterised as modern (digital), variable but generally small-scale, networked, focused on idea generation and pre-disposed to collective effort (hacker ethos).

Most of the distinguishing features separating FOI and OGD organisations are the product of their philosophical background (legal rights-based vs hacker ethos) as well as the differential influence of ICT. However, some of the features (size, level of bureaucratisation) might be also the product of the stage of organisational life. The potential change of OGD organisations into large bureaucratised entities as they grow over time, together with the adaptation of FOI[29] organisations to digital dominated information environments, are all features that still need to be explored. The assumptions about the nature of legal-oriented groups are challenged by some of the groups working on FOI that were created less than a decade ago. The ICT influence over these newly created FOI organisations was too difficult to ignore, resulting in organisations with a more flexible structure. In contrast in most OGD groups, created post-2005, the main factor of differentiation is the approach to the topic.

Acknowledgements

This chapter condenses ideas from my PhD thesis (University of Tasmania) and relies on some concepts published elsewhere while I was conducting research for my thesis. A version of this article is included in the proceedings of the 18th Annual International Conference on Digital Government Research. I would like to thank Marcos Mendiburu and Fabrizio Scrollini for their valuable comments and I would like to acknowledge the support of the Institute for the Study of Social Change (University of Tasmania). However, the views in this chapter are the sole responsibility of the author.

About the author

SILVANA FUMEGA is originally from Buenos Aires, Argentina. She obtained her doctorate from the University of Tasmania. This article is a product of her doctoral thesis on the intersections of open government data and freedom of information policies. She also holds a masters degree in public policy from Victoria University of Wellington (New Zealand) and a bachelor degree in political science from the University of Buenos Aires (Argentina). She is currently the Research and Policy Lead of ILDA (Latin American Open Data Initiative). E-mail: silfumega@gmail.com

---

29 The key point, which requires further exploration for future researchers, is how these FOI organisations adapt to the new channels of communications and information management. Despite the importance of having FOI legislation and the more traditional advocacy approach, it is important to question the ability to adapt. The principles behind the right that allows the public to access and use government-held and produced information and data will probably remain unaffected for the next few years. However, the channels and tools to access and make use of those resources are rapidly changing. The ability of the rights-based FOI organisations, in particular, to adapt to this changing environment and to adopt new tools and channels will determine the future of the field, or at least their role in the informational resources ecosystem.

RREFERENCES

Access Info and Open Knowledge Foundation (2010). *Beyond Access: Open government data and the right to (re)use public information.* Access Info and Open Knowledge Foundation

Agrawal, S., Deshmukh, J. & S. Srinivasa (2013). *A Survey of Indian Open Data.* IIT Delhi and IIIT-Delhi, Delhi, India

Ariza-Montes, J. & A. Lucia-Casademunt (eds) (2014). *ICT Management in Non-Profit Organizations.* Hershey, PA: IGI Global

Article 19 (1999). The Public's Right to Know: Principles on freedom of information legislation. *International Standards Series.* London: Article 19

Banisar, D. (2006). *Freedom of Information Around the World 2006: A global survey of access to government information laws.* London: Privacy International

Bates, J. 2012. This is what modern deregulation looks like: Co-optation and contestation in the shaping of the UK's Open Government Data Initiative. *The Journal of Community Informatics* 8(2)

Beck, U. (1992). *Risk Society: Towards a new modernity.* London: Sage

Belbis, J. (2015). Estudio de caso. Apertura legislativa en el Cono Sur ¿ Y los datos? ILDA. Documento de Trabajo. http://idatosabiertos.org/wp-content/uploads/2015/09/3.-Apertura-legislativa-Belbis.pdf

Berliner, D. (2011). The strength of freedom of information laws after passage: The role of transnational advocacy networks. *1st Global Conference on Transparency Research.* Rutgers University-Newark, 19-20 May, Newark, New Jersey

Berliner, D. (2012). Institutionalizing transparency: The global spread of freedom of information in law and practice. Doctoral dissertation, University of Washington

Berliner, D. (2014). The political origins of transparency. *The Journal of Politics* 76(2): 479-491

Bonina, C. (2015). Co-creación, Innovación y Datos Abiertos en Ciudades de América Latina: Lecciones de Buenos Aires, Ciudad de México y Montevideo. ILDA. Documento de Trabajo. http://idatosabiertos.org/wp-content/uploads/2015/09/1.-Cocreacion-innovacion-y-datos-abiertos-Bonina.pdf

Canares, M. (2014). Opening the gates: Will open data initiatives make local governments in the Philippines more transparent? Manila: Step Up

Castells, M. (1996). *The Rise of the Network Society.* Oxford, UK: Blackwell

Coleman, G. (2011). Hacker politics and publics. *Public Culture* 23(365): 511-516. http://publicculture.dukejournals.org/content/23/3_65/511.full.pdf

Coleman, G. (2013). *Coding Freedom: The Ethics and Aesthetics of Hacking.* Princeton, NJ: Princeton University Press. http://gabriellacoleman.org/Coleman-Coding-Freedom.pdf.

Contractor, N., Wasseman, S. & Faust, K. (2006). Testing multitheoretical, multilevel hypotheses about organizational networks: An analytic framework and empirical example. *Academy of Management Review* 31(3): 681-703

Coronel, S. (2001). Fighting for the right to know. In: Coronel, S. (ed.), *The Right to Know: Access-to-information in Southeast Asia.* Quezon City, Philippines: Philippine Center for Investigative Journalism. pp. 1-20

Darch, C. & Underwood, P. (2010). *Freedom of Information and the Developing World: The citizen, the state, and models of openness.* Oxford: Chandos

Davies, T. & D. Edwards (2012). Emerging implications of open and linked data for knowledge sharing in development. *IDS Bulletin* 43(5): 117-127. http://dx.doi.org/10.1111/j.1759-5436.2012.00372.x

Davies, T. & Fumega, S. (2014). Mixed incentives: Adopting ICT innovations for transparency, accountability, and anti-corruption. *U4* (4). Bergen: Michelsen Institute

Davies, A. & D. Lithwick (2010). *Government 2.0 and Access to Information: Recent developments in proactive disclosure and open data in the United States and other countries*. Ottawa: Library of Parliament. http://www.lop.parl.gc.ca/content/lop/researchpublications/2010-15-e.pdf

Davis, J. (1998). Access to and transmission of information: Position of the media. In Deckmyn, V. & I. Thomson (eds), *Openness and Transparency in the European Union*. Maastricht: European Institute of Public Administration. pp. 121-126.

De Chiara, F. (2013). Tracking the diffusion of open data policy in the EU. IPSA. World Congress of Political Science, 8–12 July, Madrid

Deloitte Analytics (2012). *Open Data. Driving Growth, Ingenuity and Innovation*. London, UK: Deloitte LLP. https://www2.deloitte.com/content/dam/Deloitte/uk/Documents/deloitte-analytics/open-data-driving-growth-ingenuity-and-innovation.pdf

Den Hengst, M. & Sol, H. (2001). The impact of information and communication technology on interorganizational coordination: Guidelines from theory. *Informing Science Journal* 4: 129-138

DiFranzo, D., Graves, A., Erickson, J., et al. (2011). The web is my back-end: Creating mashups with linked open government data. In D. Wood (ed.), *Linking Government Data*, Doredrecht: Springer. pp. 205-219

Drucker, P. (1988). *The Coming of the New Organization*. Boston, MA: Harvard Business School Press

Eagles, I., Taggart, M. & Liddell, G. (1992). *Freedom of Information in New Zealand*. Auckland: Oxford University Press.

Fioretti, M. (2010). *Open Data, Open Society. A research project about openness of public data in EU local administration*. Pisa, Italy: Laboratory of Economics and Management of Scuola Superiore Sant'Anna. http://www.dime-eu.org/files/active/0/ODOS_report_1.pdf

Foerstel, H.N. (1999). *Freedom of Information and the Right to Know: The Origins and Applications of the Freedom of Information Act*. Connecticut: Greenwood

Foss, N. (2002). New organizational forms: Critical perspectives. *International Journal of the Economics of Business* 9(1): 1-8

Fraser, R. (2001). Freedom of information: Commonwealth developments. *Australian Journal of Administrative Law* 9(1): 34-41

Fulk, J. & DeSanctis, G. (1995). Electronic communication and changing organizational forms. *Organization Science* 6(4): 337-349

Fumega, S. (2015). Understanding Two Mechanisms for Accessing Government Information and Data around the World. Washington: World Wide Web Foundation

Fumega, S. (2014b). Opening the cities: City of Buenos Aires open government data initiative. Exploring the Emerging Impacts of Open Data in Developing Countries. Web Foundation and IDRC. http://www.opendataresearch.org/content/2014/663/city-buenos-aires-open-government-data-initiative

Fumega, S. & Scrollini, F. (2014). Designing open data policies in Latin America. In Breuer, A. & Welp, Y. (eds), *Digital Technologies for Democratic Governance in Latin America: Opportunities and Risks*. London: Routledge

Giddens, A. (1991). *Modernity and Self-Identity: Self and society in the Late Modern Age*. Stanford, CA: Stanford University Press

Gonzalez-Zapata, F. & Heeks, R. (2015). The multiple meanings of open government data: Understanding different stakeholders and their perspectives. *Government Information Quarterly* 32(4): 441-452

Gooderham, P.N. & Ulset, S. (2002). 'Beyond the M-form': Towards a critical test of the new form. *International Journal of the Economics of Business* 9(1): 117–138

Government 2.0 Taskforce (2009). *Engage: Getting on with Government 2.0*. Canberra, AU: Department of Finance and Deregulation, Government of Australia. http://www.finance.gov.au/sites/default/files/Government20TaskforceReport.pdf?v=1

Grey, C. & Garsten, C. (2001). Trust, control and post-bureaucracy. *Organization Studies* 22(2): 229-250

Gurbaxani, V. & Whang, S. (1991). The impact of information systems on organizations and markets. *Communications of the ACM* 34(1): 59-73

Gustafsson, P., Ulrik, F., & Pontus, J. (2008). Identifying IT impacts on organizational structure and business value. *Proceedings of the Third International Workshop on Business/ IT Alignment and Interoperability*. pp. 44-57

Hall, K. (2013). *Making the Matrix Work: How matrix managers engage people and cut through complexity*. London: Nicholas Brealey

Harvey, D. (1989). *The Condition of Postmodernity: An enquiry into the origins of cultural change*. New York: Blackwell

Hazell, R. (1991). Freedom of information: Lessons from Canada, Australia and New Zealand. *Policy Studies* 12(3): 38-46

Hazell, R. & Worthy, B. (2010). Assessing the performance of freedom of information. *Government Information Quarterly* 27(4): 352-359

Heckscher, C. & Donnellon, A. (eds) (1994). *The Post-bureaucratic Organization: New perspectives on organizational change*. London: Sage

Hedlund, G. (1994). A model of knowledge management and the N-form corporation. *Strategic Management Journal* 15(S2): 73-90

Heinz, M. (2006). Network organizational forms. Santa Barbara, CA: University of California. Presentation. http://www.cs.ucsb.edu/~almeroth/classes/tech-soc/2006-Spring/may-31-p1.ppt

Hines, A. (2007, 20 August). Get Your International Business Terms Right. *CBS News*.

Hogge, B. (2010). *Open Data Study: New technologies*. London: Transparency & Accountability Initiative

Hoxha, J. & Brahaj, A. (2011). Open government data on the web: A semantic approach. *Proceedings of the 2011 International Conference on Emerging Intelligent Data and Web Technologies*. Los Alamitos, CA: IEEE

Huber, G. (1984). The nature and design of post-industrial organizations. *Management Science* 30(8): 928-951.

Janssen, K. (2011). The influence of the PSI directive on open government data: An overview of recent developments. *Government Information Quarterly* 28(4): 446-456

Janssen, K. (2012). Open government data and the right to information: Opportunities and obstacles. The *Journal of Community Informatics* 8(2)

Josserand, E. (2004). *The Network Organization: The experience of leading French multinationals*. Cheltenham, UK: Edward Elgar

Josserand, E., Stephen Teo, S. & Clegg, S. (2006). From bureaucratic to post-bureaucratic: The difficulties of transition. *Journal of Organizational Change Management* 19(1): 54-64

Kalampokis, E., et al. (2011). A classification scheme for open government data: towards linking decentralised data. *International Journal of Web Engineering and Technology* 6(3): 266-285

Kasuya, Y. (2013). How Does Transparency Advocacy Arise and Thrive? Formation, Organization, Activities, and Networking of Access to Information NGOs around the World. *3rd Global Conference on Transparency Research*. HEC Paris, 24-26 October, Paris

Kasuya, Y. & Takahashi, Y. (2013). Streamlining accountability: Concepts, subtypes, and empirical analyses. *SSRN*. http://papers.ssrn.com/sol3/papers.cfm?abstract_id=2493654

Kernaghan, K. (2000). The post-bureaucratic organization and public service values. *International Review of Administrative Sciences* 66(1): 91-104

Khelladi, Y. (2015). Datos abiertos en educación, primeros alcances y lecciones. ILDA. Documento de Trabajo. http://idatosabiertos.org/datos-abiertos-y-educacionprimeras-lecciones/

Klein, M. (2016, 4 January). A message from Michael Klein, co-founder and chairman of the Sunlight Foundation. Sunlight Foundation. https://sunlightfoundation. com/2016/01/04/a-message-from-michael-klein-co-founder-and-chairman-of-the-sunlight-foundation/

Kranenborg, H. & Voermans, W. (2005). *Access to Information in the European Union: A comparative analysis of EC and Member State Legislation.* Groningen: Europa Law

Levy, S. (1984). *Hackers: Heroes of the computer revolution.* New York, NY: Penguin

Lewis, J.R. (1995). Reinventing (open) government: State and federal trends. *Government Information Quarterly* 12(4): 427-455

Lipnack, J. & Stamps, J. (1994). *The Age of the Network: Organizing principles for the 21st century.* Essex Junction, VT: Oliver Wight

Maali, F., et al. (2010). Enabling interoperability of government data catalogues. *Electronic Government* (vol. 6228). Dordrecht: Springer. 339-350.

Markus, M., Manville, B. & Agres, C. (2000). What makes a virtual organization work? *Sloan Management Review* 42(1): 13-26. http://sloanreview.mit.edu/article/what-makes-a-virtual-organization-work-lessons-from-the-opensource-world/

Matheus, R. & Ribeiro, M. (2014). Open government data in Rio de Janeiro City. Exploring the Emerging Impacts of Open Data in Developing Countries. World Wide Web Foundation and IDRC. http://www.opendataresearch.org/content/2014/664/open-government-data-rio-de-janeiro-city

Mayo, E. & Steinberg, T. (2007). *The Power of Information.* London: Cabinet Office.

McChrystal, S., Collins, T., Silverman, D. & Fussell, C. (2015). *Team of Teams: New rules of engagement for a complex world.* New York: Penguin

McClean, T. (2011). Shackling leviathan: A comparative historical study of institutions and the adoption of freedom of information. Doctoral dissertation, London School of Economics and Political Science. http://etheses.lse.ac.uk/3102/

Mejabi, O.V., Azeez, A.L., Adedoyin, A. & Oluwaseyi Oloyede, M. (2014). Case study report on investigation of the use of the online national budget of Nigeria. Open Data Research Network. http://beta.opendataresearch.org/sites/default/files/publications/Investigation%20of%20Open%20Budget%20Data%20in%20Nigeria-print.pdf

Mendel, T. (2003). *Freedom of Information: A comparative legal survey.* Paris: UNESCO

Michener, G. (2010). Surrendering secrecy: Explaining the emergence of strong access to information laws in Latin America. Doctoral dissertation, University of Texas Austin

Miles, R. & Snow, C. (1986). Organizations: New concepts for new forms. *California Management Review* 28(3): 62-73

Mintzberg, H. (1980). Structure in 5s: A synthesis of the research on organization design. *Management Science* 26(3): 322-341

Morozov, E. (2013). The Meme Hustler: Tim O'Reilly's crazy talk. *The Baffle 22.* http://thebaffler.com/salvos/the-meme-hustler

Napoli, P.M. & Karaganis, J. (2007). Toward a federal data agenda for communications policymaking. *CommLaw Conspectus* 16: 53. http://scholarship.law.edu/commlaw/vol16/iss1/4/

Neuman, L. (2004). Access to Information Laws: Pieces of the Puzzle. An Analysis of the International Norms. Carter Center website. https://www.cartercenter.org/resources/pdfs/peace/americas/ati_pieces_of_puzzle.pdf

Nohria, N. (1992). Introduction: Is a network perspective a useful way of studying organizations. In Nohria, N & Eccles, R.G. (eds), *Networks and Organizations: Structure, form, and action.* Boston, MA: Harvard Business School Press. pp. 1-22

Nonaka, I. (1994). A dynamic theory of organizational knowledge creation. *Organization Science* 5(1): 14-37

One World Foundation India (2011). *ICT Facilitated Access to Information Innovations: A compendium of case studies from South Asia*. New Delhi, India: World Bank Institute. http://southasia.oneworld.net/Files/ict_facilitated_access_to_information_innovations.pdf

Open Knowledge (2014, 18 September). Announcing a leadership update at Open Knowledge. Open Knowledge Blog. https://blog.okfn.org/2014/09/18/announcing-a-leadership-update-at-open-knowledge/

Open Knowledge (2015, 29 April). Open Knowledge appoints Pavel Richter as new CEO. Open Knowledge Blog. https://blog.okfn.org/2015/04/29/open-knowledge-appoints-pavel-richter-as-new-ceo/

Pane, J. et al. (2015). Dengue open data. ILDA. Documento de Trabajo. http://idatosabiertos.org/wp-content/uploads/2015/10/7.Dengue-Pane-Ojeda-Valdez.pdf

Paterson, M. (1998). Privacy protection in Australia: The need for an effective private-sector regime. *Federal Law Review* 26: 371

Pentland, A. (2014). *Social Physics: How good ideas spread-the lessons from a new science*. London, UK: Penguin

Perritt, H. (1997). Open government. *Government Information Quarterly* 14(4): 397-406

Perritt, H. (1994). Commercialization of government information: Comparisons between the European Union and the United States. *Internet Research* 4(2): 7-23

Pollock, R. (2008). The economics of public sector information. University of Cambridge. http://rufuspollock.org/economics/papers/economics_of_psi.pdf

Powell, W. (1990). Neither market nor hierarchy. *Research in Organizational Behavior* 12: 295-336

Power of Information Taskforce (2009). *Power of Information Taskforce Report*. London, UK: Cabinet Office.

Puddephatt, A. (2009). Exploring the role of civil society in the formulation and adoption of access to information laws: The cases of Bulgaria, India, Mexico, South Africa, and the United Kingdom. *Access to Information Working Paper Series*. Washington, DC: World Bank. http://siteresources.worldbank.org/EXTGOVACC/Resources/atICivSocietyFinalWeb.pdf

Pyrozhenko, V. (2011). Implementing open government: Exploring the ideological links between open government and the free and open source software movement. *The 11th Annual Public Management Research Conference*, 2-4 June, Syracuse, New York

Rahemtulla, H., Kaplan, J., Gigler, B., Cluster, S., Kiess, J. & Brigham, C. (2012). Open Data Kenya. Case study of the underlying drivers, principal objectives and evolution of one of the first open data initiatives in Africa. Washington DC: Open Development Technology Alliance

Rees, A. (1995). Recent developments regarding the Freedom of Information Act: A prologue to a farce or a tragedy; or perhaps both. *Duke Law Journal* 46(6): 1183-1223

Roberts, A. (2006). *Blacked Out: Government secrecy in the information age*. Cambridge: Cambridge University Press

Rubinstein, M. (2014). Hackers, advocates and politicians: Civic society groups and their role in open government data. MSc thesis, Wolfson College, Oxford University.

Scrollini, F. (2014). Opening the cities: The case of Montevideo. Exploring the Emerging Impacts of Open Data in Developing Countries. World Wide Web Foundation and IDRC. http://www.opendataresearch.org/content/2014/662/open-cities-case-montevideo

Sheridan, J. & Tennison, J. (2010). Linking UK government data. *LDOW-2010: Proceedings of the WWW2010 Workshop on Linked Data on the Web*, 27 April, Raleigh, North Carolina

Snell, R. (2002). FOI and the delivery of diminishing returns, or how spin-doctors and journalists have mistreated a volatile reform. *The Drawing Board: An Australian Review of Public Affairs* 3(2): 187-207. http://papers.ssrn.com/sol3/papers.cfm?abstract_id=2539402

Snell, R. (2001). Freedom of information: The experience of the Australian states: An eEpiphany. *Federal Law Review* 29: 343

Snell, R. (2000). Kiwi paradox: A comparison of freedom of information in Australia and New Zealand. *Federal Law Review* 28(3): 575-616

Snell, R. &. Macdonald, R. (2015). Customising freedom of information law reform in South Pacific micro-states. *The Round Table* 104(6): 687-701

Srivastava, N., et al. (2014). Open government data for regulation of energy resources in India. The Energy and Resources Institute

Stankowska, M. (2014). Good governance and the non-governmental organizations. *International Journal of Governmental Financial Management* 14(1): 43-47

Starbuck, W. (1992). Learning by knowledge-intensive firms. *Journal of Management Studies* 29(6): 713-740

Steinberg, T. (2015, 2 March). My Society's director Tom Steinberg to step down – new leadership position will be advertised soon. My Society website. https://www.mysociety.org/2015/03/02/mysocietys-director-tom-steinberg-to-step-down-new-leadership-position-will-be-advertised-soon/

Stone, D. (2004). Transfer agents and global networks in the transnationalization of policy. *Journal of European Public Policy* 11(3): 545-566

Stubbs, R. (2012). A case study in the rise of public sector transparency: Understanding the global diffusion of freedom of information law. Doctoral dissertation, University of Tasmania

Symon, G. (2000). Information and communication technologies and network organization: A critical analysis. *Journal of Occupational and Organizational Psychology* 73: 389

Tkacz, N. (2012). From open ssource to open government: A critique of open politics. *Ephemera: Theory and Politics in Organization* 12(4): 386-405. http://search.proquest.com/openview/7d7da87b26e6f558971778c2c21ffb68/1?pq-origsite=gscholar

Ubaldi, B. (2013). *Open Government Data: Towards Empirical Analysis of Open Government Data Initiatives.* Paris: OECD

Udell, J. (2006, 28 June). Open government meets IT. *InfoWorld*. https://www.pcworld.idg.com.au/article/161979/open_government_meets_it/

Van Schalkwyk, F. (2013). Supply-side variants in the supply of open data in university governance. *ICEGOV'13 Proceedings of the 7th International Conference on Theory and Practice of Electronic Governance*, 22–25 October, Seoul. pp. 334-337

Villazón-Terrazas, B. et al. (2011). Methodological guidelines for publishing government linked data. Linking Government Data. New York: Springer. pp. 27-49

Wang, Q.-R. et al. (2011). Design and implementation of open user model service platform. *Jisuanji Yingyong/ Journal of Computer Applications* 31(3): 818-821

Weber, M. (1954). *Max Weber on Law in Economy and Society*. Cambridge, MA: Harvard University Press

Xiao, W. (2011). *Freedom of Information Reform in China: Information flow analysis*. Oxford: Routledge

7.

Open your data and will 'they' build it? A case of open data co-production in health service delivery

Fabrizio Scrollini

Introduction

Open data policies are currently in fashion across both developed and developing countries. The assumption behind these policies is that the release of public data in structured formats will create a set of benefits such as increased transparency, efficiency and effectiveness in the public sector. The assumption of merely opening up data and waiting for members of the public to use it, is problematic. There are barriers users must face such as reliability and accessibility, quality of data, and understanding of its potential and effective use, to name the most obvious and documented barriers. Opening up data, while an important step, will not often deliver the promised value. In short, if one releases data, 'they' (whoever they are) may well not use it. Thus, a key question is: What kind of mechanisms allow government and users to cooperate in order to deliver on the promised value of open data?

In this chapter, I explore the case of Atuservicio.uy, an application designed in a partnership between Data Uruguay (a civil society organisation) and the Ministry of Public Health in Uruguay. The application allowed 60 000 citizens (in 2016) to compare information about health service providers in Uruguay during the annual window when citizens choose their health service provider.[1] I argue Atuservicio.uy is an example of co-production between civil society and a government regulator through the release of open data. First, I explore the connection between open data and co-production in the current literature. Second, I provide an explanation of the methodology I followed and I provide a thick description of the case. Third, based on the case, I provide a framework to

---

1   This project was financed by the Ministry of Health in Uruguay and the programme Open Data for Development (OD4D) supported by IDRC and Avina Foundation through ILDA.

understand and evaluate key elements of co-production in the realm of open data. I identify a set of capacities and resources available to key stakeholders to advance co-production processes. I also argue that a clear set of rules of engagement is needed for these processes, and that this requires a new set of administrative arrangements in the public sector. Finally, I lay out a set of conclusions about the field and identify points for further research. In particular, I warn about the current 'conceptual stretching' that this field is facing, differentiating the concept of co-production from participation and co-creation. I argue for an agenda where co-production in the open data field serves the creation of public value, noting that merely publishing data will not be enough.

Co-production and open data:
Enabling a new type of co-production?

The current state of the art in public administration between government and citizens assumes several forms. From co-creation of public policies and public services (Bason 2010), government labs (Price 2015) to open policy-making (UK Government n.d). In particular, co-production, a concept often poorly defined or understood, is considered to be a cornerstone of public policy reform across the globe (Osborne et al. 2016; OECD 2011). Co-production, broadly defined as citizens collaborating in the implementation of public services, is supposed to address several pitfalls in the current state of affairs in public management, such as democratic deficit, and is seen as a way of enhancing active citizenship.

Co-production as a concept has been around for at least 40 years in the social sciences, particularly in public administration. The work done by Ostrom and colleagues in the late 1970s pioneered the concept (Alford 2014) and was further developed through the 1980s (Whitaker 1980, 1981, Levine & Fisher 1984, Brudney & England 1983). In the days of 'traditional' public administration, co-production was conceived of as a way to maximise public participation in service delivery. Whitaker (1980) defines co-production as 'the active involvement of the general public and specially of those who are beneficiaries of the service'. As the new public management paradigm emerged in public administration, co-production was also associated with 'consumerism', and eventually with new public governance (Osborne 2006) or with the digital era government paradigm (Dunleavy et al. 2006) as new modes through which citizens could participate in service delivery. It is important to note that most of the co-production literature describes co-production as an activity that often takes place at the delivery stage (Alford 2014). According to Osborne et al. (2016) and Pestoff (2006), the notion of co-production in the public sector does not challenge the orthodoxy that public servants are in charge of designing and providing services to citizens, who eventually demand, consume and evaluate them (Pestoff 2006, Osborne et al. 2016).

The public administration literature on co-production does not connect with the work developed in service delivery literature around co-production.

According to Osborne et al. (2016), in this approach the basic assumption is that co-production is an inalienable core component of service delivery: one cannot have service delivery without co-production. Thus, co-production assumes the participation (voluntary or otherwise) of the user at the point where the service is delivered. In this sense, co-production always involves the user (even if the user does not willingly participate). Following Osborne et al.'s (2016) framework, voluntary co-production can take place at a service level (as in most of what the public administration literature describes) or at the systemic level, leading to what they define as co-innovation which implies reshaping an entire service sector. Most of the co-production literature pre-dates the digital revolution in public services and, in particular, the open data movement. Therefore, it is appropriate to consider how open data practices link to co-production.

The notion of open data is fairly simple. It refers to data (or more appropriately, datasets) available in open formats for anyone to freely use and re-use.[2] There is a legal and a technical aspect embedded in this definition. Initially advocated by Tim Berners-Lee (2006) as a way to promote the evolution of the web, the field gained traction and evolved into a movement demanding open data from governments, multilaterals and the private sector. The mantra in those feverish early days was 'give us raw data' (Pollock 2007). Government engaged in building open data portals to provide data for citizens to use. Early apps using data for transport services and urban issues emerged (Warman 2010). Advocates demanded a 'flood of data from governments' to fuel citizen interest and participation (Eaves 2010). Open data portals proved themselves good repositories, but demand for datasets has remained fairly low to-date. There were (and are) several constraints on the provision of data such as availability, quality, timeliness of the provision and will to open data in the first place (World Wide Web Foundation 2016). Furthermore, not all countries have in place the legal framework and the capacity to release open data in ways that are meaningful. The recently launched International Open Data Charter aims to streamline the principles open data policies should espouse.

Open data is associated with many positive outcomes such as transparency, accountability, efficiency and efficacy in service delivery, among others (Davies 2010). But the way open data leads to these outcomes is seldom straightforward. A few practitioners have argued since the early days of the open data movement that available data should be seen as public digital infrastructure (Moncecchi 2012). Like roads, bridges or railroads, open data allows others to build on the existing infrastructure. In this way, when releasing open data, its use would contribute to public value. I have argued elsewhere (Scrollini 2015) that this would be a 'living infrastructure'. The more actors who use the data, the more data would improve and more value would be created. The ebb and flow of publication and use leads to more accurate and useful data, improving the entire system in a given

---

2   For a full definition see the Open Definition (OKFN 2011).

context (Scrollini 2015). Assuming that the use of data for political, social and economic outcomes is valuable, government agencies and the private sector across the developing world started to promote the use of data through events such as hackathons, datathons, and the like. Events would often gather technologists and policy experts to tackle complex issues. These events showed the potential to set up new types of communities and explore new ideas, and even promote political mobilisation, but they did not support sustained innovation as several stakeholders expected (Mochnacki 2015). Given these limits, open data (mostly published by governments) is still used to produce social and economic value across the world. The key question is how this is done and, in the particular case of this chapter, whether co-production is a useful approach.

In one of the few papers explicitly addressing the connection between open data and co-production, Juell-Skielse et al. (2014) note that re-users of data have intrinsic motivations such as intellectual challenge, joy and prestige, among others, to become re-users of open data. Examining the case of open data in public transportation in Sweden and the events organised to foster the use of data, they argue that is necessary to increase the understanding of collaborative production of digital services and design, and to evaluate new mechanisms for supporting the later phases of digital service execution and monitoring. In other words, they argue that it is necessary to refine our understanding of these processes as there is no established methodology to ensure the effective and sustainable use of open data.

In this chapter, I provide an example of a particular type of co-production based on the use of open government data. By co-production I mean the voluntary participation of different civil society organisations in co-producing and co-innovating (using Osborne et al.'s [2016] terms) services, using open government data. This type of co-production assumes an active role of public servants but it challenges the orthodoxy that public servants are completely in charge of the process (Pestoff 2006), as once data is released, actors can potentially re-use the data in unexpected ways, beyond the direct control of government.

On methods and case selection

The Latin American Open Data Initiative (or 'ILDA' in Spanish) is a research initiative seeking to understand and promote the use of open data in Latin America. The initiative is hosted by Avina Foundation and supported by the International Development Research Centre (IDRC) as part of its Open Data for Development programme (OD4D). ILDA developed a set of strategic initiatives to test and explore the value of open data, as well as conducting basic research on the topic. The health service delivery sector was considered strategic by stakeholders consulted at several Latin American open data conferences (*Abrelatam-Condatos*), and thus the initiative decided to steer its research in that direction.

To explore the value and use of open data, ILDA took a participatory action research approach. Participatory action research assumes the researcher works alongside members of a given community to develop a solution or knowledge about a certain issue. In this way, the researchers work with counterparts to generate evidence and potentially develop new approaches to tackle practical issues (Herr & Anderson 2005). The cycle ILDA followed in this particular case was to agree with core stakeholders on the desirable objectives, develop an intervention in order to achieve those objectives, and then reflect on this practice, feeding back to relevant partners the knowledge that was collectively created.

The web-based Atuservicio.uy application was developed by DATA Uruguay, a civic technology, non-government organisation, and the Ministry of Health, supported by ILDA as part of its strategic initiatives programme. The application allows Uruguayan citizens to access and understand information about health service providers at a critical time when they choose a health service provider for the year.

Researchers at NYU's Governance Lab (GovLab) who initially documented and evaluated the case, noted that '[i]t shows the vital function of intermediaries and civil society in promoting open data, facilitating discussions with the state, and nudging government agencies to release more and higher quality data' (Sangokoya et al. 2016: 6). The researchers propose that the web application had impact in terms of use and awareness, data quality, and on other data projects. Table 1 provides a synthesis of the impact noted by the GovLab researchers.

Table 1 Beneficiaries and impact of Atuservicio.uy

INTENDED BENEFICIARIES	IMPACT
Average citizens	1. Enabling the people of Uruguay to make better-informed health decisions as a result of actionable information. 2. Equipping citizens with data-driven evidence and tools to make better decisions on health care choice. 3. Catalysing citizens to act as agents of monitoring and evaluation around the health services they receive.
Health providers	1. Making clear to citizens which health options are best suited to their needs. 2. Improving the quality and responsiveness of service based on data-driven demand from citizens.
Government agencies	Improving the public health system through greater efficiency, transparency and accountability.
Media	Encouraging better data journalism efforts and data driven arguments for public debate on health care.
Civil society and unions	Enabling better informed argumentation and advocacy around the status of the health care system.

Source: Sangakoya et al. (2016)

As a result of this initial evaluation and the evolution of the case, sharing the way the case was developed and identifying key variables that could be used to foster co-production in other domains, make the case of Atuservicio.uy relevant to the open data field. Naturally, this approach has limits in terms of the generalisability of the findings and the potential replication of the case in other cases.

The co-production process of Atuservicio.uy

Context

Every February Uruguayans get to choose whether to stay with or change their health service provider. This opportunity is the result of a series of major reforms in the Uruguayan national health system that led to almost full coverage of the population. Significant amounts of public funding go into the system, which offers a mix of public, semi-public and private health providers. The more users one provider attracts, the more funding the provider gets from the government.[3] As a result, competition is stiff. Providers develop marketing campaigns and even offer cash to users if they switch providers, which is an illegal practice. The Ministry of Public Health, worried about these practices, started publishing information about the performance of the system in 2008. The Ministry published this information on its website in tabular Excel format. The press used these tables to produce news stories about the system, but users seldom retrieved the tables.[4] The language was difficult to understand, it assumed users had access to proprietary software, the information was not displayed in a user-friendly manner, and was difficult to compare among providers.

In 2013 the civil society organisation, DATA, identified an opportunity to work with the data published by the ministry. DATA partnered with a local online media outlet and developed a tool to visualise and rank health service providers according to user preferences. The tool was aptly named 'Transfer Window', referring to the short time-frame Uruguayans had to choose a service provider. DATA extracted the datasets from the ministry websites, cleaned them and designed an interface through which users were able to easily understand the data. The online media outlet helped to spread the word and the website received approximately 6 000 visits in February 2014. The project was based on open-source software, and treatment data received was transparent. The process did not involve the Ministry of Public Health, but authorities were aware of it.

The evolution of the case

In the context of Uruguayan Open Government Partnership[5] process, DATA and the Ministry of Public Health explored how to team up. The ministry intended

---

3   Number of users is not the only criteria to disburse funds, but it is an important one.
4   An estimate from the ministry indicates that they received no more than 400 visits per year.
5   The Open Government Partnership is an international initiative promoting open, transparent and accountable governments. Uruguay joined this initiative in 2011 and has since then kept providing spaces for open government initiatives.

to create a website similar to what DATA created, but it was not possible to find a suitable provider. DATA had the expertise to carry forward this mission, but had only a basic understanding of the technical and policy nuances of health data. Eventually the ministry and DATA set up a formal partnership to co-create and co-produce the application. The partnership included a commitment from the ministry in terms of human and financial resources to assist DATA, and DATA would also commit financial and human resources to assist the ministry.[6] Furthermore, DATA pushed for developing the application on open-source software to allow eventual replication and transparency of the process.

The process was emergent and bottom-up. DATA engaged with a group of mid-level managers with political support to proceed. DATA and the ministry's team held meetings to define the scope of the information to include. DATA would always push for more information to be published and the ministry would always be more cautious about what to publish. The ministry had initially classified part of the information they released as 'reserved' under provisions contained in the access to information law. DATA and the ministry constructively bargained for which information to include.[7]

DATA initially had a bias towards user choice. In DATA's view, the more people exercised the right to switch providers, the better. The ministry argued that switching was not the ultimate goal of the application as it could jeopardise the stability of the system. The ultimate goal for the ministry was to enable citizens' voice and to improve the system. DATA agreed to work in the framework of broader policy objectives set up by the ministry in order to move forward. This discussion was important as it affected several decisions about how information was represented, as well about what indicators users could eventually compare on the website.

Once there was agreement on what information to include, the ministry's team embarked on identifying the data sources for the required information to be published by the application. The team found that most of the data was compartmentalised across the ministry and was not in open formats. Further, collection processes were often manual. Through the identification and collection process the ministry discovered that some of the data sources had quality problems. Furthermore, the ministry noted conflicts in data from different sources. The process of collecting data helped the ministry to understand its own sources of data and to put them in order.

On DATA's side, the team initially developed the back-end of the application to import and process the data. Tests were run using the datasets from the ministry to ensure compatibility. This process was lengthy and technically challenging for both parties. Problems with data standardisation haunted the project until its first launch.

6 DATA received funding from the ILDA, supported by *Avina Americas*.
7 One particular debated issue was the number of affiliates each provider had.

As the project evolved, DATA developed the first 'mock-ups' of the website and started the validation process with the ministry team. Middle managers working on the project were usually on board with the design choices. The process also involved other managers and political appointees who were data providers. Most of them wanted to make sure that the data they collected or created would not be misrepresented on the website. Discussions revealed the asymmetry of technical knowledge that existed between managers and technologists. Members of DATA would act as 'translators' to ensure that all parties were on the same page. Also, at this stage, some managers of the ministry (not involved in the core team) viewed DATA was another 'service provider' rather than as a co-creator. As a result, they would initially interact with DATA by giving orders in a client-provider mode of interaction. DATA pushed back, noting that the process was effectively a partnership and that decisions were made by agreement. Eventually, most managers came to understand this logic.

DATA and the ministry made a set of basic decisions on what information to show and how to present the information to users. Users would be able to see information about waiting times, prices, users' rights, location of services, and performance targets on the home page. Users would be able to compare up to three providers from their administrative jurisdiction, allowing users to delve extensively into the data.

Dataset standardisation on the ministry's side and technical capacity on both sides were a threat to the project. The final stage was a sprint to get the site published before 1 February when Uruguayans would have an opportunity to choose a health service provider. Finally, both parties delivered, allowing more than 35 000 Uruguayans to access valuable information.[8] In the second year, Atuservicio's audience increased to 60 000 users.

Furthermore, the website was used in public debates and the information was re-used by several media outlets (Sangakoya et al. 2016). Even politicians from government and the opposition used Atuservicio.uy to debate health policy in parliament. The project survived a change of government and in the ministry's team, and in 2016 increased its audience and impact. All the data collected was also made available via the Uruguayan national open data catalogue.

In light of the evidence available, public servants and politicians could also be considered as beneficiaries of the project. Politicians have access to another monitoring tool to check on the performance of the health system. Public servants improved their data collection processes and developed innovative techniques to engage with civil society. In the case of the Ministry of Public Health, it enhanced its position as a regulator.

Evidence indicates that in the case of the second edition of Atuserivicio.uy, the ministry received most of the data from providers on time and with more detail.

---

8   Users spent about five minutes on the website.

Recent evidence also indicates that transparency in price and services has led to adjustments in the prices offered by service providers.[9]

Factors to consider in open data co-production

I now turn to the four main factors that contributed to the co-production process: enabling environment, broadly shared policy objectives, partners' capacity and positive feedback loops. Table 2 provides a set of possible indicators to measure these factors or variables.

Table 2: Factors and possible indicators

Factor	Possible indicators
Enabling environment	1. Which are the available governance indicators in a given country? How does the country rank in these indicators? 2. Is there a policy forum such as the Open Government Partnership to discuss open data and potential joint projects? 3. How does the country rank in open data measurement instruments such as the Open Data Barometer of the OKFN Open Data index?
Broadly shared policy objectives and coordination mechanisms	1. Do partners have a common policy goal? 2. Is there a coordination mechanism that allows partners to engage in defining these goals? 3. Are there institutional and legal arrangements to execute the delivery of agreed policy objectives?
Partners' capacity	Policy capacity: 1. Are partners able to engage in field specific and open data policy issues?
	Technical capacity: 1. Is the data available? 2. Is it open? 3. Are partners able to contribute specific technical skills to the process to open, clean and use the data?
	Financial capacity 1. Are both partners able to contribute to the project? If so, to what degree?
Positive feedback loop	1. Is there any sign of positive feedback loop once the product or service was developed? If so, according to which indicators?

Enabling environment

Government–civil society relationships differ from country to country. Even in democratic countries, with legitimate governments, such relationships can be more or less cooperative. Further, there are no 'obvious' policy forums to discuss the co-production of public services. The Uruguayan case provided fertile ground for this particular co-production initiative. Uruguay is well ranked in terms of perception of government transparency (Transparency International

---

9 According to public servants in the ministry, this is due to health services providers trying to avoid being considered the most expensive provider listed on the website.

2015) and is considered a full democracy (EIU 2015). Uruguay engaged in the Open Government Partnership (OGP) process, which opened a window of opportunity to formalise previous work Uruguayans did around open data. The OGP process managed to set up a continuous dialogue among key government and civil society stakeholders (Guillen 2015). Uruguay is also one of the regional leaders in terms of open data policies as measured by the Global Open Data Index (OKFN 2015) and the Open Data Barometer (Web Foundation 2016). Thus, an environment that promotes open government with a certain degree of formalisation, plus certain institutional conditions (a democratic and transparent government), provides a good basis for co-production processes.

Broadly shared policy objectives and a mechanism to coordinate

Partners need to have a shared policy objective and mechanism to coordinate. The Uruguayan case shows that while initially DATA had a focus on promoting choice and the ministry a focus of information dissemination, there was a larger policy objective, which was the improvement of the national health system. If partners do not share the same objective, and are not able to clarify this through a dialogue mechanism, then it is likely to be difficult to engage in a co-production process. These mechanisms need to include institutional and legal arrangements on how partners will proceed. To truly share a policy objective, partners need higher-level political support to proceed. For instance, in Uruguay, the website www.quesabes.uy allows users to make freedom of information (FOI) requests. The website was developed by the same organisation with no involvement from the government, and often found resistance from several government offices (Fumega & Scrollini 2017). There was a shared objective, but no coordination mechanism with government officials. In a similar vein, the first version of Atuservicio.uy developed in isolation by DATA, had no coordination mechanism.

Partners' capacity

To engage in co-production, partners need a combination of policy, technical and financial capacity. Both organisations need to understand both the field-specific policy (in this case health) and open data policy. Early involvement of the Uruguayan E-Government Agency secured an understanding of the open data policy at the Ministry of Public Health, which evolved through the project. Also, the project organisations balanced this capacity by exchanging knowledge between field-specific policy issues and open data policy issues. Through such exchanges, partners are likely to bargain around the final form of the product.

By technical capacity I mean a set of basic systems that collect, process and publish data, as well as human resources able to work with such data at a professional level. This aspect is crucial. The government partner needs to have the technical expertise on board as well as basic systems in place to collect data. In the case of Atuservicio.uy there were not sophisticated information systems in place; on the contrary, most of the data came from Excel sheets that were transformed into open data. Furthermore, technical capacity on the government partner's side is also helpful in the co-creation stage where issues around design choices, UX interface and hosting are likely to emerge.

On the civil society side, there is a need for capacity to work with the available data, occasionally to clean it and to structure it to serve the product's purposes. Furthermore, civil society organisations will assume responsibility for delivering the information in ways that the government could not. Design and UX interface become crucial capacities in addition to back-end and front-end development.

A co-production process assumes that government is able to invest resources in co-producing. This requires planning in advance and making available sufficient budget, which mostly goes to support the technical work done by the civil society origination. On the other hand, it also assumes that civil society organisations have their own funds to cover the costs for part of the project. To fully engage in a co-production process, civil society must be able to bring some resources to the table, either as junior, equal or major partner in the co-production process. Civil society resources allow CSOs to be more flexible with the use of resources, and to engage in activities that governments might not have the capacity or feel comfortable with (for example, social media advertising). In the Uruguayan case, civil society and the ministry contributed the same level of funding to the prototype, and government mostly covered the second version of the application.

Positive feedback loops

The co-production process needs to deliver a product or service that adds value to the existing situation. In the Uruguayan case, the impacts documented through the evolution of Atuservicio.uy provided motive to the ministry to continue its efforts. The positive feedback loop opens a conversation on how to make the co-production process sustainable. This is something Atuservicio.uy has partially succeeded in as the ministry committed to support the application until 2020.

Open data and co-production: A new way forward?

This case provided an opportunity to explore how to foster the use of open data through co-production between government and civil society organisations. First, this case shows that co-production between civil society and a government organisation is possible. As defined in the first section of this chapter, this kind of co-production is voluntary and demands specific ways in which civil society organisations and governments engage. Dialogue and engagement with the right set of capacities led (in the Atuservicio.uy case) to a particular kind of co-production which contributes to an innovative way of enabling choice for Uruguayan healthcare users. The focus is on the voluntary and active aspect of this co-production process. In this way, while it is theoretically possible for users to engage directly with the data at the point of service (via the national open data portal), it is the engagement process that leads to genuine innovation and an improvement of the service being delivered, as well as the democratisation of the data so that users can benefit from it. These users are able to co-produce (in the sense described by Osborne et al. [2016]), as they can monitor and act to improve the service. To put this in other way: this type of co-production enables other types of co-production with a different set of users.

Second, this case shows that use of data by civil society, business or other stakeholders can also be disruptive. This was the case when the 'Transfer Window' application was produced – a type of co-production that does not require any kind of involvement of public authorities. Nevertheless, this disruption is what created an opportunity for the public sector to engage in a co-production process as described in this chapter. Disruption can be uncomfortable for public authorities, but it can also be a source of public innovation. However, Juell-Skielse et al. (2014) suggest more resources are needed if these disruptions are going to transform public services. In this chapter, I have argued that certain factors should be considered to set up sustainable co-production processes.

This understanding of co-production also has a larger implication for the open data field. Bates (2014) notes that open data is another way of fostering modern deregulation where the private sector would be in charge of leading the field. Citizens should be consumers of these new products and services and not necessarily engaged in co-producing them. Open data would be at service of the neo-liberal state. This case shows a different picture. The co-production process in the open data field offers an opportunity to pull resources towards a new relationship between government and citizens. It involves external and public oriented agents in the co-production efforts, often backed by public or philanthropic resources. Thus, co-production processes that will change the way government works (or create new services), will need an active government on board, rather than absent one.

The case also highlights that more research is needed in this area. Civic associations such as DATA are new and rare. While there is no official data, evidence from the last five years suggests that open data focused organisations form a relatively small group in Latin America (Abrelatam 2014). These organisations often lack the means to engage governments and other social organisations in co-production processes. The Uruguayan case shows that only a few organisations in the public sector have the ability to engage in co-production processes. How the public sector acquires this new set of skills is also problematic. And how and whether the Atuservicio.uy case can scale, is something that is yet to be proven. Nevertheless, co-production in the open data space provides a promising avenue to explore ways in which the public sector can partner with other actors to produce a new kind of value. If the process scales, it could contribute to a living 'data infrastructure' that supports participation, transparency and better social outcomes. The concept needs further theoretical development and more systematic evidence. This case helps to highlight that while opening data is a step in the right direction, impact requires institutional, technical and financial resources provided by government, while not being totally in control of the process. Developing such arrangements, goes beyond the technical mantra of opening data and moves into the realm of policy and politics in ways that are often not explored.

Acknowledgements

The research presented in this chapter was supported by the International Development Research Centre and Avina Foundation. A first version of this paper was presented at the IIAS Study Group on Co-production of Public Services. I am thankful for all the comments received.

About the author

FABRIZIO SCROLLINI is the lead researcher of the Latin American Open Data Initiative (ILDA). Fabrizio holds a PhD in government from the London School of Economics and Political Science. E-mail: fabrizio.scrollini@gmail.com

REFERENCES

Alford, J. (2014). The multiple facets of co-production: Building on the work of Elinor Ostrom. *Public Management Review* 15(3): 299-316

Abrelatam (2014). Abrelatam map. http://www.abrelatam.org

Bates, J. (2014). The strategic importance of information policy for the contemporary neoliberal state: The case of open government data in the United Kingdom. *Government Information Quarterly* 31(3): 388-395

Brandsen, T. & Pestoff, V. (2006). Co-production, the third sector and the delivery of public services: An introduction. *Public Management Review* 8(4): 493-501

Bason, C. (2010). Co-creation is key to innovation in government. *Understanding Society* Winter. Ipsos Mori. http://mind-lab.dk/wp-content/uploads/2014/09/Understanding_Society_Winter_2010_CBason.pdf

Davies, T. (2010). Open data, democracy and public sector reform: A look at open government data use from data.gov.uk. Edited version of unpublished masters thesis, University of Oxford. http://www.opendataimpacts.net/report/wp-content/uploads/2010/08/How-is-open-government-data-being-used-in-practice.pdf

Dunleavy, P., Margetts, H., Bastow, S. & Tinkler, J. (2006). New public management is dead – long live digital-era governance. *Journal of Public Administration Research and Theory* 16(3): 467-494

Eaves, D. (2010, 15 June). Learning from libraries: The literacy challenge of open data. Open Knowledge International Blog. http://blog.okfn.org/2010/06/15/learning-from-libraries-the-literacy-challenge-of-open-data/

Economist Intelligence Unit (2014). *Democracy Index.* https://www.eiu.com/public/topical_report.aspx?campaignid=Democracy0115

Fumega, S. & Scrollini, F. (2017). You've got mail: The role of digital civil society platforms in improving Right to Information regimes. In Hinnant, C.C. & Ojo, A. (eds), *Proceedings of the 18th Annual International Conference on Digital Government Research* (dg.o '17). New York: ACM. pp. 387-396

Herr, K. & Anderson, G. (2005). *The Action Research Dissertation: A guide for students and faculty*. Thousand Oaks, CA: Sage

Juell-Skielse, G., Hjalmarsson, A., Johannesson, P. & Rudmark, D. (2014). Is the public motivated to engage in open data innovation? In: M. Janssen, H.J. Scholl, M.A. Wimmer & F. Bannister (eds), *Electronic Government. EGOV 2014. Lecture Notes in Computer Science* 8653. Berlin: Springer

Levine, C.H. & Fisher, G. (1984). Citizenship and service delivery: The promise of coproduction. *Public Administration Review* 44: 178-189

Moncecchi, G. (2012). Towards a public digital infrastructure: Why do governments have a responsibility to go open? Open Knowledge International Blog. http://blog.okfn. org/2012/11/01/towards-a-public-digital-infrastructure-why-do-governments-have-a-responsibility-to-go-open/

Mochnacki, A. (2015) Organizational templates, performative claims-making and expert work in open data advocacy: Mobilizing grassroots participation in Toronto. Paper presented at the Open Data Research Symposium, Ottawa, 27 May. http://www. opendataresearch.org/dl/symposium2015/odrs2015-paper35.pdf

OECD (2011). *Together for Better Public Services: Partnering with citizens*. Paris: OECD

Price, A. (2015, 19 May). World of labs. Nesta. http://www.nesta.org.uk/blog/world-labs

Pestoff, V. (2006). Citizens and co-production of welfare services: Childcare in eight European countries. *Public Management Review* 8(4): 503-519

Pollock, R. (2007, 7 November). Gives us raw data and give it to us now! Open Knowledge International Blog. http://blog.okfn.org/2007/11/07/give-us-the-data-raw-and-give-it-to-us-now/

Pollock, R. (2013, 24 April). Frictionless data: Making it radically easier to get stuff done with data. Open Knowledge International Blog. http://blog.okfn.org/2013/04/24/frictionless-data-making-it-radically-easier-to-get-stuff-done-with-data/

Open Knowledge Foundation (2011). The Open Definition. https://github.com/okfn/opendefinition

Osborne, S.P., Radnor, Z. & Strokosch, K. (2016). Co-production and the co-creation of value in public services: A suitable case for treatment? *Public Management Review* 18(5): 639-653

Sangokoya, D., Clare, A., Verhulst, S. & Young, A. (2015). *Uruguay's A tu Servicio: Empowering citizens to make data-driven decisions on health care*. New York: GovLab. http://odimpact.org/files/case-study-uruguay.pdf

Scrollini, F. (2015, 24 May). The emerging impact of open data in Latin America. ILDA. http://idatosabiertos.org/the-emerging-impact-of-open-data-in-latin-america/

UK Government (n.d.). About open policy making. Policy Lab. https://openpolicy.blog. gov.uk/what-is-open-policy-making/

Warman, M. (2010, 22 January). Data.gov.uk: Top ten apps so far. *The Telegraph*. http:// www.telegraph.co.uk/technology/news/7044147/Data.gov.uk-Top-Ten-Apps-so-far.html

Whitaker, G. (1980). Co-production: citizen participation in service delivery. *Public Administration Review* 40: 240-246

World Wide Web Foundation (2016). Open Data Barometer. http://www. opendatabarometer.org

Transparency International (2015). *Corruption Perception Index*. https://www.transparency. org/cpi2015

8.

The relational impact of open data intermediation: Experience from Indonesia and the Philippines

Arthur Glenn Maail

Introduction

Understanding the impact of open data initiatives requires in-depth investigation of the relationships between data publishers, intermediaries and end-users of open data (Davies et al. 2013). This relationship is central in justifying whether the emerging impacts of open data are sustainable and stable, or whether they are vulnerable due to the absence of intermediary groups (Van Schalkwyk et al. 2016a). However, there is still a lack of understanding of how these relationships change as a result of the implementation of an open data initiative.

This research aims to understand the impact of open data projects in terms of changes in the relationship between an intermediary organisation and a data supplier (government), and between the intermediary and the end-user. The primary research question put forward in this research is: How does the participation in an open data project change the working relationship between intermediary organisations, data suppliers and end-users of open data?

Empirical data was gathered on a citizen-led budget transparency open data project (OD4Transparency), an initiative run by the Open Data Lab Jakarta, in two countries: Indonesia and the Philippines. Several qualitative data collection techniques were used in the case-study approach, including in-depth semi-structured interviews and document/archival analysis of the project documentation, reports, project websites and social media.

The results of the study provide evidence that support the findings of prior studies regarding the impact of intermediary organisations in open data initiatives. In complementing prior studies, this research documents the best practices from the case studies on how participation in an open data project changes the working relationship between the intermediary and other key stakeholders. This chapter shows how trust among intermediary and other stakeholders developed over the course of the project while at the same time introducing synergies in pursuing government transparency and accountability. Both trust and a synergistic relationship contribute to the institutionalisation of open data in government. As for the relationship with end-users, the study shows that continuous interaction is key to improving scalability and sustaining public awareness. Finally, the study shows that improving public participation begins with the effective use of open data to address those socio-economic and development issues affecting communities.

Open data intermediaries

An open data intermediary 'is an agent positioned at some point in a data supply chain that incorporates an open dataset, is positioned between two agents in the supply chain, and facilitates the use of data that may otherwise not have been the case' (Van Schalkwyk et al. 2016a). From this definition, previous studies have described different roles to intermediaries in open data ecosystems. First, intermediaries are critical to ensuring data use, especially in developing countries where awareness regarding the existing data may be low, and where the capacity of users to make use of and derive results from data are limited (Cañares & Shekhar 2016, Chattapadhyay 2014). Second, intermediaries can play an important role as advocates for open government data. They can play a significant role in increasing visibility of the open data movement and in advocating for better transparency in government (Cañares et al. 2014). Intermediaries can also play the role of convener or catalyst by, for example, bridging the relationship between data supplier and potential end-users (Andrason & Van Schalkwyk 2017). Intermediary organisations need not necessarily be open data savvy; there are cases where local chiefs, community centers, churches and mosques function as intermediaries between governments and citizens (Mutuku & Mahihu 2014).

Therefore, intermediaries are vital to both the supply and the use of open data to translate data into information, knowledge and workable action. Prior research has underlined the important role (both technical and social) of intermediaries in ensuring 'effective use' and re-use of data as well as in ensuring a match between data supply and demand (Gurstein 2011). There are, however, several steps that need to be taken before open data interventions can deliver long-term political, social and economic impacts (Craveiro et al. 2014, Davies 2014, Zuiderwijk & Janssen 2014). Moreover, the interaction between intermediaries with both data suppliers and data users is necessary to transform data into measurable outcomes and impacts. The availability of good-quality datasets, the appropriate legal frameworks and technical skills are all important. Integration of these resources can transform datasets into several usable outputs. Nevertheless, whether the outputs drive home their intended impact will depend on how the outputs are used to change practices, behaviour and systems within governments (Van Schalkwyk et al. 2016b), and also among citizens and citizen groups.

Research design

The choice of approach and method is shaped by the research aim and associated research question (Neuman 2006). The research employed a qualitative approach using a case study method, which is suitable because the nature of the study required the inclusion of the context in which the study takes place and an in-depth understanding of the phenomenon to be observed (Yin 2009).

Case study 1: Perkumpulan IDEA Indonesia

The OD4Transparency project in the city of Yogyakarta aims to encourage public participation in monitoring city budget by providing budget data in a machine-readable format, allowing for further analysis by the public. The project also produces tools and budget analysis, in both online and offline formats (e.g. the budget newspaper).

The city budget open data portal was launched in February 2015. Before the launch, several preparatory activities were conducted by Perkumpulan IDEA, including data requests from the city government, data scraping and data cleaning. At the time of writing, the portal provided budget data for the fiscal years 2012 to 2014 for all ten government offices, including (1) the regional tax and financial management office, (2) the department of health, (3) the regional public hospital, (4) the department of education, (5) the settlement and regional infrastructure office, (6) the department of social welfare and labour, (7) the department of trade, industry, cooperatives and agriculture, (8) the market management office, (9) the tourism office, and (10) the women and community office. There is also provision to download the data in several open formats such as JSON, .sql, .csv and .xls. In addition to providing budget data, the portal also offers several analyses and visualisations of budget data. Examples of analysis include revenue trends, expenditure trends (totals and by government office/department) and trends of the budget balance.

Besides online formats, the analysis of budget data was also disseminated in print in the form of a two-page newspaper called the 'budget newspaper'. A total of 2500 copies of the budget newspaper were printed and distributed to CSOs, individuals and communities in several sub-districts in the city of Yogyakarta. The budget newspaper also contains illustrations to aid readers in their understanding of the analysis presented.

In this project, Perkumpulan IDEA is the open data intermediary. They have been advocating for transparency, participation and local budget accountability for almost ten years. Perkumpulan IDEA works closely with the city government,

155

particularly the regional tax office and financial management (*Dinas Pendapatan Daerah dan Pengelolaan Keuangan* [DPDPK]). DPDPK is the data supplier. The DPDPK provided city budget data for the years 2012 to 2014, including budget realisation data for the year 2012. In disseminating the results, Perkumpulan IDEA worked with several CSOs and individual users who are the end-users of open data. The CSOs work on various issues including women and reproductive health, children, disability, and community information. Individuals who have an interest in the city budget were also invited to participate in the project.

Case study 2: E-Net Philippines

The E-Net Philippines is a network of CSOs in the Philippines working on education reforms to ensure that quality education becomes a basic human right for all. Its main activities are focused on education financing, strengthening of alternative learning systems and civil society partnership with governments to achieve better education outcomes.

E-Net Philippines advocates for better use of the Special Education Fund (SEF). These funds are administered by local school boards (LSB), of which 40% of the members are from civil society. The SEF can be used to meet the supplementary needs of the public-school system. Funds are equivalent to 1% of the assessed value of every real property and collected together with property taxes paid to the local government.

Through this project, E-Net sparked the development of a process where LSBs can monitor the budgeting and utilisation of the SEF, using open data made available through the Full Disclosure Policy Portal (FDPP). The FDPP is a government portal where local government units are mandated to upload plans, budgets, financial reports and other related financial documents in machine-readable formats. Their pilot project took place in two sites in Northern Mindanao, namely Kidapawan and Alamada.

Before this project, monitoring of the SEF in the pilot sites was very low due to lack of awareness and information on the role of LSBs, and the lack of data available to be used for monitoring the use of the funds. Currently, local government units are required to post SEF utilisation reports on the FDPP, and civil society members can access the report to monitor spending. With increased awareness on these topics, more than 100 CSO members of the school boards from the two municipalities are now in a better position to monitor the use of public funds and to ask local governments questions regarding how the funds are used to improve education outcomes at the local level. With access to data and knowledge on how to analyse the data, CSOs feel more empowered to engage with government to discuss their demands for better spending on education. To document lessons learned from this process, E-Net is currently preparing an Open Data and SEF Toolkit that LSBs can use in ensuring the transparent utilisation of the education budget.

Several qualitative data collection techniques were utilised, including in-depth semi-structured interviews and document/archival analysis (project documentation, report, website and Twitter/Facebook).

A semi-structured questionnaire was used to gather data from selected participants within the (1) intermediary organisation, (2) government agencies as the suppliers of data, and (3) CSOs and citizens as end-users. Participants were identified together with Perkumpulan IDEA and E-Net. The case study participants are listed in Table 1. Individual (one-on-one) interviews employed in the case study allowed for a detailed examination of each individual's (i.e. participant's) opinion about the phenomenon under study (Kvale 1996).

Table 1 Case study participants

Stakeholders	Position and affiliation (Perkumpulan IDEA, Indonesia)	Position and affiliation (E-NET, Philippines)
Data supplier	Head of the regional tax office and financial management City Government of Yogyakarta: Section head, financial management City Government of Yogyakarta: Regional tax office and financial management	Chair, Committee on Education of the Local Government Unit (LGU) Kidapawan Local school board member of LGU Kidapawan
Intermediary	Perkumpulan IDEA Executive Director Programme coordinator for OD4Transparency project Programme staff	E-Net Philippines Staff members Members of the Board of Trustees
End user	CSOs: Sapda[1] (Sentra Advokasi Perempuan, Difabel, dan anak) Komunitas Angkringan Yogyakarta[2] KMIPY (Koalisi Masyarakat Informasi Publik Yogyakarta); CRI[3] (Combine Resource Institution); CIQAL[4] (Center for Improving Qualified Activity in Life People with Disabilities); Aksara[5] Individual users: Archival consultant, lecturer, housewives (2), lecturer/activist	Participants of the two-day workshop on special education fund (March 2015) from the CSO community

Notes
1   http://www.sapdajogja.org/
2   http://angkringan.web.id/
3   http://www.combine.or.id/
4   http://ciqal.blogspot.co.id/
5   http://www.aksara-jogja.net/

In addition to the semi-structured interview, this study used document analysis as a secondary source of information. These secondary sources serve a data triangulation purpose to corroborate and augment evidence obtained from the interviews. The sources include (1) project proposals and annual progress reports, (2) formal studies or evaluations of the same cases, (3) news clippings and other articles appearing in the media or newspapers, (4) blog posts and website, and (5) Twitter and Facebook posts.

In the analysis stage, the data were analysed according to the themes emerging from transcripts of the interviews and other data sources. The focus of data analysis is to discover regularities and patterns within the empirical data with an established rigor to answer the research question (Miles & Huberman 1994).

Findings

This section discusses the impact of the implementation of the OD4Transparency project on several aspects concerning stakeholders' relationships in open data initiatives. The first three sub-sections review the impact of project implementation on the relationship between the data supplier and the intermediary. The last two sub-sections present the findings related to the impact on the relationship between the intermediary and the end-users.

Opportunity to build trust

The open data initiatives had the potential to create a new space for government and civil society organisations to work together in building trust. The trust-building process develops as each stakeholder understands what constitutes the open data project. The project also creates an opportunity for each stakeholder to share their prior experiences.

At Perkumpulan IDEA, the evidence from the case study reveals that prior to OD4Transparency project, government officials at the DPDPK had fears about the integrity of data. As a result, DPDPK always provided the data in hardcopy or PDF to whoever requested the data. The head of DPDPK indicated that once he learned more about the project and followed the activities organised by Perkumpulan IDEA, none of the original concerns materialised.

Besides an understanding of the current project, knowledge about prior activities and the track record of the organisation contributed to building trust between both parties. Perkumpulan IDEA's OD4Transparency project is the first project in ten years done in cooperation with the city government of Yogyakarta. However, government officials commented that they have known Perkumpulan IDEA for several years and understood the credibility of the organisation.

At E-Net Philippines, the LGU acknowledged the challenges in implementing the open data initiative, even within the LSB. It also realised that CSOs, like E-Net, should be seen as connectors and promoters of education and should operate further downstream to explore structures that can be used for monitoring and evaluation, and to inform them how to hold the government accountable. An example of such a downstream structure is the Parents-Teachers Association.

One of the outputs of the open data workshop facilitated by E-Net was a plan drafted by the participants detailing what can be done to promote open data on the SEF. Given the reality that LGUs are not conscious of how specific budget allocations should be spent and hence how budgets may be diverted, one of the measures formulated was a directive on the proper use of the SEF which could then serve as a 'bible' for the LGU to follow. In the workshop, it was explained that there are only certain projects which can be funded by the SEF, as specified by law (for example, for school improvement but not for the travel expenses of senior school administrators). To date, the LGU claims significant success. They have curtailed the inappropriate use of the SEF and identified additional subsidies for teachers and students. A strict implementation of the RPT collection and information, education, communication (IEC) campaigns were also successfully implemented to reduce the number of delinquent taxpayers.

LGU Kidapawan is open to CSO participation as it considers the number of CSOs in the City Development Council (CDC) as its barometer for maximum citizen participation. The CDC of LGU Kidapawan allows 20 CSOs as official members but urges others to participate as observers. It recognises the critical role of E-Net as a leader in education issues. It encourages E-Net to sit in the CDC and be part of the planning processes.

Some politicking is inevitable. A case in point is the LSB composition which mandates for a representative from the Parents-Teacher Association and a non-teaching personnel representative; however neither was rightfully represented. This was corrected later on through creative campaigning and the work of the advocates for transparency. This demonstrates the evolving landscape of the LSB in the LGU. As a whole, what helped in the struggle for transparency in the budgeting process and in advocating for open data, was awakening the sectors and consulting with stakeholders, such as putting in place the rightful composition of the LSB.

Synergy to pursue government accountability and effectiveness

Both case studies also reveal that open data projects can enable synergy among all stakeholders to pursue government accountability and effectiveness. This was accomplished through the availability of a new communication channel for information exchange that allows for public participation in the monitoring and evaluation of the governance process.

In the case of Perkumpulan IDEA, government officials noted that budget transparency, including publication of budget data, had been their priority. Several regulations concerning publication of budget data include:

- Regulation of the Minister of Home Affairs Number 13 of 2006 regarding Guidelines for Management Regional Finance.
- Law No. 14 of 2008 on Disclosure of Public Information.
- Instruction of the Minister of the Interior of the Republic of Indonesia Number 188.52/1797/ SJ dated May 9, 2012 on Enhancing Transparency Budget Management Area.

The city government of Yogyakarta also has an action plan for eradicating corruption (*Rencana Aksi Daerah untuk Pemberantasan Korupsi* [RADPK]) with one of the action points being to provide budget data in a transparent way. For this purpose, the government has utilised several channels of communication. Publication of the budget data on the official government website has been done continuously since 2012. Responses from citizens are channeled through the (1) Musrembang (*Musyawarah Rencana Pembangunan*/Multi-Stakeholder Consultation Forum for Development Planning); (2) UPIK[1] (*Unit Pelayanan Informasi dan Keluhan*/Information and Complaints Service Unit) where citizens can send queries via SMS, phone or the website; and (3) *Walikota Menyapa* (Mayor Greets), a weekly local radio talkshow featuring the mayor of the city.

However, the head of DPDPK admitted that publication of the budget data is still far from effective. He noted 'we also tried to publish APBD data to the public. But for me, it (publication) is not interesting because it is still very narrative. All this time, related to the budget, the public only knows the value of the budget alone. The public does not know about the government's priorities. For me, the publication was not effective. So when Perkumpulan IDEA came up with this project, to provide the data in different ways, we certainly agreed.'

The initiative to publish budget data in machine-readable formats on an online portal and in the printed budget newspaper was seen by the city government of Yogyakarta as an innovative way to provide budget transparency to the public.

Perkumpulan IDEA also noted that the OD4Transparency project has allowed for synergy between government and CSOs to change how the government used the data and presented it to the public.

Similarly, E-Net views the OD4Transparency project as an opportunity for CSOs to engage creatively with the government, especially in the development landscape where there are many opportunities to make data user-friendly and accessible. It has intensified its attention and collaboration with LGUs as a strategic partner in budget transparency initiatives by making its presence more visible in areas where it can influence public fiscal processes such as the proper utilisation of the SEFS.

The OD4Transparency project framework has intensified E-Net's working approach towards the LGU regarding dealing with the education budget. It has shifted from focusing on use alone to involvement in the whole budgeting process. This is demonstrated in the network members' strong advocacy for public audit, transparency and accountability via Social-Watch and other alternative budget initiatives, for instance on how much tax has been collected. Whereas before this information could bot cannot be generated easily, the government now exercises more prudent responses to those seeking access to data. Such local-level advocacy expands to the broader advocacy effort of monitoring treasury at the national level. This also connects with the continuing effort of E-Net in

---

1   http://upik.jogjakota.go.id/index.php/home

pushing for the amendment of the Local Government Code (LGC), specifically on the LSB and SEF. E-Net hopes that this will also trickle down to its advocacy for stronger School Governing Boards (SGBs) and increase participation in drafting the School Improvement Plan (SIP).

Institutionalisation of the open data initiative

Participation in an open data project can change how government creates, prepares and uses its data. These changes, in turn, affect the institutionalisation of open data within government. It also affects the long-term sustainability of the open data initiative.

Two important observations were noted from the Perkumpulan IDEA's project. First, the DPDPK is willing to sign a memorandum of understanding (MoU) with Perkumpulan IDEA to ensure the long-term sustainability of the initiative. Starting from 2016, DPDPK will submit the city budget to allow for publication of budget newspaper as supplementary pages attached to the local daily newspaper. DPDPK is also in discussion with the IT department of the city government to link the APBD open data portal to the city government's website.

Second, Perkumpulan IDEA will continue to support the analysis of budget data. During the workshop held by Perkumpulan IDEA, government officials began to think how to better provide budget information to the community after hearing the aspirations from the workshop participants. In terms of the analysis of the datasets, besides the current budget plan, DPDPK will add two more aspects of budgeting data, including a budget realisation report which shows in detail actual spending in a fiscal year and a budget administration report which records the city's actual revenue and expenditure for the fiscal year.

In the case study of E-Net project, DepEd Kidapawan as a partner agency understands that the open data project is just starting out, but the principles it advocated for have been in practice within DepEd, with the exception of technological data management capacity-building which is still in the works. But DepEd also recognises this effort as parallel with its EPA 2015 which mandates performance indicators for the agency such as access, quality and governance.

There is also an acknowledgment that transparency increases the level of understanding of the stakeholders and that an informed citizenry can make a significant contribution. DepEd Kidapawan also revealed that IEC is embedded in all its units. It also has its information system (the Enhanced Basic Education Information System[2]) where all information about education is available.[3]

---

2 http://ebeis.deped.gov.ph/
3 The information system is not as 'open' as E-Net revealed, as access still requires a password.

Continuous interactions are necessary for public awareness

Awareness represents the knowledge or perception of a situation or fact. In a simple term, awareness means knowing what is going on (Gutwin & Greenberg 2002). The implementation of the OD4Transparency project has certainly brought awareness to the CSOs and individuals of the potential of open data to promote budget transparency. Two important insights regarding public awareness revealed from both case studies are scalability and sustainability of public awareness.

On the scalability of public awareness, all stakeholders in the case study of Perkumpulan IDEA were aware of the limitation of public awareness towards the use of public funds in the city of Yogyakarta. Several channels were used by Perkumpulan IDEA including:

- Website: www.perkumpulanidea.or.id
- http://128.199.127.141:8000/, for visualisations of the analysis of the local budget.
- Twitter: @perkumpulanidea, followers: 54, tweets:100
- Facebook: Idea Yogyakarta, friends: 2 817
- Dissemination and public discussions between Open Data APBD Kota Yogyakarta and the government, citizens, CSOs, NGOs, the media and academics.
- Budget newspapers.

However, all stakeholders agreed that more needs to be done before the OD4Transparency project can create ripple effects to increase public awareness on budget transparency in the city of Yogyakarta. As mentioned above, starting in 2016, the DPDPK will publish the results of budget analysis in leading local newspapers to reach a wider audience. The CSOs and individual users intend to continue promoting the portal and budget newspaper in their communities. Perkumpulan IDEA think that the limited project duration affected the number of audiences they are able to reach. In the future, their work will focus on the development of current open data for the budget transparency programme to reach lower income communities. They are also looking for the development of mobile apps to cater for middle to upper-income communities.

For E-Net Philippines, the most immediate yet important gain of the OD4Transparency project is that the end-users recognised and appreciated the effort of E-Net in highlighting the importance of transparency and all its concomitant processes, in that simply, corruption in government can be detected when there is access to data. End-users who participated in the Open Data Workshop felt strongly that their ideas on transparency were reinforced with the OD4Transparency project. This is to the extent that the concept of open data as espoused by E-Net is equated by end-users to transparency and accountability given the current initiative of the government on Full Disclosure and Open

Data which advocates for transparency and accountability. The common reaction elicited from encountering the concept of open data is the perception of honesty. This downplays a focus on 'open data formats' and the technological aspects of open data. But overall, end-users viewed positively the initial outputs of the open data workshop, particularly that they learned more about SEF and LSB mechanisms. They also learned about the vital importance of CSO participation in the LSB, the rightful composition of the LSB and targets for lobbying.

The second concern regarding public awareness is the continuity of the awareness. As the social and political environments are continually changing, public awareness must constantly be maintained. Perkumpulan IDEA is aware that the nature of OD4Transparency project was not conducive to maintaining public awareness since it was done within a short period of time. The difficulties in maintaining the interaction can be seen from the Twitter response during the project: the data shows that the end-users only interact (i.e. re-tweet) when there was a tweet from Perkumpulan IDEA. Hence, sustaining end users' awareness is still challenging for open data initiative when done through the social media.

In the case of the E-Net project, further interaction between E-Net and stakeholder-partners after the workshop was limited to emails. In these emails, E-Net asked for further data on the area as well for inputs on the Toolkit for SEF Open Data. Per E-Net's May 2015 Terminal Report, the number of people reached through communication materials and information activities has yet to reach a critical mass. The open data initiative is viewed as still in its 'birthing stage'. When asked how much change can be attributed to the OD4Transparency project, end-users stated that such anticipated changes would take time as the most difficult thing to do is to change the mindset of the people. The project has only been downloaded this year, and the key components of the open data shall have to be disseminated further. The data management aspect of the work also still needs more work.

Public participation is an outcome of the effective use of open data

The term participation in the context of development is often viewed as a process of giving relevant knowledge and experience from the public that could potentially serve as important inputs for effective development (Olphert & Damodaran 2007, Puri & Sahay 2007, Puri & Sahay 2003). Citizen participation tends to create links with the issue of social inclusion. From the viewpoint of the data, information and knowledge framework, public participation is the output of knowledge creation and usage.

The findings from the IDEA project show that more work is needed to improve information use before the OD4Transparency project could bring significant public participation in promoting transparency in the use of public funds at LGU. Thus far, in the city of Yogyakarta, the work has only been done by Perkumpulan IDEA.

In the case study of E-NET Philippines, the increased awareness of open data translated into actionable points such as when a workshop participant approached the LGU and the DepEd, and made use of the SEF data which was user-friendly and released fairly quickly. As a result of the positive experience in accessing data, this participant went on to teach other *ustadz* (Islamic teachers) how to access the SEF. They formed the North Cotabato Federation of Madrasa Community Ustadz in July 2015. The group requested that the salaries of their *ustadz* be funded by the SEF. Two of the eight requests have been earmarked for funding. This lobbying extended to another success: access to the budget for uniforms of the *ustadz*. They are hopeful that their initiative will have a multiplier effect and can empower more *ustadz* to demand increased access to the SEF.

With the abovementioned example, it can be said that the use and practice of open data are already gaining currency. However, broader participation of the end-users in public fiscal transparency issues is still something to be desired. Stakeholders in the education system and in this initiative are multiple; and are not confined to internal stakeholders such as teachers and students. External stakeholders include the Parents-Teachers Associations, School Governing Councils, government agencies, NGOs, the private sector and marginalised groups. These stakeholders need data for evidence-based planning. Citizen participation serves as the balancing factor for any government action, but open data inititiatives have consistently been a solitary struggle, such as the initiative pushing for the rightful composition of the LSB in the LGU. While there was a point when the network of church organisations and militant organisations in the area were still strong and this kept alive watchdog initiatives, the culture of citizen participation has waned. There is a need for a push from media and CSOs for more consciousness-raising on the issue. This is where E-Net plays a pivotal role in injecting more dynamism through its wide and existing network members in what has been perceived as a diminished activism on the part of CSOs in the area.

Conclusion

The results of this study offer evidence to support the findings from prior studies and further document best practices regarding the importance of intermediaries for both the supply and use of open data (Chattapadhyay 2014, Van Schalkwyk et al. 2016a). The findings suggest that intermediary organisations view open data favorably as it acts as a novel tool and intermediation channel for advocacy work (Davies 2014). Digital technology, which is an intrinsic part of open data, provides efficient information sharing, analysis and retrieval. However, these advantages come with specific requirements which are now becoming challenges for the intermediary organisations given their limited resources (Chattapadhyay 2014, Zuiderwijk & Janssen 2014).

164

The findings also show that open data initiatives offer a new intermediation channel based on information technology (Davies 2014). Not only can the public receive the information, but it can also re-use the information created by the intermediary organisations for their own analysis, integrating data and information to address different questions, issues and concerns that are significant in their community.

In addition to confirming the role of intermediaries in open data initiatives, the study also provides detailed descriptions on how participation in open data initiative changes relational working process between intermediary organisations and other stakeholders. Open data initiatives created a new space for government and civil society organisations to work together to build trust. The sustainability of open data initiatives is achievable as long as intermediaries can build their credibility as a trusted partner of the government. The ability to identify a gap in the current transparency programmes of the city government and simultaneously propose solutions to address the gap are critical to ensuring the match between the needs of the data supplier and end users. Hence, synergy in the working process between data supplier, intermediary and the end users is critical.

The conversations with the intermediary organisations that participated in this study also reveal that open data projects allowed for synergies to be exploited by government and the intermediary in order to change how government uses data and how it presents data to the public. Therefore, working on an open data project can change how government creates, prepares and uses its data. This outcome, in turn, affects the institutionalisation of open data within government practices. It will also affect the long-term sustainability of the open data initiatives.

For the open data initiatives to sustain public awareness towards the critical issue in the society, a long-term interaction between the intermediaries and the end-users must be maintained. Similarly, better information quality and the high capacity of end-users are necessary prerequisites for widespread effective user participation since end-user participation should be viewed as an output of effective use of open data. Effective inputs from the end users can only be achieved if society is constantly working to produce knowledge that can be used to address socio-economic and development issues.

About the author

GLENN GLENN MAAIL is the Open Data Lab Jakarta's lead researcher. He has several years of experience in the telecommunications industry in Indonesia as a technical project manager and a consultant for the planning and optimisation of mobile networks. Glenn holds a bachelor degree in electrical engineering from Telkom University in Indonesia. He also holds a masters degree in Digital Communication Systems and Technology from the Chalmers University of

Technology in Sweden, and a Doctorate in Engineering (Information Systems) from the University of Melbourne in Australia.
E-mail: glenn@jakarta.labs.webfoundation.org

REFERENCES

Andrason, A. & Van Schalkwyk, F. (2017). Opportune niches in data ecosystems: Open data intermediaries in the agriculture sector in Ghana. *SSRN*. https://ssrn.com/abstract=2949722

Canares, M.P., De Guia, J., Narca, M. & Arawiran, J. (2014). Opening the gates: Will open data initiatives make local governments in the Philippines more transparent? Opendataresearch.org

Cañares, M. & Shekhar, S. (2016). Open data and sub-national governments: Lessons from developing countries. *The Journal of Community Informatics* 12(2): 99-119

Chattapadhyay, S. (2014). Opening government data through mediation: Exploring the roles, practices and strategies of data intermediary organisations in India. ODDC

Craveiro, G.S., Machado, J.A.S., Martano, A.M.R. & Souza, T.J. (2014). Exploring the impacts of web publishing budgetary information at the sub-national level in Brazil. Sao Paulo: Colab-USP

Davies, T. (2014). Open data in developing countries: Emerging insights from Phase 1. Washington DC: World Wide Web Foundation

Davies, T., Perini, F. & Alonso, J.M. (2013). Researching the emerging impacts of open data: ODDC conceptual framework. Washington DC: World Wide Web Foundation.

Gurstein, M. (2011). Open data: Empowering the empowered or effective data use for everyone? *First Monday* 16(2): 1-7

Gutwin, C. & Greenberg, S. (2002). A descriptive framework of workspace awareness for real-time groupware. *Computer Supported Cooperative Work* 11(3-4): 411-446

Kvale, S. (1996). *Interviews: An introduction to qualitative research writing.* Thousand Oaks: Sage

Miles, M.B. & Huberman, A.M. (1994). *Qualitative Data Analysis: An expanded sourcebook*: Thousand Oaks: Sage

Mutuku, L. & Mahihu, C.M. (2014). Open data in developing countries. Opendataresearch.org

Neuman, W.L. (2006). *Social Research Methods: Qualitative and quantitative approaches.* 6th edn. London: Pearson Education

Olphert, W. & Damodaran, L. (2007). Citizen participation and engagement in the design of e-government services: The missing link in effective ICT design and delivery. *Journal of the Association for Information Systems* 8(9): 491

Puri, S.K. & Sahay, S. (2007). Role of ICTs in participatory development: An Indian experience. *Information technology for Development* 13(2): 133-160

Puri, S.K. & Sahay, S. (2003). Participation through communicative action: A case study of GIS for addressing land/water development in India. *Information Technology for Development* 10(3): 179–199

Van Schalkwyk, F., Cañares, M., Chattapadhyay, S. & Andrason, A. (2016a). Open data intermediaries in developing countries. *The Journal of Community Informatics* 12(2): 9-25

Van Schalkwyk, F., Willmers, M. & Schonwetter, T. (2016b). Institutionalising open data in government. *SSRN*. http://dx.doi.org/10.2139/ssrn.2925834

Yin, R.K. (2009). *Case Study Research: Design and methods.* 4th edn. Thousand Oaks: Sage

Zuiderwijk, A. & Janssen, M. (2014). Barriers and development directions for the publication and usage of open data: A socio-technical view. In Gascó-Hernández, M., *Open Government: Opportunities and challenges for public governance.* New York: Springer

9.

Smart cities need to be open:
The case of Jakarta, Indonesia

Michael P Cañares

If the city could speak, what would it say to us?
– Beauregard, 1959

Introduction: The appeal of smart cities

In recent years, the re-conceptualisation of the city as more than just a physical, geographic space has dominated the discourse of urban planners, politicians, academics and the private sector, among other stakeholders. This process of redefinition is not novel and is largely brought about because cities have increasingly become the biggest catchment area of the population. It was reported that 'the year 2008 marked the first time in history that majority of the world's people live in cities' (Peirce & Johnson 2008: 18). More recent figures report that 54% of the world's population now live in urban areas (UN 2014) and with this reality come the attendant challenges of housing, water and sanitation; health and education; transport and communication; and food and agriculture, among others.

Making cities smart is one of the strategies to deal with these growing urban challenges. Washburn et al. (2010) identify five emerging challenges that provide the impetus for making cities smart: the scarcity of resources; inadequate infrastructure; energy shortages and price instability; global warming and human health concerns; and the demand for economic opportunities and social benefits. The core of the strategy is to use information systems to address these five challenges, which are the result of the process of urbanisation (Harrison & Donnelly 2011).

What exactly is a smart city? Many definitions have been put forward and tested by different authors. In a triple helix model proposed by Nam and Pardo (2011), three fundamental components of a smart city are defined: the smart city is conceived as being composed of technological (digital, intelligent, ubiquitous, wired, hybrid, information), institutional (smart community, smart growth) and human (creative, learning, humane, knowledge) factors (see, also Chourabi et al. 2012). The definitions focus on the adjective 'smart', generally concern themselves with the means to become smart (for example, communications technology), what a smart city does (for example, combines infrastructure and information), or on what a smart city can achieve (for example, efficiency in public service delivery). While several definitions include aspects such as participatory governance, natural resource management and sustainable economic growth (see Caragliu et al. 2009), the smart city concept has 'evolved to mean any form of technology-based innovation in the planning, development, and operation of cities' (Harrison & Donnely 2011: 3). This chapter will use Nam and Pardo's (2011) conceptualisation of a smart city. For them, a smart city is one which

> infuses information into its physical infrastructure to improve conveniences, facilitate mobility, add efficiencies, conserve energy, improve the quality of air and water, identify problems and fix them quickly, recover rapidly from disasters, collect data to make better decisions, deploy resources effectively, and share data to enable collaboration across entities and domains. (Nam & Pardo 2011: 284)

The use of information technology is at the centre of this process. Not surprisingly, the phrase has been adopted by major technology companies (such as Siemens and IBM) to characterise new ways of managing big-city concerns such as crime, service delivery, transport, communication, water, business and energy use (Batty et al. 2012). In fact, in a review of articles on smart cities, Meijer and Bolivar (2015) find that most definitions focus on the use of technology in cities.

Here lies the appeal of the smart city. The smart city as an operational construct is intended to make city living more comfortable, productive, efficient, responsive and resilient through the use of technology. The International Standards Organisation, for example, reported that smart cities are targeted towards ensuring convenience in public services; livability of the living environment; smartness of infrastructure; long-term effectiveness of network security; and delicacy in city management (ISO 2015). Thus, it is not surprising that in Asia, the Indian government has invested in the building of one hundred smart cities by 2020,[1] and that Indonesia engages in an annual ranking of smart cities based on economic, social and environmental indicators.[2]

---

1 http://indianexpress.com/article/india/india-others/100-smart-cities-project-gets-cabinet-nod/
2 http://lipsus.kompas.com/kotacerdas/about

Literature review

Lombardi et al. (2012) and Batty et al. (2012) have also identified five characteristics of smart cities, namely: smart governance (related to participation), smart human capital (related to people), smart environment (related to natural resources), smart living (related to quality of life) and smart economy (related to competitiveness).

In this chapter, the focus is on the concept of smart governance which underpins the smart city concept. So far, the most extensive work on the governance of smart cities has been done by Meijer and Bolivar (2015). They categorise four ideal or typical conceptualisations of smart city governance as summarised in Table 1.

Table 1 Prevailing concepts in the governance of smart cities

Conceptualisation	Characterisation	Implication
Governance of a smart city	• Making the right policy choices, implementing the policy choices in an effective and efficient manner; • Traditional governance of the city when the city promotes itself as 'smart'	• No need for transformation of existing governmental structures and processes; • The promotion of smart city initiatives
Smart decision-making processes	• Focused on the process of decision-making and how these decisions are implemented; • Decision-making is innovative through the use of technology and information	• Government rationality is enhanced through the collection and analysis of data; • Data are used for government decision-making processes
Smart administration	• Electronic governance that uses information and communication technologies to connect and integrate information, processes, institutions, and physical infrastructure to better serve citizens and communities (internal transformation)	• Coordination of the many different components of a smart city; • Integrating different information from various sources
Smart urban collaboration	• Collaboration between government, citizens, private sector and communities to achieve citizen-centric governance (external transformation)	• Highlights the need of citizen participation, multi-stakeholder collaboration; • Data is accessible and used by citizens

However, neither the conceptualisation nor the operationalisation of smart cities involves essential aspects of access to information, civic participation, public accountability, and technology and innovation for openness and accountability – critical aspects of what can be considered as principles of open governance (OGP

169

2012). As per the Open Government Partnership (OGP) guiding document, these four areas are defined as follows:

1. *Transparency* – access to information and the disclosure of governmental activities at every level of government.
2. *Accountability* – the highest standards of professional integrity.
3. *Citizen participation* – the public participation of all people; equally and without discrimination.
4. *Technology and innovation* – the use of technology for information sharing, public participation, collaboration and innovation.

The OGP characterisation of open government comes from a sound conceptual base. In a review of the historical evolution of the concept, Yu and Robinson (2012) argue that at the very core, open government denotes accountability, which can be the result of transparency. Harrison et al. (2011) argue that the basic concepts of transparency, participation and collaboration which characterise democratic theory all underpin the foundations of open government. However, are these open government principles reflected in the conceptualisation of smart cities?

As can be seen in Table 1, there is no mention of any of the principles of open governance as a key feature in smart governance; specifically transparency, accountability and citizen participation. Access to data by citizens is considered as part of the process, but this has only happened at the most advanced level in smart governance. Likewise, there is no mention of public accountability – though the overarching thought behind why smart cities are conceptualised as end-states or as strategies is to be responsive to citizens.

When viewed as a continuum, data, with accessibility and not necessarily openness, are only available at advanced stages in smart governance, while early stages only denote data use by government, without necessarily making this available to the public. This is because the smart city, as an operational construct, is largely predicated by the notion of efficiency within government, while in more advanced stages (i.e. smart urban collaboration), the involvement of stakeholders beyond government is contemplated. However, this is not akin to the open government principles where the participation of all – equally and without discrimination – is assured. Thus, it can be said that within the early stages of smart city initiatives, public consultations (and other activities that promote citizen involvement in smart city processes) are not an important and necessary process. Likewise, citizen access to information is not a fundamental factor either.

Meijer and Bolivar's (2015) analogy seems to suggest that cities strengthen their internal processes first (hence the term 'internal transformation' at the third level) before they actually open themselves for public participation and scrutiny (referred to as 'external transformation').

In proposing a theory of smart cities, Harrison and Donnely (2011) highlight that people-systems are at the topmost layer of the urban information model – this represents a person's experience of the city, and part of this experience is citizens' ability to participate in the city's management and governance (Chourabi et al. 2012). The smart city should allow this process of communication between citizens and government, as well as among citizens, to improve the quality of urban life, and for citizens to contribute and exercise full control over their data, and have access to data that matters to them (Batty et al. 2012). As such, Meijer and Bolivar (2015) argue that the smart city discussion should not only focus on technology and its associated impacts on city residents' convenience, but also on how it affects the distribution of social power.

In a review of smart cities and the role of citizen participation, Offenhuber (2015) presents five layers through which citizens participate in smart cities. He presents what he calls the ladder of participation in civic technologies. The concept is presented in Figure 1.

Figure 1 Ladder of participation in civic technologies (adapted from Offenhuber 2015)

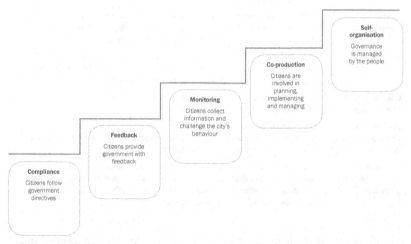

The lowest forms of participation – those of compliance, feedback and monitoring – position the citizen as an outsider to the smart city process. In these levels, they are sources rather than users of data, and are end-receivers of government information. But for citizens to be able to assert how the smart governance of their city should take shape, they should have access to data and be able to use it. As stated earlier, for smart urban collaboration to work at the highest level in the smart governance process, citizens, civil society organisations, the private sector, media and other stakeholders need to have access to data that government collects and aggregates. Without this access, citizens are but outsiders to the smart city process.

A framework for open cities

As shown in the section above, there is a need to introduce a framework of openness to the smart city narrative. But how can this be done? The International Open Data Charter – launched in 2015 and adopted by 10 national governments and 12 local governments, and endorsed by 28 international organisations – can play a significant role. The Charter has six principles, namely: open by default; timely and comprehensive; accessible and usable; comparable and interoperable; for improved governance and citizen engagement; and for inclusive development and innovation. Table 2 shows what these principles mean and their implications for a smart city narrative.

Table 2 International Open Data Charter Principles

Principle	Meaning
Open by default	All government data should be open to the public, except those where not opening up is justified.
Timely and comprehensive	Release of data without delay, in its original form, disaggregated to the lowest levels, with opportunity for user comment and feedback, and with complete documentation of the process of collection and publication.
Accessible and usable	Data are published on a central portal, in open formats, free of charge and in unrestrictive licence, and without the need for payment or registration. Users should be made aware of and capacitated to engage with the data.
Comparable and interoperable	Data should be easy to compare with, and between, sectors; and presented in structured and standardised formats.
For improved governance and citizen engagement	Open data should allow the space for civil society organisations, private sector, media, research institutions, and other stakeholders to strive for better governance, transparency and accountability.
For inclusive development and innovation	Open data can be used to stimulate innovation and promote inclusive development and this requires collaborative work with different stakeholders including multi-lateral institutions, civil society organisations, schools, research institutes, technologists, among others.

As indicated earlier, there are at least three areas where the concept of smart governance of smart cities is wanting – transparency, accountability and citizen participation. Adopting the principles of the International Open Data Charter can hasten this process, starting off by making data about how the smart city is governed accessible to the public – in open formats, and for citizen use and reuse. This could be a building block in ensuring that smart cities are not only about public service delivery, but also about citizen engagement, better governance and inclusive development. But the disclosure of data is only an initial step – more is required.

Table 2 suggests that opening up smart cities requires the broadening of smart city goals – from the rather individualistic and personal experience of living in a city to more inclusive development and governance processes. This requires that governments not only be responsive to citizens' complaints, but that they are obliged to answer questions too – things that citizens can only ask if they have access to data and information (*transparency*). It requires that initiatives are designed not only to provide citizen information or opportunities to provide feedback, but also to ensure that citizens are given a space to define what their cities, smart or not, should look like (*citizen participation*). It requires that technology is not just used for the purposes of 'smartness' or efficiency, but for making governments more transparent and accountable to citizens (*technology and innovation*). Finally, it requires that governments provide citizens in a smart city with the information on how its officials adhere to the highest standards of professional integrity, and how its systems and processes are making this happen (*accountability*). In summary, how the smart city is visualised, how it should be achieved, and what role citizens should have in this process of production needs to change.

This chapter sets outs to lay the groundwork for developing a framework for open cities. The rhetoric of smart cities, despite its popularity, has become centred on the use of technology and in making the governance of the city more efficient. While it does seem that the argument on opening up cities is data-centric, as illustrated in the previous sub-section, it can be argued that opening up cities needs to target citizens as the ultimate outcome. The underlying reason why we want open cities is to, in the aspirational words of the OGP, 'foster a global culture of open government that empowers and delivers for citizens' (OGP 2012).

Accordingly, open cities are those cities that deliver services to and empower citizens. This definition firmly places the political dimension of the city into the discourse, as well as the city's responsibility to the constituents it is supposed to serve. It puts the purpose and responsibility of a city and city governments over and above the means by which such purposes are achieved. Citizen empowerment is not only about providing the tools (technology), but also the resources (data) and the capability (skills) to engage in an open space where debate and contestation are invited and encouraged. Open cities would then deliver relevant services and public infrastructure – because citizens are asked how they would like their cities to take shape and are involved in the manner in which the vision will be implemented.

Figure 2 shows open government principles as the core concepts of open cities, intertwined with open data and smart city principles. Data provision and, in this case, open data, should be undertaken in the name of transparency to encourage citizen participation. Government decision-making should be conducted in a transparent and accountable manner. Government administration should be accountable, harnessing the power of technology to encourage reform and innovation. Finally, citizen participation is required to allow meaningful collaboration in the use of technology to improve governance, recognising that governments do not have a monopoly on innovation and insight. Moving the discussion further, transparency and citizen participation are essential preconditions for empowerment while accountable governments make effective and efficient use of technology and innovation to improve service delivery.

Figure 2 Open cities: A framework

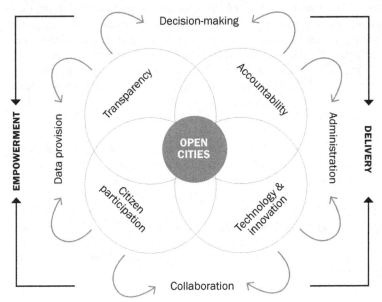

Nam and Pardo's (2011) three dimensions of smart cities – technology, institutions and the human – can aptly apply to this conceptualisation, but the emphasis is largely on how people can effectively and efficiently participate in using technology to build stronger institutions. Technology, in this case, should not be regarded as superior to other dimensions, and its use should be fit for purpose and appropriate to context. Moreover, the processes and the means used to make cities liveable should be couched in the terms and principles of openness – the use of open data, deployment of open technology and the use of open processes – that allow the participation of different sectors and stakeholders in order to achieve the goals which citizens themselves have identified.

This initial step at conceptualisation is intended to challenge current thinking on how urban spaces (cities) are organised. In the same way, this step continues to question the conceptualisation and popularity of the smart city concept, which, as this chapter suggests, is more government-centric than focused on citizens. While far from perfectly iterated, this chapter and the proposed framework hopes to start the debate on how smart cities, as they are shaped now, can be made more open in the future.

Methodology

To explore the concept of the smart city and its relationship to an openness, the quantitative and qualitative data used in a case study conducted by the Center for Innovation Policy and Governance (CIPG) on the Smart City Programme of Jakarta, Indonesia, was used (see Putri et al. 2016). The analysis was supplemented by profiling the Smart City Programme through interviews and focus groups. The results were analysed qualitatively using the lens of the Open Government Principles and their intersection with Meijer and Bolivar's (2015) conceptualisation of smart governance, as elucidated in the proposed Open Cities Framework presented in Figure 2. In analysing the levels of participation within the Jakarta Smart City Programme, Offenhuber's (2012) ladder of participation in civic technologies was used.

The primary questions of interest are the following:

1. How does the Jakarta Smart City Programme allow citizen participation in the implementation of its projects and activities?
2. How do open government principles of transparency, accountability, technology and innovation, and citizen participation fit into the Jakarta Smart City narrative?
3. What options are available for the Jakarta Smart City Programme to transition into a Jakarta Open City Programme?

Findings and discussion:
The Jakarta Smart City Programme

The Indonesian city of Jakarta has the most integrated public service delivery information system in the country. Jakarta is also one of the first cities to have its own dedicated citizen reporting application. Under the leadership of Governor Basuki Tjahaja Purnama (Ahok), Jakarta has promoted and implemented open government initiatives since 2012 through different activities such as hackathons and the launch of the Jakarta Smart City Programme in 2014.

Initiated in December 2014, Jakarta Smart City was developed to create one platform that provides public information about the city to citizens. The Jakarta Smart City Technical Executive Unit (UPT – *Unit Pelaksana Teknis*) was officially established in January 2015 to coordinate the needs and demands for data from both government and citizens.

One of the first key programmes of Jakarta Smart City was designed to provide information to citizens on traffic conditions, public service delivery and flood occurrence, with data obtained through crowd-sourcing platforms Waze and Qlue, and the twitter account PetaJakarta, respectively. The citizen-generated data from these channels are managed by private companies. Waze collects and reports data on traffic conditions for motorists. Qlue is a public complaints system that feeds into a complaint–response system on behalf of city government agencies, while PetaJakarta collects and disseminates data on flood conditions across the city. Information collected on these platforms serve the private companies that aggregate them (for Qlue and Waze) and the researchers that initiated the project (in the case of PetaJakarta). These non-public stakeholders share the data collected with government. However, based on a study conducted by the CIPG (Putri et al. 2016), the actual use of the data made available to government is still very low. There are fundamental problems with data governance in the city: a lack of data analysis skills; little appreciation of how data can affect operational decisions or policy choices; and the basic lack of understanding on how to manage and use the trove of data produced through this initiative.

Online platforms such as these are appropriate for Jakarta where internet penetration reaches as far as 56% (APJII & UI 2015), and the mobile-phone ownership is as high as 97.24% (BPS 2015). The three applications mentioned above are all accessible via internet-enabled smartphones.

The results of the survey conducted among users of the different applications indicate that none of them are aware that Jakarta Smart City exists, and that they use Waze extensively as compared to the other platforms. The primary considerations in using the applications are ease-of-use, relevance to citizen interests or needs, and the ability to search for information. It is therefore not surprising that Waze topped the list, considering that traffic is one of Jakarta's worst problems, affecting residents on a daily basis.

Jakarta Smart City and participation

All of the Jakarta Smart City initiatives encourage only low levels of participation. Qlue, Petajakarta and Waze all fall within the feedback and monitoring steps on the ladder of participation.

Qlue is an application that connects individuals with their neighbourhood and city officials by reporting on the conditions of their surroundings. The idea for this application came from the desire to figure out how problems in Jakarta could be managed and solved with citizens' participation. Qlue was launched in December 2014, and it has a sister application called Crop (*Cepat Respon Opini Publik*) that officials use to respond to reports from Qlue. The two applications facilitate the efficient handling of citizen complaints and the required response from the city government. Qlue crowd-sources the data and delivers real-time reports directly to city officials.

Waze is an application that provides a mapping service to enable its users to share real-time traffic and road information. Traffic information provided by Waze circulates mainly among citizens. In this case, direct interaction between citizens and the government is not necessary. Citizens report traffic and road conditions to other 'wazers' (the term used to identify a Waze user). In return, they get an aggregated map with traffic information and use the information according to their needs. But Waze provides access to its data to the Jakarta Smart City team for its use while at the same time providing external validation of the data that the city government collects on road and traffic information.

Finally, the motivation behind PetaJakarta is to use an existing platform (in this case Twitter) to spread useful information on flood conditions. During monsoon season, citizens actively share information on flood conditions through Twitter. When citizens observe flooding, they can tweet using the hashtag #banjir and mention the Twitter account @PetaJakarta. The administrator of PetaJakarta will confirm the report to the respective citizen/Twitter user. Once the report is confirmed, it is retweeted by PetaJakarta and automatically displayed as a flood map. Citizens can access this flood map and the tweets in order to monitor flood conditions in the city. The disaster agency also monitors this flood map as some of the tweets are requests for help and evacuation support.

In these applications, citizens are not participants in co-creation. In the case of Qlue, citizens are treated as sources of feedback and complaints, while in the case of both Waze and PetaJakarta citizens collect or provide a third-party organisation, which later provides government, with information on traffic and flooding respectively. While not necessarily intended to challenge government behaviour, the participation of citizens in providing information on traffic or flooding condition challenges the city government in transport and spatial planning, to avoid heavy traffic congestion in the case of Waze and incessant flooding in the case of PetaJakarta.

Jakarta Smart City and notions of openness

Using the experience of the Jakarta Smart City Programme as a concrete example of the operationalisation of the smart city concept, it can be argued that for the early stages of smart cities, openness is not necessarily a factor. This is fundamentally because, as argued above, the conceptualisation of what makes a city smart is about transforming internal processes within the bureaucracy. What makes the Smart City Programme in Jakarta impressive, however, is the collaboration between government and researchers (PetaJakarta) and the private sector (Qlue, Crop, Waze). However, such collaboration, which is a feature of advanced smart cities, is largely initiated by external stakeholders rather than by the city government.

Using open government principles as a lens, the prominent feature of the Jakarta Smart City Programme initiative is the use of technology and innovation. However, it lacks the important elements of transparency and accountability. While accountability is sought using Qlue and Crop, it does not go beyond the concept of public service delivery to consider difficult questions such as corruption in public spending and the outsourcing of public services, or how the government prioritises investment in public service delivery.

177

Reflecting on Meijer and Bolivar's (2015) characterisation of smart governance, the Jakarta Smart City Programme is still stuck at the level of 'governance of a smart city', where the focus is largely on the promotion of smart city initiatives. The different initiatives were viewed as ways to enhance public service delivery by responding to citizen reports (for example, Qlue and Crop). At its current stage, Waze remains unutilised within city government, especially with regard to reconfiguring transport planning to solve current traffic problems. Similarly, there is no evidence to show that PetaJakarta is used to solve persistent flooding problems in the city.

As indicated above, the lowest forms of participation – those of compliance, feedback and monitoring – position the citizen as an outsider to the smart city process. At these levels, they are sources rather than users of data, and are end-receivers of government information. But for citizens to be able to effectively assert how smart governance of their city should take shape, they should have access to data and be able to use them. As stated above, for smart urban collaboration to work at the highest level in the smart governance process, citizens, civil society organisations, the private sector, media and other stakeholders need to have access to data that government collects and aggregates. Without this access, citizens are outsiders to the smart city process.

The Jakarta Smart City Programme benefits from information largely provided by citizens through getting real-time information on flooding conditions as well as interventions needed for more vulnerable areas; generating feedback in the delivery of public services and providing the appropriate response; and in determining bottlenecks and problems in traffic and roads for use in the planning and management of traffic. In these cases, citizens are mere providers of data, with little opportunity to use or reuse the data they contribute to smart governance. Indeed, citizens, have access to the user-interface capabilities of Waze and PetaJakarta, meaning they will know the traffic conditions or flood conditions in a particular area, but they will not have access to the data that will help them either analyse other things – such as the connectedness of flooding and traffic, the plans and resource allocations related to flooding and traffic – or conduct a comparative analysis of flooding or traffic across geographical space and time.

One dataset that the Jakarta government has used extensively is the public reporting/complaint data gathered through Qlue, and which is subsequently relayed to concerned government agencies through Crop. While citizens can submit complaints and check their status, they do not have access to all the other complains posted to Qlue, or to government responses posted through Crop. The government-to-citizen interaction is limited to an individual level, and Crop and Qlue data are only available for use by government and no one else.

This chapter argues that there is a strong value proposition in opening up datasets collected, acquired or gathered through smart city initiatives for three primary reasons. First, the data that smart city initiatives have been able to collect are citizen-generated data, and citizens should have right of access. Second, opening up data from smart city initiatives allows for public scrutiny and deeper transparency. In the case of the Jakarta Smart City initiative, for example, restricting access to Qlue and Crop data to government will not allow people to see government's level of responsiveness or allow them to develop a sense of accountability. Finally, data use will likely become more pervasive if widely shared. There is sufficient evidence to show that once data are opened publicly, they can become a vital resource in empowering citizens, improving government, creating opportunity and solving public problems (Verhulst & Young 2016).

Conclusion

Using the Jakarta Smart City Programme as a test-case for analysing whether a smart city mirrors principles of open governance, this chapter has shown that the current conceptualisation is not leading to greater transparency and accountability, and while the smart city initiative uses technology and innovation to presumably make public services better, it limits the participation of citizens in decision-making processes, making them passive participants in defining what their cities should look like.

What does it take to inject openness into smart city discourses? It requires that all data collected, produced and aggregated by smart city platforms, including those that were generated through third-party agreements should be published in real-time, with meaningful disaggregation and with complete documentation, in open format, free of charge and with an unrestrictive licence. Users should have the opportunity to interact with the data and provide feedback, and to do this, the city government should actively promote awareness and capacity, not only in using smart city applications, but also in accessing and using the data that are generated by these applications. In the same way, city governments should strengthen accountability mechanisms to ensure that those agencies that are at the back-end of these platforms and applications will be responsive to citizens' demands and aspirations.

Smart city initiatives should not only endeavour to achieve goals of convenience, liveability and smartness of infrastructure, but also the better participation of citizens in governance and the increased accountability and transparency of governments. Smart city initiatives should harness the power of multi-stakeholder collaboration to solve urban challenges, promote equal access to opportunities and spur innovation. Benefits of smart city initiatives should not only accrue to those already empowered but to all residents of the city, especially those who are excluded in the development process.

While these observations have arisen from a single case study of the Jakarta Smart City initiative, the critique that it presents is not peculiar to this case alone. Others have written, using other case studies and country contexts, that smart cities as they are planned and implemented ignore the principles of social justice and inhibit the participation of excluded groups in, say, India (Datta 2015), and ignore the underlying power dynamics that make the poor more powerless in, say, African cities (Watson 2015), and reproduce the same kinds of narratives in urban formation that place a premium on technology rather than on people and human networks and relationships (Soderstrom et al. 2014). An area of future work is to apply the same frame of analysis used in this chapter to other similar cases in the Global South in order to widen the discussion on how smart city initiatives can be influenced to transition towards greater openness.

About the author

Michael Cañares is Open Data Lab Jakarta's Regional Research Manager for Asia. He is a graduate of law and accountancy at Holy Name University and holds an MSc in Development Studies from the London School of Economics and Political Science. Before joining the Lab, Michael taught for over ten years, served as a monitoring and evaluation specialist for infrastructure governance and local economic development, and managed various open data research projects in the Philippines.

REFERENCES

APJII & P. UI (2015). *Profil Pengguna Internet Indonesia 2014*. Jakarta: APJII

Batty, M., Axhause, K.W., Giannotti, F., Pozdnoukhov, A., Bazani, A., Wachowicz, M., Ouzounis, G. & Portugali, Y. (2012). Smart cities of the future. *The European Physical Journal Special Topics* 214: 481-518

BPS (2015) *Statistik Indonesia 2015*. Jakarta: Badan Pusat Statistik

Caragliu, A., Del Bo, C. & Nijkamp, P. (2009). Smart cities in Europe. In *Proceedings of the 3rd Central European Conference in Regional Science – CERS 2009*. pp. 49-59

Chourabi, H., Nam, T., Walker, S., Gil-Garcia, J.R., Mellouli, S., Nahon, K., Pardo, T. & Scholl, H.J. (2012). Understanding smart cities: An integrative framework. In *Proceedings of 45th Hawaii International Conference on System Sciences*. Washington DC: IEEE Computer Society

Cohen, J. & Uphoff, N. (1980). Participation's place in rural development: Seeking clarity through specificity. *World Development* 8: 213-235

Datta, A. (2015). New urban utopias of postcolonial India: 'Entrepreneurial urbanization'. *Dialogues in Human Geography* 5(1): 36-39

Harrison, C. & Donnely, I.A. (2011). Theory of smart cities. In *Proceedings of the 55th Annual Meeting of the ISSS*. The University of Hull, UK, 17–22 July. http://journals.isss.org/index.php/proceedings55th/article/view/1703/572

Harrisson, T., Guerrero, S., Burke, G.B., Cooke, M., Cresswell, A., Helbig, N., Hardinova, J. & Pardo, T. (2011). Open government and e-government: Democratic challenges from a public value perspective. *Proceedings of the 12th Annual International Digital Government Research Conference: Digital government innovation in challenging times*. New York: ACM

Hollsteiner, M.R. (1979). *Mobilizing the Rural Poor through Community Organization*. Manila: Institute of Philippine Culture

International Open Data Charter (2016). http://opendatacharter.net/wp-content/uploads/2015/10/opendatacharter-charter_F.pdf

ISO/IEC (2015) *Smart Cities: Preliminary Report 2014*. ISO: Switzerland. http://www.iso.org/iso/smart_cities_report-jtc1.pdf

Lombardi, P., Giordano, S., Farouh, H. & Yousef, W. (2011). An analytic network model for smart cities. Paper presented at the International Symposium on the Analytic Hierarchy Process, Sorrento, Italy, 15–18 June

Maail, G. (2016). A comparison of open cities and smart cities. Unpublished document.

Mansbridge, J. (1995). Does participation make better citizens? *Political Economy of a Good Society Conference*, February

Marris, P. & Rein, M. (1967). *Dilemmas of Social Reform: Poverty and community action in the United States*. New York: Atherton

Meijer, J. & Bolivar, M.P.R. (2015). Governing the smart city: A review of literature on smart urban governance. *International Review of Administrative Sciences* 82(2): 1-17. http://journals.sagepub.com/doi/abs/10.1177/0020852314564308

Nam, T. & Pardo, A. (2011). Conceptualizing smart city with dimensions of technology, people, and institutions. *Proceedings of the 12th Annual International Digital Government Research Conference: Digital government innovation in challenging times*. New York: ACM

Offenhuber, D. (2015). Civic technologies: tools or therapy? Keynote lecture at Ars Electronica 2015. https://medium.com/@dietoff/civic-technologies-tools-or-therapy-20f2e596ac23#.ct16sp9ji

Open Government Partnership (2012). Open Government Partnership: Articles of Governance. http://www.opengovpartnership.org/sites/default/files/attachments/OGP%2520ArticlesGov%2520Apr%252021%25202015_0%5B1%5D.pdf

Peirce, N. & Johnson, C. (2008). *Century of the City: No time to lose*. New York: Rockefeller Foundation. https://www.rockefellerfoundation.org/report/century-of-the-city/

Putri, D.A., Karlina, M., Tanaya, J. & Canares, M. (2016). How do citizens benefit from a smart city? Case Study of Jakarta, Indonesia. Jakarta: Open Data Lab Jakarta

Soderstrom, O., Paasche, T. & Klauser, F. (2014). Smart cities as corporate storytelling. *City* 18(3): 307-320

United Nations (2014). *World Urbanization Prospects 2014*. UN DESA. https://esa.un.org/unpd/wup/publications/files/wup2014-highlights.pdf

Verhulst, S. & Young, A. (2016). *Open Data Impact: When demand and supply meet*. New York: The GovLab and Omidyar Network. http://odimpact.org/static/files/open-data-impact-key-findings.pdf

Washburn, D., Sindhu, U., Balaouras, S., Dines, R.A., Hayes, N.M. & Nelson, L.E. (2010). Helping CIOs understand 'Smart City' initiatives: Defining the smart city, its drivers, and the role of the CIO. Cambridge, MA: Forrester Research

Watson, V. (2015). The allure of 'smart city' rhetoric: India and Africa. *Dialogues in Human Geography* 5(1): 36-39

Yu, H. & Robinson, D. (2012). The new ambiguity of 'open government'. *UCLA Review Discourse*. http://papers.ssrn.com/sol3/Papers.cfm?abstract_id=2012489

10.

Protecting privacy while releasing data: Strategies to maximise benefits and mitigate risks

Joel Gurin, Matt Rumsey, Audrey Ariss & Katherine Garcia

Introduction

Privacy has become an urgent issue in data use. Traditionally, 'open government data' has been thought of as free, public data that anyone could use and republish. Now, the discussion is shifting to include data that may not be appropriate for wide, unfettered access, but can still be of use to non-government communities.[1] Data containing personally identifiable information (PII) cannot be released widely, but there are certain circumstances that could allow for its use in restricted or de-identified forms. By considering various levels of sensitivity in the datasets they manage, data stewards can provide several levels of openness and release datasets in different ways accordingly (Open Data Institute n.d.).

As more open government data has become available, data users in business, academia, and the non-profit community have come up against a conundrum. Many datasets in health, education, housing and other areas may have the most value when they are released with 'microdata' that can be analysed at the level of individual records. But releasing data at that level carries the risk of exposing PII that could threaten individuals' privacy if it were released openly. Government agencies must address the risks and sensitivities of making data available while at the same time maximising its accessibility and use.

---

1   Academic observers have been considering how best to balance open data and privacy concerns for several years. More recently, as the concept of open data is becoming accepted at all levels of government and the 'low hanging fruit' is released, government policy-makers and open data advocates have turned their attention to useful data that may be more difficult to release for a variety of reasons – including privacy concerns. Examples cited elsewhere in this chapter include the Open Data Institute's Data Spectrum; the Sunlight Foundation's work on 'microdata', privacy and criminal justice data; and the Center for Open Data Enterprise and White House Office of Science and Technology Policy's Open Data Roundtable Series.

Approaches to privacy are inevitably affected by political goals and considerations. In the US, for example, President Obama recognised the need for clear guidelines by establishing the Federal Privacy Council in February 2016 (Obama 2016), and the Federal Communications Commission under Obama instituted privacy protections for data collected by internet service providers. A few months into the Trump Administration, the Republican Congress eliminated those FCC protections. It remains to be seen how changing political dynamics in the US, and potentially other countries, will affect approaches to privacy policy. This chapter presents an analysis that should be helpful to any policy-maker who wants to study and address this issue.

Research context

'Microdata' is data released in its most granular, unaggregated form (Shaw 2014). The key question is: How can we maximise public access to and value from open granular information while protecting privacy? To answer this question, data and privacy experts have explored issues such as:

- What are the potential benefits of using unaggregated data (or microdata) for the public good?[2]
- What are the risks of using these datasets if they contain or could lead to the discovery of personally identifiable information, and how can those risks be minimised?[3]
- What are the best technical, policy and pragmatic approaches to ensure strong privacy protections while maximising the benefits of open data?[4]

Benefits of releasing microdata

Analyses of government-held microdata can advance public policy and social benefit through insight into public issues, better informed decision-making and improved delivery of public services. Microdata is already being used to improve the health and safety of citizens, the national transportation infrastructure, the criminal justice system, the quality of education, and the equity and stability of the country's housing market, among other uses. Here are examples of the benefits that highly detailed data can support.

---

2   See examples from transportation (Center for Open Data Enterprise 2015) and education (Park & Shelton 2012).
3   See, for example, Ortellado (2016).
4   See, for example, Altman et al. (2015); Borgesius et al. (2015); Dwork & Roth (2014); Ohm (2010).

Healthcare

A revolution in healthcare is underway, with data at its core. However, advances in this arena are also demonstrating the challenges and risks of greater health data utilisation. Health data has long been recognised as especially personal and sensitive information: it is already protected by the Health Insurance Portability and Accountability Act (HIPAA), and some experts believe that additional protections may be necessary (Podesta et al. 2014).

With proper privacy and security mechanisms in place, health and medical research institutions are able to share de-identified patient health information with doctors, allowing them to diagnose and treat disease more effectively. Large health datasets may be used to target services to underserved populations (Federal Trade Commission 2016). Research centers, drug companies, hospitals, and other institutions can analyse patient data to improve services and develop new treatments (Podesta et al. 2014).

The Precision Medicine Initiative (PMI) exemplifies the opportunities in analysing health microdata. Launched in 2015, the PMI is a US federal effort to 'enable a new era of medicine through research, technology, and policies that empower patients, researchers, and providers to work together toward development of individualised treatments' (The White House n.d.). If successful, it will allow for highly targeted treatments based on a range of inputs including personal medical histories and genetic analysis.

The PMI does not aim to make health data fully open to the public, but it relies heavily on data-sharing among clinicians and researchers with appropriate restrictions and safeguards. As the White House explains: 'to get there, we need to incorporate many different types of data [... including] data about the patient collected by health care providers and the patients themselves. Success will require that health data is portable, that it can be easily shared between providers, researchers, and most importantly, patients and research participants' (The White House n.d.).

Transportation

Around the world, untold numbers of commuters now check their mobile phones every day to see when the next bus will arrive. This information is at their fingertips thanks to open data (Press 2010). Ubiquitous travel apps have shown how open transportation data can improve public transit access, ease traffic congestion, and make citizens' lives easier.

Transportation microdata has potentially powerful applications when combined with other types of microdata. At a 2015 roundtable held with the US Department of Transportation and users of its data, participants flagged the need for crash data to be combined with hospital data 'to understand the long-term impacts of vehicle crashes and how different kinds of safety equipment can mitigate injury' (Center for Open Data Enterprise 2015). Microdata from different sources can also be particularly useful for transit planners. For example, microdata on both travel patterns and commuters' income levels helps planners understand the obstacles faced by low income workers as they travel to their jobs, allowing for more efficient service delivery and equitable planning decisions (Tierney 2012).

Increasingly popular 'bike sharing' systems are another example of using transit microdata. These programmes generate mountains of data which are often released publicly, allowing advocates to push for expanded service, authorities to better target infrastructure investment, and researchers to ask tough questions about system equality. For example, a recent analysis of 22 million trips taken using New York City's Citi Bike system revealed that the bikes were heavily used for commuting purposes and rides were often concentrated in areas with robust bike lane infrastructure (Thomas 2016).

Criminal justice

Microdata can help improve the criminal justice process at several stages. It can be used to develop effective public policies, improve community relations, and correct unfair practices.

Recent high-profile efforts have focused on opening data about police practices and operations (Shaw 2015). The Sunlight Foundation has found that previous data releases 'have already paid off by improving outcomes that communities perceived as unfair. The case of released stop-and-frisk data provides an important example of this, where New York's public release of granular pedestrian stop data, and the analysis it permitted, led to the discovery that almost 9 out of every 10 people stopped were entirely innocent, and that 9 out of every 10 people stopped were non-white' (The Sunlight Foundation 2014). Stop-and-frisk is a controversial practice during which police would stop and search pedestrians without a warrant. Allowing for better understanding of this data helped kick-start the repeal of what proved to be an ineffective and discriminatory policy.

Housing

Microdata on housing can help identify discriminatory lending patterns, surface structural vulnerabilities, and help policy makers prevent a future housing crisis. After the global financial crisis, the United States Congress took a number of steps to safeguard the country's financial system. Congress mandated the public release of data showing trends in the mortgage industry, in the interest of avoiding another housing bubble. As part of that effort, Congress strengthened requirements for publishing data under the Home Mortgage Disclosure Act (HMDA), a 1975 law designed to help prevent housing discrimination (Consumer Financial Protection Bureau 2015).

Data collected under HMDA, which is now implemented by the Consumer Financial Protection Bureau (CFPB), is released publicly every September. The data 'help show whether lenders are serving the housing needs of their communities; they give public officials information that helps them make decisions and policies; and they shed light on lending patterns that could be discriminatory' (Consumer Financial Protection Bureau n.d.). The CFPB is statutorily mandated to publicly disclose data under HMDA while developing appropriate protections for borrower privacy in light of HMDA's purposes.

Education

Microdata on student performance can help educational institutions provide students with the tools and support they need to build useful knowledge and skills. Data can be combined with mobile technologies and education software to personalise education (Podesta et al. 2014). To this end, the Obama administration took a number of steps to ensure that education data is properly leveraged, and pledged to 'work to develop a common trust mechanism for schools that want to exchange student data with each other and other qualified parties' (Park & Shelton 2012). So far, however, the difficulty of establishing that trust has been an obstacle to working with student data.

Risks of releasing microdata

The risks of releasing microdata from datasets containing PII are real and well documented. There is concern that releasing microdata from these sources could result in privacy violations, even if efforts have been made to 'anonymise' or 'de-identify' the data by stripping it of PII.

For many years it was thought that if a database was scrubbed of identifying information such as name, address, or social security number that privacy could be effectively protected. However, a growing body of research shows that this is often not sufficient to guarantee privacy. Furthermore, the increasing influence of big data has turned previously non-existent or inconceivable pieces of data into potentially identifying ones. There is also no standard definition of PII and wide variance in the way that various laws define the concept (Polonetsky et al. 2016).

The 'Mosaic Effect' is a common term for the idea that disparate datasets and information can be combined to expose sensitive information and negate attempts to protect privacy. Some high-profile examples have fueled these concerns. Latanya Sweeney's work showing that de-identified medical data can often be re-identified through linking or matching with other datasets is perhaps the most well-known instance (Sweeney 1997). In another well-known example, researchers were able to identify individuals from supposedly anonymised Netflix rating information a high percentage of the time with only the help of publicly available information from another source, the Internet Movie Database

187

(Narayanan & Shmatikov 2008). Another commonly cited example emerged when America Online (AOL) released 'anonymised' search results from 650 000 of its users. This turned out to be a case of very weak anonymisation, since AOL failed to consider the fact that individuals often perform web searches for their own names, rapidly allowing interested individuals to significantly narrow the list of potential names (Arrington 2006). While the Netflix and AOL examples took place several years ago, they exemplify a continuing concern.

Privacy concerns go beyond the technical difficulty of anonymising data. In a recent paper, Borgesius et al. (2016) highlight 'three kinds of concerns about releasing personal information as open data: (1) the chilling effects on people interacting with the public sector, (2) a lack of individual control over personal information, and (3) the use of open data for social sorting or discriminatory practices'. There is general consensus that there is no foolproof way to completely anonymise a dataset, because linking de-identified data to other sources of data can often give enough information to identify individuals (O'Hara 2011).

Loss of public trust

The chilling effects detailed by Borgesius et al. (2016) can be tied to a loss of public trust. As O'Hara put it, 'not only are privacy and transparency compatible, privacy is a necessary condition for a successful transparency programme' (O'Hara 2011). If individuals in a study don't trust that their privacy is being taken seriously, the programme in question will run into serious problems.[5]

Experience shows that it is critically important for the public to feel that privacy has been considered in the decision-making process around data release and sharing (O'Hara 2011). InBloom was a private data analytics company working with educational data from a number of states. The company's goal was to help teachers tailor assignments to better suit the needs of individual students. While 'there weren't any documented cases of InBloom misusing the information' that the company held, InBloom did not demonstrate to the community's satisfaction that the company was taking privacy seriously. There was serious pushback from parents and privacy advocates and the company was eventually forced to shut down (Kharif 2014). This lesson is applicable to government agencies and companies working with sensitive information.

Discriminatory practices

Scassa (2014) explains this risk in more detail as 'the potential for open government data – even if anonymised – to contribute to the big data environment in which citizens and their activities are increasingly monitored and profiled'. In January 2016, the US Federal Trade Commission (FTC) released a report looking at the

---

5   See, for example, Kharif (2014).

potential for big data to be used for discrimination (Federal Trade Commission 2016). That report followed a 2014 document released by the White House that assessed opportunities and risks associated with big data (Podesta et al. 2016).

Predictive policing has been cited as a data-driven area that has significant built-in risks of discrimination. For example, police reports may be used for predictive purposes, but neighborhoods with 'lots of police calls aren't necessarily the same places the most crime is happening. They are, rather, where the most police attention is – though where that attention focuses' is often directed by gender and racial biases (Isaac & Dixon 2017).

The 2014 White House report on big data and privacy, released right after InBloom announced that it was shutting down, used educational data as an example of this concern. 'As students begin to share information with educational institutions,' the report said, 'they expect that they are doing so in order to develop knowledge and skills, not to have their data used to build extensive profiles about their strengths and weaknesses that could be used to their disadvantage in later years' (Podesta et al. 2014).

Current legal and policy frameworks

A number of laws and guidelines provide a framework for ensuring privacy for individuals who share information with the government, and for communicating about privacy safeguards. Some of the broader legal and policy frameworks include the following:

Freedom of information laws

Freedom of information laws 'provide inspiration on how to strike a balance between privacy and transparency in the open data context [... they] typically aim to accommodate privacy interests, for example by reserving access to personal information to parties with particular interests, or by only making records available in secure reading rooms' (Borgesius et al. 2016). That said, these laws may have narrow privacy restrictions that do not protect against all the risks of misusing personal information.

Organization for Economic Cooperation and Development (OECD) Privacy Guidelines

First published in 1980, the OECD Privacy Guidelines were the first set of internationally agreed upon privacy principles (Kuschewsky 2013). They were updated and expanded in 2013. The Framework is widely utilised, but has been criticised for its 'risk-based approach [... as well as] for promoting business over privacy' (Borgesius et al. 2016).

Privacy impact assessments

US federal law requires government agencies to consider individual privacy broadly by requiring them to conduct Privacy Impact Assessments about their electronic information systems and data that may contain PII. These assessments can be useful when balancing the relative costs and benefits of releasing a dataset (Altman et al. 2015).

Fair Information Practice Principles

The Fair Information Practice Principles are 'a set of principles and practices that describe how an information-based society may approach information handling, storage, management, and flows with a view toward maintaining fairness, privacy, and security in a rapidly evolving global technology environment' (Dixon 2008). The principles are internationally recognised and were developed over decades by a number of international bodies including the US Departments of Health, Education, and Welfare, and the OECD (Dixon 2008). These principles have been lauded for their 'balance [between] privacy-related interests and other interests, such as those of business and the public sector' (Borgesius et al. 2016).

Methodology

The Center for Open Data Enterprise used a multimethod approach to identifying strategies to best manage data release and privacy protection. This included desk research; an Open Data Roundtable with legal, policy and technical experts on open data and policy; solicitation of expert feedback; and interviews. The sequence of work was as follows:

(1) Review of existing literature on data and privacy issues. From this, an initial framework for identifying the challneges, solutions, and experts was developed.

(2) Information collection through an online public survey. Questions assessed:
   • Respondents' evaluation of the key issues in open data and privacy
   • Effectiveness of current approaches used to address challenges in open data and privacy
   • Respondents' interest in participating in the roundtable

The survey received 61 responses, which were used to inform the plan for the roundtable and preparation of background materials.

190

	Legal	Policy	Technical	Total
Academic	1	1	2	4
Company	1	1	6	8
Government	8	14	16	38
Non-profit	2	5	4	11
Total	**12**	**21**	**28**	**61**

(3)   Preparation of a briefing paper for background to the Open Data Roundtable, based on literature review and survey responses.

(4)   An all-day Open Data Roundtable, held on 24 March 2016, to address the issue: how to open granular information while protecting privacy. The roundtable brought together 75 participants from federal agencies, academia, the private sector, and non-profit organisations with technical, policy, and legal expertise. This facilitated discussion included presentations, small-group breakout sessions, reports back to the full group, and synthesis of findings by the Center for Open Data Enterprise.

	Legal	Policy	Technical	Total
Academic		1		1
Company	2	4	5	11
Government	13	21	13	47
Non-profit	2	11	3	16
Total	**17**	**36**	**21**	**75**

Roundtable participants were not asked to develop consensus recommendations but to provide individual observations and suggestions.

(5)   Additional interviews with roundtable participants to provide additional details on existing projects and strategies.

Strategies for managing data release and privacy protection

While many government agencies are concerned about the privacy risk of opening data, policy-makers can create programmes and assessment tools that reduce these risks to release data for the public good. In developing their open data programmes, agencies should consider a range of strategies, and consider using them in combination to develop a holistic approach to data management. When truly sensitive data is at stake, agencies or cross-agency programmes will need to develop thorough, coordinated plans for privacy protection.

The responses to the survey, and the discussions at the roundtable itself, showed the need for a portfolio of strategies in addressing data privacy concerns. Some of the issues highlighted in the survey responses included the need to balance privacy risks against the public value of opening data; controlled access as a strategy for handling sensitive data; the importance of community engagement; education about how data will be used; and building trust in the organisation that holds the data.

Participants at the roundtable also stressed the importance of including legal, policy, and data experts, as well as stakeholders including industry and civil society, to bring different perspectives to bear in devising privacy-protection strategies. The ultimate goal, they agreed, is to develop a portfolio of approaches for different situations. As one survey respondent put it, 'One size does *not* fit all use cases. The most appropriate method to protect data privacy and confidentiality depends on one's goals and objectives, risk tolerance, and audience.'

It is important to note that there is no one global view on privacy. Different areas of the world have different approaches, understandings, legal frameworks, and risk tolerances.[6] However, many of the strategies discussed in this paper should be useful for governments trying to strike a balance between privacy and openness, regardless of the local context.

Develop balancing tests

Agencies can balance the risks of releasing data against the potential for public good. They can thereby create customised privacy-protection programmes based on risk assessment for each type of data involved, recognising and assessing the actual risk for releasing a given dataset under different conditions. While the exact tradeoffs may be difficult to work out, the use of a 'balancing test' can be a useful framework for handling the risks and benefits of data release.

This is the approach the Consumer Financial Protection Bureau (CFPB) is planning to use to release data under the Home Mortgage Disclosure Act (HMDA). The CFPB is statutorily mandated to publicly disclose data under the HMDA while developing appropriate protections for borrower privacy in light of the HMDA's purposes. Following a recent rulemaking, the CFPB will use a balancing test with public input to determine the right balance of serving the public good and protecting individual privacy in this data release. The test, which has not yet been developed, will be used 'to determine whether and how HMDA data should be modified prior to its disclosure to the public in order to protect applicant and borrower privacy while also fulfilling the disclosure purposes of the statute' (Consumer Financial Protection Bureau 2014).

Balancing tests have also been explored in the academic literature around privacy and open data. Borgesius et al. (2016) propose a 'balancing framework to help public authorities address this question in different contexts. The framework takes into account different varying of privacy risks for different types of data. It also separates decisions about access and re-use, and highlights a range of

---

6   For a better understanding of the different views taken in Europe and the United States, see Van der Sloot (2011).

disclosure routes. A circumstance catalogue lists factors that might be considered when assessing whether, under which conditions, and how a dataset can be released.'

Customise privacy protection based on risk assessment for each agency or programme

Although there are risks to opening data, policy-makers can create programmes and assessment tools that reduce these risks. Data-sharing culture should recognise and assess the actual risk for releasing a given dataset under different conditions. The potential damage from someone breaking the code and learning where an individual went to college, for example, is much less than the potential harm from revealing that same person's medical history. For that reason, each agency should assess the true risk for every dataset that contains PII and choose strategies for managing those datasets accordingly.

When truly sensitive data is at stake, agencies or cross-agency programmes will need to develop thorough, coordinated plans for privacy protection. For example, the US Precision Medicine Initiative (PMI), which is intended to help patients personalise their health care, has developed a framework for protecting privacy without inhibiting this scientific work. The PMI is part of a new approach to disease treatment and prevention that 'takes into account individual variability in genes, environment, and lifestyle for each person'. The success of the PMI – and precision medicine more broadly – will require researchers, providers and patients to 'work together to develop individualised care' and will rely heavily on patient participation (National Institutes of Health n.d.). The PMI Privacy and Trust Principles 'articulate a set of core values and responsible strategies for sustaining public trust and maximising the benefits of precision medicine'. Developed by an inter-agency working group with expert consultation, they are broken down into six key areas: governance, transparency, respecting participant preferences, participant empowerment through access to information, data sharing, access, use, and data quality and integrity (The White House 2015).

Data governance in each agency should also consider a range of possible conditions and risks. Governance approaches make a distinction between 'good actors' and 'bad actors'. When data is released to good actors, such as qualified researchers, re-identification risk can be limited through agreements on conditions of data use. These kinds of agreements can provide a 'trust framework' to govern the use of data effectively. At the same time, trust frameworks are useless against 'bad actors' who want to breach privacy protections on purpose.

Agencies may want to use 'threat modeling' to identify worst-case scenarios and decide what measures they need to prevent them. Threat modeling is a concept applied to network security, where it involves identifying system objectives, vulnerabilities, and countermeasures to prevent or reduce the impact of potential threats to the system. The same concept can be applied to privacy issues by developing scenarios where bad actors might try to break through security safeguards to identify individuals in a database, and planning effective preventive measures.

Apply differential access

It may be necessary to consider gradations of openness under different circumstances. For example, some kinds of data could be made 'open' only for sharing between federal agencies under certain conditions, or sharing only with qualified and vetted researchers, rather than opening it to the public at large. Approaches include:

- Inter-agency transfer of data that is controlled and kept securely between the two agencies involved.
- Federated model using a cloud repository and limiting access to trusted users. This model requires a secure way to upload data as well as secure ways to share it.
- Tiered access data-sharing programmes to allow levels of access to multiple types of users.
- Opt-in and permission-based mechanisms that enable individuals to make their data more widely available if they choose to. For example, individual patients have an incentive to share data about their condition in the hope that it will be used to find better treatments.

One of the first priorities of the Precision Medicine Initiative was a set of Privacy and Trust Principles that 'articulate a set of core values and responsible strategies for sustaining public trust and maximising the benefits of precision medicine'. They aim to ensure transparency, strong governance, and data quality while empowering patients and protecting privacy (The White House 2014). The principles for data sharing, access, and use, for example, include using methods to preserve the privacy of patients' records, prohibiting unauthorised re-identification of patients, and establishing multiple tiers of data access, from open to controlled, depending on the nature of the data. Overall, the Privacy and Trust Principles outline a strong framework for applying many current approaches to balancing data sharing with privacy.

Employ de-identification technologies

It seems to be impossible to create a method of de-identification that removes all the privacy risks of PII from public datasets while also retaining the full value of the data for analysis.[7] However, it may be possible to provide a secure level of

---

7   For a comprehensive look at the inability of anonymisation to function as a prescription for

de-identification if researchers can accept a loss of some detail and granularity in the resulting dataset. Approaches to de-identification include:

- Identifying individuals with unique ID numbers that make it possible to connect data about them in different datasets without revealing their identity.
- Dropping non-critical information to make re-identification more difficult. For example, one regular practice is to drop the last three digits of an individual's zip code.
- Using differential privacy and synthetic data. Differential privacy applies algorithmic research to the problem of data privacy. At its best, it 'can make confidential data widely available for accurate data analysis'. Over time, however, this method can also become vulnerable to re-identification. Therefore, 'the goal of algorithmic research on differential privacy is to postpone this inevitability as long as possible' (Dwork & Roth 2014). Synthetic data relies on 'a complex statistical model that generates a simulated population that has the same general features as the original data'. While it has several existing applications, there is no consensus on its broad usefulness (Callier 2015). These are both sophisticated tools that require resources and data science expertise to apply.

The technical challenge of de-identifying data is becoming increasingly complex. De-identification technology is difficult to apply to the range of data now available, including geospatial, medical and genomic, body-camera and other data. Finally, even if it is possible to de-identify data today, it could become possible to re-identify individuals as technology evolves in the future. If de-identification or related strategies are being used as part of a broader privacy protection strategy, 'The decision of how or if to de-identify data should thus be made in conjunction with decisions of how the de-identified data will be used, shared or released' (Garfinkel 2015).

Enhance data governance structures

New data governance structures can help manage privacy concerns. In the US, many agencies now handle privacy issues through a chief privacy officer, a disclosure review board, or other offices and organisational structures. To make privacy protection as effective as possible, governance structures and safeguards need to be integrated and aligned with goals for data release. Options include:

- Identifying a single agency leader (for example, a chief data officer) to centralise each agency's management of open government data and address privacy concerns.

---

privacy concerns, see Ohm (2010).

- Develop core sets of policies and procedures that can be customised for each agency.
- Create model infrastructure – a virtual central data hub where access to data and APIs is managed by a common set of metadata (security, definitional, sharing licences) and user agreements.

Build trust with the community

Individual privacy should be treated in the context of public good. Many datasets that include PII also include information that can have great public benefit. In these cases, it will be essential to craft approaches to privacy protection that respect individuals' rights while also making data available to the public, or to selected researchers, in a way that supports social and scientific goals.

It is also essential to communicate the goals of open data, and privacy safeguards for the data, to the community and individuals that have provided it. Individuals are understandably concerned that data about their health, education, employment, financial status, or other sensitive data should not be exposed or misused. Agencies and others that plan to use the data with appropriate privacy protections will need to be sure that the communities involved understand and are satisfied with their approach.

One successful example from the U.S. has been the Police Data Initiative (PDI), launched in May 2015 with an initial group of 21 police departments from across the country, along with a range of partners. Through the PDI, police departments are working with data and technology partners to overcome technical and other hurdles and improve data sharing and analysis. Working with police data poses challenges to security and privacy, including concerns about releasing data on potential perpetrators, victims, and individual officers' actions. Several police departments have taken this challenge as an opportunity to work with the community to find solutions together. For example, 'the New Orleans Police Department...previewed policing datasets with a group of young coders and their tech mentors [and] the Orlando Police Department worked with sexual assault and domestic violence victim advocates to figure out how to balance transparency with victim privacy'. By taking this kind of approach, a number of 'communities and police departments [are] using data as a way to engage in dialogue and build trust' (Wardell & Ross 2016).

Conclusion

There is no single, foolproof solution to the challenge of protecting privacy when open data is released. However, a combination of strategies can make it possible to tap the value of granular, detailed data while managing privacy risks. While some strategies involve technical approaches, others are based on policy, data governance, community outreach and communication. These strategies should be applicable not only in the US, where this research was based, but in other countries and contexts around the world.

As technology and policy around privacy evolve, more research will help open data programmes optimise their strategies for privacy protection. Researchers may choose to focus on the potential and limits of different technical approaches; the conditions for success of different privacy-protection strategies; protocols for releasing data with different 'degrees of openness'; cultural and social expectations of privacy in different communities; or other topics that help to develop a multifaceted approach to privacy protection in the context of open data.

Acknowledgements

The Center for Open Data Enterprise thanks its open data partner Microsoft and open data supporter Booz Allen Hamilton for supporting the Center's work on the 2016 Open Data Roundtables and related research. We also thank participants in the Open Data Roundtable on Privacy, the White House Office of Science and Technology Policy for providing input and feedback throughout the process, and the Center team, fellows, and interns who have all contributed to this effort throughout 2016. Parts of this paper have also been published in the 'Open Data and Privacy' Briefing Paper (2016) and the Roundtable Report (2016) published by the Center for Open Data Enterprise.

About the authors

JOEL GURIN is President and Founder of the Center for Open Data Enterprise, a Washington-based non-profit that works to maximise the value of open data as a public resource. Before launching the Center in January 2015, he wrote the book *Open Data Now* and led the launch team for the GovLab's Open Data 500 study and Open Data Roundtables. He was Chair of the White House Task Force on Smart Disclosure and has served as Chief of the Consumer and Governmental Affairs Bureau of the US Federal Communications Commission and as Executive Vice-President of Consumer Reports. E-mail: joel@odenterprise.org

MATT RUMSEY is a researcher and consultant focused on government data and information policy. He previously worked at the Sunlight Foundation, where he helped develop and implement federal policy initiatives. He holds a Bachelors in History from the American University in Washington DC.

AUDREY ARISS is the Director of Research and Design at the Center for Open Data Enterprise in Washington DC, where she co-leads international initiatives. Audrey has spent the past five years focusing on the use of data and technology for economic development. Audrey holds a masters in International Affairs and Quantitative Methods from Columbia University and a bachelors degree in

Modern History and French from the University of Oxford. She was a 2013 Google Policy Fellow.

KATHERINE GARCIA is a communications professional and consultant focused on open data and sustainability. Previously, Katherine was a member of the founding team for the Center for Open Data Enterprise, where she managed communications and outreach. She earned her Master of Public Administration degree with an emphasis in policy analysis from Baruch College and her Bachelors in Communication at the University of California, Santa Barbara.

REFERENCES

Altman, M., Wood, A., O'Brien, D.R., Vadhan, S. & Gasser, U. (2015). Towards a modern approach to privacy aware government data releases. *Berkeley Technology Law Journal* 30(30). http://btlj.org/data/articles2015/vol30/30_3/1967-2072%20Altman.pdf

Arrington, M. (2006, 6 August). AOL Proudly Releases Massive Amounts of Private Data. *TechCrunch*. http://techcrunch.com/2006/08/06/aol-proudly-releases-massive-amounts-of-user-search-data/

Borgesius, F., Van Eechoud, M. & Gray, J. (2015). Open data, privacy, and fair information practice principles: Towards a balancing framework. *Berkeley Technology Law Journal* 30(3): 2074-2099. http://btlj.org/data/articles2015/vol30/30_3/2073-2132%20Borgesius.pdf

Callier, V. (2015, 30 July). How fake data could protect real people's privacy. *The Atlantic*. http://www.theatlantic.com/technology/archive/2015/07/fake-data-privacy-census/399974/

Center for Open Data Enterprise (2016). Briefing paper on open data and privacy'. http://www.opendataenterprise.org/convene.html

Center for Open Data Enterprise (2015). Improving safety data: A Roundtable with the US Department of Transportation. https://s3.amazonaws.com/odenterprise/DoT+Roundtable+Report.pdf

Consumer Financial Protection Bureau (2014). *Final Rule Home Mortgage Disclosure Regulation, Docket No. CFPB-20140-0019.* http://files.consumerfinance.gov/f/201510_cfpb_final-rule_home-mortgage-disclosure_regulation-c.pdf

Consumer Financial Protection Bureau (n.d.). *The Home Mortgage Disclosure Act: About HMDA.* http://www.consumerfinance.gov/hmda/learn-more

Consumer Financial Protection Bureau (2015) *CFPB Finalizes Rule to Improve Information About Access to Credit in the Mortgage Market* http://www.consumerfinance.gov/about-us/newsroom/cfpb-finalizes-rule-to-improve-information-about-access-to-credit-in-the-mortgage-market/

Data.gov (n.d.). Project Open Data Dashboard. http://labs.data.gov/dashboard/offices

Dixon, P. (2008). *A Brief Introduction to Fair Information Practices.* World Privacy Forum. https://www.worldprivacyforum.org/2008/01/report-a-brief-introduction-to-fair-information-practices/

Dwork, C. & Roth, A. (2014). The algorithmic foundations of differential privacy. *Foundations and Trends in Theoretical Computer Science* 9(3–4): 211-407. http://www.nowpublishers.com/article/DownloadSummary/TCS-042, 5

Federal Trade Commission (2016). Big data: A tool for exclusion or inclusion? https://www.ftc.gov/system/files/documents/reports/big-data-tool-inclusion-or-exclusion-understanding-issues/160106big-data-rpt.pdf

Garfinkel, S. (2015). De-identification of personal information. National Institute of Standards and Technology, 8053. http://nvlpubs.nist.gov/nistpubs/ir/2015/NIST.IR.8053.pdf

Isaac, W. & Dixon, A. (2017, 10 May). Why big-data analysis of police activity is inherently biased, *The Conversation*, https://theconversation.com/why-big-data-analysis-of-police-activity-is-inherently-biased-72640

Kharif, O. (2014, 1 May). Privacy fears over student data tracking lead to InBloom's shutdown. *Bloomberg Business*. http://www.bloomberg.com/bw/articles/2014-05-01/inbloom-shuts-down-amid-privacy-fears-over-student-data-tracking

Kuschewsky, M. (2013, 23 September). Revised OECD privacy guidelines strengthen accountability principle. *Inside Privacy*. https://www.insideprivacy.com/international/revised-oecd-privacy-guidelines-strengthen-accountability-principle/

Narayanan, A. & Shmatikov, V. (2008). Robust de-anonymization of large datasets (How to break the anonymity of the Netflix prize dataset. University of Texas at Austin. http://arxiv.org/PS_cache/cs/pdf/0610/0610105v2.pdf

National Institutes of Health (n.d.). Precision Medicine Initiative Cohort Program https://www.nih.gov/precision-medicine-initiative-cohort-program

Obama, B. (2016, 9 February). Establishing the Federal Privacy Council Executive Order. The White House. https://www.whitehouse.gov/the-press-office/2016/02/09/executive-order-establishment-federal-privacy-council

O'Hara, K. (2011). Transparent government, not transparent citizens: A report on privacy and transparency for the Cabinet Office. London: Cabinet Office. http://eprints.soton.ac.uk/272769/

Ohm, P. (2010). Broken promises of privacy: Responding to the surprising failure of anonymization. *UCLA Law Review* 57: 1701-1777. www.uclalawreview.org/pdf/57-6-3.pdf

Open Government Guide (n.d.). Privacy and data protection. http://www.opengovguide.com/topics/privacy-and-data-protection/

Ortellado, D. (2016, 16 February). Reconciling criminal history open data and expungement. The Sunlight Foundation. http://sunlightfoundation.com/blog/2016/02/03/reconciling-criminal-history-open-data-and-expungement/

Park, T. & Shelton, J. (2012, 8 June). The power of open education data. The White House. https://www.whitehouse.gov/blog/2012/06/08/power-open-education-data-0

Press, E. (2010, 29 July). A case for Open Data in Transit. *Streetfilms.org.* http://www.streetfilms.org/a-case-for-open-data-in-transit/

Podesta, J., Pritzker, P., Moniz, E., Holdren, J., & Zients, J. (2014, 1 May). Big data: Seizing opportunities, preserving values. The White House Executive Office of the President. https://www.whitehouse.gov/sites/default/files/docs/big_data_privacy_report_may_1_2014.pdf

Polonetsky, J., Tene, O., & Finch, K. (2016). Shades of gray: Seeing the full spectrum of practical data de-identification. *Santa Clara Law Review* 593. http://digitalcommons.law.scu.edu/lawreview/vol56/iss3/3

Scassa, T. (2014). Privacy and open government. *Future Internet* 6(2): 397–413. http://doi.org/10.3390/fi6020397

Shaw, E. (2015, 22 January). What do we want? Data about police practice! The Sunlight Foundation. http://sunlightfoundation.com/blog/2015/01/22/what-do-we-want-data-about-police-practice/

Shaw, E. (2014, 24 October). Exploring open data's microdata frontier. The Sunlight

Foundation. https://sunlightfoundation.com/blog/2014/10/24/exploring-open-datas-microdata-frontier/

Sweeney, L. (1997). Weaving technology and policy together to maintain confidentiality. *Journal of Law, Medicine & Ethics* 25(2&3): 98-110

The Open Data Institute (n.d.). Data spectrum: The data spectrum helps you understand the language of data. https://theodi.org/data-spectrum.

Sunlight Foundation (2014). The benefits of criminal justice data: Policing and beyond. The Sunlight Foundation. http://assets.sunlightfoundation.com/criminaljustice/sunlight-policy-brief-the-benefits-of-criminal-justice-data-policing-and-beyond.pdf

The White House (2015, 9 November). Precision Medicine Initiative: Privacy and trust principles. https://www.whitehouse.gov/sites/default/files/microsites/finalpmiprivacyandtrustprinciples.pdf

The White House (n.d.). The Precision Medicine Initiative. https://www.whitehouse.gov/precision-medicine

Thomas, K.E. (2016, 28 January) What 22 million rides tell us about NYC bike-share. *Next City*. https://nextcity.org/daily/entry/citi-bike-new-york-city-bike-share-data

Tierney, K.F. (2012). Use of the US Census Bureau's Public Use Microdata Sample (PUMS) by State Departments of Transportation and Metropolitan Planning Organizations. Transportation Research Board of the National Academies. http://onlinepubs.trb.org/onlinepubs/nchrp/nchrp_syn_434.pdf

Van der Sloot, B. (2011). On the fabrication of sausages, or of open government and private data. *eJournal of eDemocracy and Open Government* 3(2). http://papers.ssrn.com/sol3/papers.cfm?abstract_id=2323771

Wardell, C. & Ross, D. (2016, 22 April). The Police Data Initiative year of progress. The White House. https://medium.com/the-white-house/the-police-data-initiative-year-of-progress-how-we-re-building-on-the-president-s-call-to-leverage-3ac86053e1a9#.58iuq5xo7

Printed in the United States
By Bookmasters